Extreme Common *Eloquence*

D1765504

Scottish Cultural Review
of Language and Literature

Volume 3

Series Editors
John Corbett
University of Glasgow

Sarah Dunnigan
University of Edinburgh

James McGonigal
University of Glasgow

Production Editor
Gavin Miller
University of Edinburgh

SCROLL

The Scottish Cultural Review of Language and Literature publishes new work in Scottish Studies, with a focus on analysis and reinterpretation of the literature and languages of Scotland, and the cultural contexts that have shaped them.

Further information on our editorial and production procedures can be found at www.rodopi.nl

Extremely Common *Eloquence*

Constructing Scottish identity through narrative

Ronald K.S. Macaulay

Amsterdam - New York, NY 2005

Cover design: Gavin Miller

The paper on which this book is printed meets the requirements of "ISO 9706: 1994, Information and documentation - Paper for documents - Requirements for permanence".

ISBN: 90-420-1764-3
©Editions Rodopi B.V., Amsterdam - New York, NY 2005
Printed in The Netherlands

ah knew a linguist wance
wanst I knew a linguist
shi used tay git oanty mi
ah wish I could talk like you
ahv lost my accent.

Tom Leonard (1984: 113)

One important way of characterizing a culture is by the narrative models it makes available for describing the course of a life.

Jerome Bruner (1987: 15)

Contents

Preface

This book has been a long time in the making. I have been working on some of the materials for twenty-five years and I have published extracts from them in a variety of places. In the present work, I have not hesitated to include examples that have been cited elsewhere because I believe that their cumulative effect justifies this decision.

One reason it has taken so long to write this book is that it does not easily fit into any recognisable category. It is about language but it is not about phonology, morphology, syntax or semantics, and it does not address questions of linguistic theory. It does not fit easily into the usual divisions of sociolinguistics. It is about language in society but it is not about language variation or language change. It is about cultural attitudes but it is not an ethnography.

In an earlier work (Macaulay 1997: 162), I quoted a remark by Charles Fillmore: "We need to distinguish between *how* people speak their language and *how well* people speak their language" (1979: 92). This book is about how well some speak their language. It might seem to be unnecessary to defend the way people speak but as the Milroys make clear in the latest edition of their book *Authority in Language* (Milroy and Milroy 1999), prejudice against categories of speakers persists. Labov (1969) convincingly defended "nonstandard English" and Tannen (1989) has shown how ordinary conversation contains many features that used to be associated only with literary works. Yet Labov's and Tannen's works are only brief illustrations of the kind of skills that speakers possess. The present work displays a much wider range of rhetorical skills, but more importantly it shows how these skills are employed to communicate important aspects of Scottish identity and culture.

In 1973, I interviewed a range of people and collected their opinions on Glasgow speech (Macaulay and Trevelyan 1973: 119–178; Macaulay 1977: 75–130). Many of the comments were negative and most of those comments referred to pronunciation and a few well-known stigmatised forms such as *I seen* and *I done*. This focus was largely the result of my questions, which were designed to investigate linguistic prejudice, and thus the form of the questions and the way they asked probably encouraged negative comments. There were few comments about speech style in general except for numerous complaints about the inarticulateness of young people. However, there were two general comments that are worth quoting here. One was made by the staff manageress of a factory:

1. (Glasgow survey, E07)
I think this is something that is lacking in Scottish people in general. I don't know whether it's a lack of confidence. They don't generally express themselves terribly well. If they're good they're very good. I find English people, people coming from abroad, can express themselves very well. But in Scotland they don't seem to– maybe it's just our dour natures, I don't quite know. (Macaulay 1977: 124)

The second comment was made by a training college lecturer:

2. (Glasgow survey, T42)
There is something in the temperament, something in the speech habits of the West of Scotland whereby it is not done for people to speak at any length. If you speak at any length normally people won't listen. (Macaulay 1977: 97)

The examples in the present work constitute a refutation of these two comments. The speakers express themselves very well and often at considerable length. In the Glasgow survey I was investigating the importance of language differences on success in education and in getting a job. Thus the respondents' comments to a large extent referred to formal contexts such as the classroom and job interviews. The materials on which the present book is based were recorded in much less hierarchical and threatening situations. One of the aims of the book, consequently, is to counteract the negative impression of Scottish speech given in Macaulay (1977) by showing how expressive and eloquent Scottish speakers can be.

A second aim is to connect the examples of language to the lives the speakers live. The political status of Scotland as a nation has fluctuated over the past four hundred years, but the sense of Scottish identity has remained strong. Part of that identity comes from a form of speech that remains distinct from that of its dominant southern neighbour. There are cultural attitudes that indicate a spirit of independence that is consistent with this linguistic separation. It is, of course, impossible to show causality either way but by examining the cultural implications of what the speakers say it is possible to show where the consistency lies.

A third aim is to show that eloquence does not depend upon education. Most of the speakers cited in this work come from a working-class background and left school at the minimum age of fourteen. Yet, as will be demonstrated again and again, they are remarkably articulate and effective speakers. They come from different backgrounds and locations, they have held different kinds of jobs, and they include both men and women. They may not be a representative sample of the population but they are certainly an impressive one.

My first expression of gratitude must go to the speakers themselves for their willingness to talk to me and the openness with which they were prepared to tell me about their lives. Although it is unlikely that any of them will ever see this book, I hope that the message it is intended to convey will be some reward for their co-operation. However, the work would not have achieved its present form without the generous encouragement and tireless efforts of John Corbett, whose many perceptive comments and suggestions helped me through the preparation of the final version. My sincere thanks go to him and also to Gavin Miller who has seen the work through the production process. Any faults that remain are my responsibility.

List of speakers

The examples in this book come from a range of recordings, my own unless otherwise stated. For ease of reference, a brief description of the speakers is provided here. All the names are pseudonyms, with the exception of Bella K. and Len M., whose names are in the public record.

Aberdeen (recorded 1979)
Bill Dalgleish. Age 59.
Nan Dalgleish. Age 56.
Pat Dalgliesh. Age 30.
Jim Dyce. Age 32.

Bill Finlay. Age 39.
Leslie Simpson. Age c. 55
Betty Simpson. Age 43.
Meg Spence. Age 41.

Ayr (recorded in 1978–79)
Ellen Caldwell. Age 72.
Hugh Gemmill. Age 78.
Wallace Gibson. Age 55.
Ella Laidlaw. Age 69.
Willie Lang. Age 56.
Andrew MacDougall. Age 35.
James MacGregor. Age 63.
Nan Menzies. Age 62.
Duncan Nicoll. Age 67.
Willie Rae. Age 54.
Mary Ritchie. Age 70.
Andrew Sinclair. Age 58.

Dundee (recorded as part of the Dundee Oral History Project, 1985)
Bella K. Age 63.
Len. M. Age 66.

Edinburgh (recorded as part of the Scottish Working People's Oral History Project, 1985)
Jock Bell. Age 66.
Harry Melrose. Age 65.
John MacDonald. Age 67.

Mary Morrison. Age 66.
Archie Munroe. Age 64.

Glasgow (recorded as part of the survey of language, education, and employment in 1973)
John Wilson. Age 47.

Chapter One

The Study of Language

Bakhtin recognized that any abstract objectivist theory of language always went hand in hand with the language of the dominant social class. High languages are imperialistic. They establish themselves as both "standard" and prestige by a variety of methods, including "objective" grammars, the prescription of norms, structural theories of language, [...] in so far as all these systematically exclude the actual speech use of the majority of people. (White 1993: 154)

The past fifty years have seen a vast expansion in the range and amount of scholarly activity devoted to different aspects of language. *The Handbook of Linguistics* (Aronoff and Rees-Miller 2001) contains thirty-two chapters ranging from "Origins of language" to "Language planning" by way of the usual topics of the basic levels of language, such as phonetics, phonology, syntax, etc., to typology, neurolinguistics, and computational linguistics. For those who wish to explore some of these topics further, there are equally large separate handbooks for Child Language, Phonological Theory, Contemporary Semantic Theory, Sociolinguistics, Phonetic Sciences, Morphology, Contemporary Syntactic Theory, Discourse Analysis, and Language Change and Variation. And all this is from the list of a single publisher; the total range of titles on linguistic topics published each year is evidence of a very active field of scholarship.

It might appear to the mythical visitor from Mars (or Venus) that there can be little left to say about human language, since everything must have been thoroughly investigated and agreement reached about its nature and function. Yet nothing could be further from the truth. Despite the proliferation of linguists and linguistic departments, there is little agreement even about the object of study or the methods to be employed in studying it. The major division follows that set out by Saussure (1922) between language as an abstract system (*langue*) and language in actual use (*parole*), and of these it is *langue* that has received by far the greater attention. This has had immense influence on the study of language. In the approach that Voloshinov (1929) labelled *abstract objectivism*:

What interests the mathematically minded rationalists is not the relationship of the sign to the actual reality it reflects nor to the individual who is its originator, but the *relationship of sign to sign within a closed system* already accepted and authorized. In other words, they are interested only in the *inner logic of the system of signs itself*, taken, as in algebra, completely independently of the ideological meanings that give the signs their content[1]. (Voloshinov [1929] 1986: 57–58, emphasis in original)

The mythical Martian visitor looking at the past fifty years or so of linguistic enquiry might think that this statement was remarkably prophetic. At about the same time, Bloomfield observed that "de Saussure's *la parole* lies beyond the power of our science" (1927: 445).

Abstract objective linguists, taking physical science as the model for the scientific study of language, have, as it were, attempted to study language through a microscope, on the assumption that the universal structural characteristics of language can be identified in this way. Just as the specimen on the slide is often a fragment separated from a larger body, the forms of language studied by linguists using this approach are isolated from any actual situation in which they might have been used and they are examined as abstract, decontextualised, static examples. This approach emphasises the importance of form over function, an emphasis which has had immense influence not only on assumptions about the nature of language but also on the ways in which language is studied and described. It has also, somewhat paradoxically, led to a privileging of the written form (Voloshinov [1929] 1986; Linell 1982, 1998; Macaulay 1997).

An alternative scientific model for the description of language is closer to that of the ethologist studying animal behaviour. In such an approach, the linguist observes how individuals in a society use language and attempts to create a coherent description of this behaviour. Instead of examining abstract, decontextualised examples, the linguist in this model is looking at the dynamic use of language in specific

---

[1] Todorov (1984) gives a slightly different translation: "It is not the relation of the sign to the concrete reality it reflects, or to the individual that generates it, but it is the *relation of sign to sign within a closed system*, once that system has been accepted and licensed, which interests the mathematically oriented mind of the rationalist. In other words they are only interested in the inner logic of the sign system itself, considered as algebra, quite independently of the ideological meanings that the signs convey" [emphasis in original].

situations. In this activity the microscope is likely to be of little use, though there are other aids to the human eye, such as binoculars. However, as any bird-watcher knows, there are occasions when the naked eye is more effective because the width of vision is greater. Perspective is crucial because of the importance of context on language use (Duranti and Goodwin 1992).

There are at least two approaches to the study of language use. One is the ethnographer's observation of communicative practices which requires that the investigator spends time in the community, observing behaviour, identifying speech events in all the complexity set out by Hymes (1974). In this way, the ethnographer can report on a wide range of speech events, limited only by the extent to which members of the community will allow access to certain settings. It has become clear from many studies (e.g., Brenneis 1978, 1986; Duranti 1981, 1994; Hanks 1990, 1996; Moerman 1988; Ochs 1988; Rickford 1987; Sankoff 1980; Schieffelin 1990; Wolfowitz 1991) that the use of language is best understood when seen in the context of the community in which it is used. Language serves many functions in addition to being the major vehicle for conveying information from one human being to another. Through language we also communicate our hopes, fears, anxieties, dreams, and to some extent our emotions (Lutz and Abu-Lughod 1990). Such notions cannot be studied in the abstract objective approach. Ethnographic studies, however, depend directly on the accuracy of the investigator's observations and interpretations, and validation of any conclusions will usually require another investigator to visit the same situation and carry out further observations to confirm or refute the original findings (e.g., Freeman's (1999) revision of Margaret Mead's (1928) description of Samoa).

Sociolinguists, on the other hand, present their results based on analysis of language samples, generally taken from recordings of speech. The recordings are usually made of a single type of speech event (e.g., an interview) to allow comparability of the samples. The results are based on items transcribed from the recordings. Although the accuracy of these transcriptions can seldom be challenged, the interpretation of the data can be checked and alternative analyses suggested (e.g., Horvath's (1985) reanalysis of an example of Labov's

(1966a) New York data showing that gender was more important than Labov's claim about the significance of social class).

Many sociolinguistic studies are based on the premiss that quantitative methods are useful for the investigation of linguistic variation (Macaulay 2002c). In this approach a linguistic variable is correlated with some extralinguistic social factor. Common to many studies is a focus on social, gender, and age differences, but some investigators have included social factors such as ethnicity (Labov 1966a; Feagin 1979; McCafferty 2001), racial isolation (Wolfram 1969), rurality (Trudgill 1974), religion (Macaulay 1977; McCafferty 2001), peer group status (Cheshire 1982; Eckert 2000), social network (Milroy 1980; Labov 2001), and education (Coupland 1988; Haeri 1996). Many studies are primarily concerned with linguistic change (e.g., Labov 1966a, 2001; Trudgill 1974; Milroy 1980).

Most sociolinguistic studies have concentrated on phonological and, to a lesser degree, morphological variables (Macaulay, forthcoming). This is hardly surprising, because these are the kind of variables for which it is easiest to obtain evidence (Labov 1966a: 49) since they occur frequently and are less likely to be suppressed. Such variables are also often salient because they are indicative of social differentiation in communities (Coupland 2001). These variables are also amenable to quantification. It is also possible to use quantitative methods to chart variation in grammatical features (Feagin 1979; Cheshire 1982; Macaulay 1991a) and discourse features (Bernstein 1962; Macaulay 1991a, 1995, 2002a, 2002b, 2002c, forthcoming), though fewer investigators have been interested in these features. While most sociolinguistic studies are based on recorded speech, different aims require different kinds of samples. For example, it is possible to gain information about pronunciation by asking people to read out a list of appropriate items, but it is not possible to investigate variation in the use of grammatical or discourse features in this way.

The study of "language within the social context of the community in which it is spoken" (Labov 1966a: 3) has come a long way since Labov's pioneering work in New York. Some of Labov's later work looked at different genres (e.g., narratives, ritual insults). Schiffrin (1987) and Labov (1984) extended this trend by examining features of discourse in context. This has revealed greater complexity in the use of language than had previously been investigated systematically. Weihun He (2001) sums up this complexity in setting out the aims of discourse analysis:

> discourse analysis seeks to describe and explain linguistic phenomena in terms of the affective, cognitive, situational, and cultural contexts of their use and to identify linguistic resources through which we (re)construct our life (our identity, role, activity, community, emotion, stance, knowledge, belief, ideology, and so forth). Essentially it asks why we use language in the way we do and how we live our lives linguistically. (Weihun He 2001: 429)

Given such an ambitious goal, it is hardly surprising that there are no examples that fulfill all the aims listed by Weihun He, and most examples of discourse analysis are more modest in their goals. Contrary to the expectations set out in Weihun He's programme, few examples of discourse analysis have been concerned with such matters as social class, identity, or ideology. *The Handbook of Discourse Analysis* (Schiffrin, Tannen, and Hamilton 2001) has forty-one chapters and runs to more than eight hundred pages, yet only nine pages are listed under social class in the index, eighteen under identity, and eighteen under ideology. It might have been expected that the work of Bakhtin would be influential in discourse analysis but he is mentioned on only four pages in the *Handbook*, and Voloshinov only once, none of the references dealing with their views in any detail. Even in the branch known as Critical Discourse Analysis "the study of the discursive reproduction of class has been rather neglected" (van Dijk 2001: 364). When I recently reviewed works on discourse variation (Macaulay 2002a) I found that the major emphasis was on gender differences; very few studies dealt with social class or ethnicity.

White (1993: 137) points out that "Bakhtin has a much more conflict-centred view of sociolect than most linguists". For Bakhtin all language use was ideological, but as Emerson explains: "For Bakhtin and his colleagues, it [ideology] meant simply an 'idea system' determined socially" (1986: 23). This is made clear in Voloshinov's phrasing:

> By ideology we will mean the set of reflections and refractions of social and natural reality that is held by the human brain and which the brain expresses and fixes

through words, drawings, lines, or whatever signifying form. (Voloshinov 1928: 53; cited in Todorov 1984: 18).

Language is the means by which we express this ideology. As Romaine has pointed out, "at the pragmatic level, all linguistic choices can be seen as indexical of a variety of social relations" (1989: 111). The present volume is an attempt to explore some of the ideological significance of certain linguistic choices for notions of Scottish identity, through an examination of some examples of the use of language in lowland Scotland.

Surprisingly, it has often been denied that language plays a significant role in Scottish identity. In the conclusion to the first edition of his book, *Understanding Scotland*, David McCrone claimed that nationalism in Scotland "draws very thinly on cultural traditions; there is virtually no *linguistic* or religious basis to nationalism" (1992: 214, emphasis added). He based this claim on the view that "there is little to distinguish Scotland linguistically from England, since Gaelic is spoken by less than 2 per cent" (1992: 211). These categorical statements have disappeared from the second edition of McCrone's book (McCrone 2001). However, he still makes the same point in more subtle phrasing: "the weak language tariff which people have to pay to be 'Scots' has been low to the point of non-existence" (McCrone 2001: 177). McCrone's position assumes that the only significant linguistic differences are those between clearly distinct languages, such as Gaelic and English. In this he is not alone. J.G. Kellas in *Modern Scotland* is even more categorical: "Scottish nationality is not linguistic, for there is no Scottish language" (1980: 3). This attitude results from a view of language that, in Allon White's words quoted in the epigraph, "systematically exclude[s] the actual speech use of the majority of people" (White 1993: 154). This attitude is probably the result of an identification of nationalism with the independence movement, in which language has not played a significant role.

In contrast to the views of McCrone and Kellas, in the over two hundred interviews I have conducted in Scotland, I have found that Scots speakers are more or less unanimous that what distinguishes the Scots from the English is the way that they speak. This view is also found outside of Scotland: "It is probable that most British people would agree that the biggest dialect differences of all, and the most obvious, are today those that divide the English and the Scots" (Trudgill 1990: 76).

McCrone and Kellas, like many of the others who write about Scotland and nationalism, appear to view many aspects of the situation from a middle-class perspective. It may be true of many middle-class Scots that they pay only "a weak language tariff" by salting their Scottish Standard English with "overt Scotticisms" (Aitken 1984: 107), but working-class Scots generally assert their identity in more marked forms of speech.

McCrone (2001: 127–48) devotes a chapter to Scottish culture, dealing with such topics as "tartanry" and the "Kailyard" school of writing. Harvie (1998a) in his book *Scotland and Nationalism* has a chapter on intellectuals in which he deals not only with the Kailyard school but also the Scottish Renaissance, headed by Hugh MacDiarmid. McClure (1988) in *Why Scots Matters* gives a brief summary of the riches of literature in Scots. None of these aspects of Scottish "culture" figures in the materials I will be dealing with and does not seem to play a significant role in the speakers' sense of identity.

Giles and Coupland (1991: 96) give four reasons for the salience of language in ethnic relations: (1) language is often a criterial attribute of group membership; (2) language can be an important cue for ethnic categorisation; (3) language is an emotional dimension of identity; and (4) language is a means of facilitating in-group cohesion. These four reasons would appear to apply to the case of lowland Scotland but there is a confounding factor. The situation is complicated by social class differences. While most Scots reveal their Scottishness through their speech, it is the working-class speakers who display the most marked features. Working-class speech in lowland Scotland thus has a double function: 1) to affirm Scottish identity and separateness from the English; and 2) to affirm working-class loyalty and distance from middle-class values.

The present work examines examples of Scottish speech that provide some evidence for the claim that there is a link between language and identity, including class loyalty and gender roles. The emphasis, however, will not be on the most salient aspect of Scottish speech, namely pronunciation. There is plenty of evidence for the phonological distinctiveness of Scottish speech (e.g., Johnston 1997; Macaulay 1977, 1991a; Stuart-Smith 1999, 2003) but that is not a primary concern here. Nor will the emphasis be on grammatical forms, although the examples discussed will include many constructions that are commonly found in Scotland and rarely elsewhere (Miller 2003). Instead the emphasis will be on the kinds of variation that can be found in more extended samples of talk-in-action, of which one of the richest sources lies in the stories that people tell about themselves and their lives. As Ochs observes:

Given the variety of modes and genres that realize narrative activity, it is an enormous task to consider how narrative is rooted in cultural systems of knowledge, beliefs, values, ideologies, action, emotion, and other dimensions of social order. (Ochs 1997: 189)

This book is based on tape-recordings of a variety of speakers in different parts of Scotland, but the speakers' words are not represented directly. Instead, the speakers' remarks and stories have been transcribed for the purposes of analysis and quotation. Since transcription is a complex process, the principles upon which the examples have been transcribed are set out in detail in Chapter Two.

Chapters Three to Eight examine a number of stories told by different speakers. The analysis shows that such stories are often constructed in complex and subtle ways. More importantly the narrators through their stories often convey information about their attitudes and values. Chapter Three, for example, presents what appears to be a simple account of going to meet someone at a railway station. The analysis shows that this brief story has a complex narrative structure that brings out the psychological significance of the event. This chapter provides an introduction to the method employed in examining more complex narratives in later chapters.

When someone is telling a story about interaction with others, it is quite common for the narrator to dramatise the scene by reporting what the participants, including the narrator, said. Chapter Four examines this use of dialogue and the problems it can present for analysis.

Three long and complex narratives are examined in Chapter Five. All three are about getting a job, two of them telling about the speaker's first job. The aims of this chapter are twofold. One aim, as in Chapter Three, is to show how these apparently simple stories are carefully constructed and structurally coherent. The second aim is to show how these stories combine the kind of cultural information described by Ochs above with the presentation of a personal identity that the speakers would probably not have asserted explicitly.

Most of the stories told in these interviews tell of situations in which the narrator was a principal participant. However, occasionally narrators tell stories of an event at which they were not present. Chapter Six examines several narratives of the kind showing the different kind of problems that they present to the analyst.

The notion of stylistic variation has been an important part of sociolinguistic investigation since Labov's New York study (Labov 1966a, 1966b). The principal focus has been on phonological and morphological features, but some attention is now being given to lexical and discourse features (Eckert and Rickford 2002; Macaulay 1995, 1991, forthcoming). Chapter Seven examines a working-class speaker whose complex mixture of registers presents a challenge to current models of stylistic variation.

Most of the materials on which this book is based were recorded in face-to-face interviews with a single speaker. Chapter Eight, however, examines two group sessions in which several family members participated. Although the sessions were recorded in the same city, Aberdeen, and both families belong to the working-class, the dynamics of interaction in each session contrast strongly. The members of one family demonstrate their eagerness to cooperate with each other in telling what happened. In the other session, the participants challenge and tease each other in a much more competitive fashion.

The focus of this work is not on phonological, morphological, or syntactic features, but it will be obvious from the transcripts that most of the speakers use some forms that are not found in Standard English or Standard Scottish English. These are **dialect** features in Coupland's (2002) sense, and they vary from community to community. For example, there are dialect forms used by the Aberdeen speakers in Chapter Eight that are not used by the speakers from other parts of the country. Chapter Nine shows how the speakers are aware of social class and regional differences of this kind. The working-class speakers

recognise the difference between their speech and that of the middle-
class but they do not manifest the kind of linguistic insecurity that has
been found in other locations (e.g., Labov 1966a).

The persistence of nonstandard varieties has puzzled many people (see, for example, Ryan 1979). In Scotland there is the added
paradox that traditional Scots forms may be valued in the works of
Burns and Scott but denigrated in the speech of children (McClure
1996). It is clear, however, from the examples in this book that most
of the working-class speakers (at the time when they were recorded)
were not inhibited in their use of dialect forms by the kind of disap-
proval shown by teachers (Macaulay 1977). Chapter Ten examines
some of the beliefs and attitudes manifested in the interviews, showing the kind of cultural understandings shared by many of the speakers, particularly those concerning equality, work, and money. These
attitudes and beliefs have an ideological significance that may help to
explain how the speakers have retained their distinctive form of
speech, despite official pressures to abandon it.

It will be obvious in the examples taken from the interviews that
the speakers use language very effectively. Nevertheless, their skill
may be underestimated because we do not usually subject speech to
the kind of detailed analysis that literary works in prose and verse receive. Chapter Eleven shows the results of looking for examples of
rhetorical figures of speech in the recorded samples. It turns out that
these speakers demonstrate the use of a surprising range of traditional
rhetorical devices.

The final chapter argues that the eloquence of the working-class
speakers has been ignored because "the myth of egalitarianism" has
assumed that all Scots speak "the same language", which consequently has to meet the standards of middle-class speech. For those
who uphold those standards, the use of nonstandard (i.e., dialect) features may have obscured the vitality of Scottish working-class speech
and prevented them from understanding its deep significance. This
volume is addressed to those who have undervalued these distinctively
Scottish voices. As I have struggled to find the right words to describe
what the speakers have done, I have been humbled by the apparent
ease with which these speakers, most of whom left school at the
minimum age of fourteen, succeed in telling their stories so effec-

tively. It is my hope that whatever shortcomings may be found in my own efforts, the success of their eloquence will shine through. They are the "onlie begetters" of this volume.

Chapter Two

The Problems of Transcription

It has become apparent to us during the last few years that the theory and practice of "transcription" as carried out by linguists leaves a great deal to be desired, especially if applied to conversational material. (Kelly and Local 1989: 197)

In the near future studies of language variation will presumably be presented in a computerised form that will allow the reader of a transcript to hear what has been transcribed and this will influence the form of transcription (Sinclair 1995).[1] Ideally, there will be more than one transcription available for the same sample of speech so that the reader can switch from one that presents a user-friendly orthographic version to one of a number of other possibilities containing phonetic, prosodic, and paralinguistic details (Johansson 1995). Until that time, however, for printed works it is necessary to choose the form in which to represent the speech that has been recorded.

Coombs in his book on the *Theory of Data* (1964) points out that there is an ambiguity in the use of the word "data": "The term is commonly used to refer both to the recorded observations and to that which is analyzed" (1964: 4). Coombs provides the following diagram (Figure 1, overleaf) to illustrate the difference. It is important to note here that Coombs' use of "recorded observations" does not refer to tape-recordings but to what the scientist pays attention to. Instead, a tape-recorded interview would constitute an example of what Coombs calls "a universe of potential observations". From the universe, the scientist will decide to pay attention to certain things and ignore others. Coombs' example is that a political pollster asking an individual who he will vote for will probably not record how long it took the individual to answer, whether there was a change in respiration, or what he did with his hands. In other words, the pollster will pay attention to some aspects of the situation (the response to the question) and

---

[1] This already being done at the University of Newcastle with *The Newcastle Electronic Corpus of Tyneside English*.

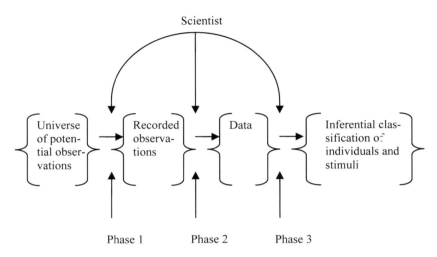

Flow diagram from the real world to inferences.
(Figure 1, from Coombs 1964: 4)

ignore others. Similarly, the linguist in attending to the tape-recording of an interview will pay attention to some details and ignore others.

For many studies of discourse, the data will consist of a transcript of a tape-recording and this is where Coombs' distinction becomes very clear. It is not unusual for linguists to refer to the tape-recording as data but that is not the way that Coombs wishes to use the term. The tape-recording only provides the basis for the data that the analyst can extract from it, and as Ochs (1979) has pointed out the choices made in preparing the transcript have significance for the inferences that can be drawn from the data.

This is very obvious in the case of transcripts produced by different investigators for different purposes, which show the features that are of interest. The conversation analysts (Sacks, Schegloff, and Jefferson 1974), for example, believe that the transcript should include a great deal of information that many analysts will prefer to ignore. They include such information as details of pausing, audible in-breaths and out-breaths, and laughter. For many analysts much of this information is irrelevant and the time involved in transcribing a whole series of interviews in this way would be enormous.

Other analysts (e.g., Coates 1996) who are interested in the dynamics of conversational exchange have chosen a format like a musical stave in which each speaker is given a single line. In this way it is easier to mark overlaps and interruptions in multi-party conversations, but it is not always easy to follow, particularly if there are several speakers engaged in animated discussion.

The conversation analysts also make extensive use of idiosyncratic **eye-dialect** to suggest a certain style of production. Linguists have generally found this unsatisfactory (Macaulay 1991b; Preston 1982, 1985) on the grounds that if details of pronunciation are to be shown it is better to use some accepted form of phonetic transcription. However, a total transcript in phonetic transcription is also impractical as was shown by Pittinger, Hockett, and Danehy (1960) in their book-length account of the first five minutes of an interview.

Transcription constitutes a particular problem for anyone dealing with a form of pronunciation that differs from the reader's, since standard English orthography can accommodate a wide variety of pronunciations. For example, the use of *r* works equally well for nonrhotic and rhotic dialects, although it is not pronounced in the former. A more restricted example, relevant to the present work, is that the spelling *gh* before *t* in a word such as *night* for speakers of most English varieties represents only a clue as to the pronunciation of the vowel *i*, but some Scots speakers retain the historical velar fricative as /nɪxt/ and the vowel is not diphthongised. The representation of vowels in English orthography has changed little since Chaucer's time, despite the widespread effects of the Great Vowel Shift. In most circumstances, this situation is not seen as problematic; readers interpret the text in terms of their own pronunciation. It becomes problematic, however, when the writer tries to suggest a dialect form that may not be familiar to the reader. This is a problem whether the speech being represented is "natural discourse" or "fictive discourse" (Smith 1978).

The difficulty of representing speech in fictive discourse is brought out very clearly by the Glasgow writer Tom Leonard:

Yi write doon a wurd, nyi sayti yirsell, that's no thi way a say it. Nif yi tryti write it doon thi way yi say it, yi end up wi thi page covered in letters stuck thigithir, nwee dots above hof thi letters, in fact yi end up wi wanna they things yi needti huv took a course in phonetics ti be able ti read. But that's no thi way a *think*, as if ad took a

course in phonetics. A doant mean that emdy that's done phonetics canny think right –
it's no a questiona right or wrong. But ifyi write down "doon" wan minute, nwrite
doon "down" the nixt, people say yir beein inconsistent. But ifyi sayti sumdy,
"Whaira yi afti?" nthey say, "Whut?" nyou say "Where are you off to?" they don't
say, "That's no whutyi said the furst time". They'll probably say sumhm like, "Doon
thi road!" anif you say, "What?" they usually say, "Down the road!" the second time–
though no always. Course, they never really say, "Doon the road!" or "Down the
road!" at all. Least they never say it the way it's spelt. Coz it *izny* spelt, when they say
it, is it? (1984: 73).

Leonard is a rare example of a poet who has succeeded in representing a nonstandard form of English effectively in his poetry
(Macaulay 1988a; 1997: 72–83). In the above extract he demonstrates
one way of dealing with elision and vowel reduction as well as nonstandard segmental features. What Leonard does in a passage like this
and in his poetry in general is to exploit the phonetic potential of normal orthography to guide the reader to an interpretation of nonstandard speech.

There is, however, in this kind of writing a great deal of what
Cole calls "code noise" that makes it more difficult to read (1986: 6).
This is not necessarily a problem in fairly short poems but in longer
works it can interfere with the reader's absorption of the text. Cole
claims that there is an implicit undertaking on the part of the writer
not to introduce such noise "without an overriding purpose". Cole and
Leonard are dealing with the representation of dialect in literary
works, but the same problem confronts the transcriber of "natural discourse".

The basis on which the transcripts in the present volume are
based were given as a set of guidelines in Macaulay 1991b: 287,
which are reproduced below:

I. A transcript should be appropriate for the specific purposes for which it is to be
used.
a. There is a difference between a transcript which is intended for the purposes of
analysis by the original researcher and one which is used to illustrate certain points in
an article to be read by people who have no access to the original.
b. The representation of particular features may be clear to those who are familiar
with the original and with the speech community in which the speech was recorded,
but the representation may be opaque to those unfamiliar with either. In the latter
case, some key to the transcription may be necessary.

c. The inclusion of a representation of features that are irrelevant for the immediate purpose may have the effect of distracting the reader's attention from the essential features.

II. The aim of any transcription is to make the reader's task a simple as possible.

a. Any feature that complicates the reader's task constitutes "noise" and should be avoided.

b. The transcription should be designed with a specific type of reader in mind, not for universal purposes.

III. It is unnecessary to indicate phonetic features which are predictable from general rules of the orthography.

a. In English it is unnecessary to indicate such features as vowel reduction, consonant-cluster simplification, and assimilation of the kind that would be "normally" employed in reading aloud a text "in conversational style".

b. Any "variant" spellings should be accompanied by a key which indicates their phonetic quality and the social significance of the variants.

IV. Indication of prosodic and paralinguistic features is best conveyed by a representation that is separate from the orthographic text.

a. Where intonation is important for a particular point, it should be shown by a representation of the contour (e.g., as in Labov and Fanshell 1977).

b. Discussion of prosodic features should include reference to the norms of interpretation in the speech community for such features.

c. Indication of paralinguistic features should be limited to those which are relevant to the point under consideration.

V. The same passage might appear in several different transcriptions, depending upon the features under consideration.

a. Any transcription can give only an indirect impression of a spoken text, and it is misleading to suggest that a complicated transcription is "more accurate" than a simple one.

b. The reader will bring certain skills to the task of interpreting an orthographic text, and the transcript should take advantage of these interpretative skills rather than disrupting them.

VI. The success of a transcription is not to be judged on how much the transcriber has managed to include but on how much the reader succeeds in getting out of it.

Obviously, many of these guidelines are controversial and do not represent the position taken by many other researchers (e.g., Chafe 1995, Edwards 1995; Dressler and Kreuz 2000; Wood and Kroger 2000) but they outline the motivation for the transcriptions used in this book. Since I am not primarily concerned with pronunciation, there will be few indications of phonetic or prosodic features, but some common phonological variants affecting lexical incidence will be shown. For example, *oot* (= *out*), *hame* (= *home*), *jeckit* (= *jacket*), and *faw* (= *fall*) can all be interpreted according to the normal rules for

English orthography. Since the digraph *gh* has other interpretations in normal orthography, the digraph *ch* is used to represent the velar fricative in words such as *nicht* (= *night*) and *bocht* (= *bought*). This should not cause problems for any reader, least of all those familiar with German (or the poetry of Robert Burns). All Scottish forms are listed in the glossary at the end of the book.

In this work, my principal focus is on patterns of language use rather than on everything that is being communicated on a particular occasion. As a consequence, I am looking mainly at aspects of language that can be reproduced in a transcript that is relatively easy to read (Macaulay 1991b; Cook 1995). In Cook's helpful metaphor, "Good map making, in linguistics as in geography, is the result of determining what to miss out rather than what to include" (Cook 1995: 45). As pointed out above, transcripts of the kind used by the conversation analysts (e.g., Sacks, Schegloff and Jefferson 1974; Atkinson and Heritage 1984) contain a large number of details that often make them difficult to read. In Cole's (1986: 6) words there is a great deal of "code noise".

This is particularly problematic when dealing with extended texts (e.g., Moerman 1988). An emphasis on what Drew and Heritage call "the interactional accomplishment of particular social activities" (1992: 17) requires attention to more than the purely linguistic aspects of the interaction. It is appropriate to focus on paralinguistic features in dealing with studies of specific instances of social interaction, though to present a comprehensive account it is probably also necessary to have some record of what is happening visually (Goodwin 1981, Kendon 1991). In the present volume, reference to paralinguistic features or non-verbal communication has been kept to a minimum, except where they are necessary for understanding particular points. The transcripts in their stripped down form ("clean text" in Sinclair's sense (1991: 21)) are a rich enough source.

Since punctuation belongs to the written language, the only punctuation marks used are question marks (to indicate questions, not intonation) and quotation marks to indicate quoted dialogue.[2] The latter are essential for clarity because quoted dialogue is an important fea-

---

[2] In Chapter Eight, the equals sign = is used to indicate **latching**, where a speaker completes a remark begun by another.

ture of oral narratives and is often signalled only by such devices as intonation or tone of voice (Macaulay 1991a: 177–203). In place of punctuation the transcript is divided into lines. There is no general agreement as to what constitutes "a line" (Gee 1999; Hymes 1996). Chafe (1994, 1995) makes a persuasive argument for basing line division on **intonation units**, but there are serious problems with this approach, since there are no simple objective measures of intonation.

Although a number of prosodic features contribute to intonation (Crystal 1969), there is general agreement that the most important factor is the perceived pitch of the speaker's voice (Brazil 1985). However, pitch is itself a perceptual phenomenon (Shapley 1989; Schuetze-Coburn, Shapley and Weber 1991), being the hearer's interpretation of fundamental frequency (F_o). The problems of tracing F_o directly are considerable (Menn and Boyce 1982; Jassem and Demenko 1986; Shapley 1989), particularly in the kind of noisy recordings made outside of the laboratory setting.

So I have not followed Chafe's example for a number of reasons. One is merely practical. As Chafe admits (1995: 61), annotating large amounts of text in this way is extremely time-consuming, and I am not sure that it would be rewarding for my purposes. But my major reason is more basic. By focusing attention on the auditory qualities of the text, the transcriber as it were asks the reader "to play the tape" in his or her head. Since most readers will not be familiar with the sound of the voices represented here, their playing of the tape would not be accurate. Moreover, it would distract their attention from the aspects of language that I wish to explore.

One of the effects of presenting the speech in lines is that "it slows down and guides the eye" (Hymes 1996: 122). My main criterion for line division is the desire to "guide the eye" and therefore line divisions in this book should not be assumed to be intonation units or marked by pauses unless this is made explicit in the text. On the occasions when prosodic or paralinguistic features are important for the understanding of the utterance a description will be given in the text. This avoids the need for the reader to master a set of typographical devices to decode this information directly from the transcript. Some of the line divisions differ from those used in earlier publications. This is in accordance with guideline II above "to make the reader's task a simple as possible". No other significance should be read into these changes.

Anyone who has attempted to make an accurate transcription of tape-recorded speech will have encountered passages that for some reason are difficult to decode. Perhaps there is some extraneous noise, there may be overlapping voices, the speaker may have turned away from the microphone or changed tempo or volume, and so on. However, even when most of the phonetic segments appear to be audible, there are occasions when a sequence is hard to interpret despite frequent rehearings. Then at some point, often at a later attempt, something "clicks" and the sense is quite clear. This presumably happens because we use our expectations and the surrounding context to help identify the linguistic units corresponding to the acoustic signal (Macaulay 1990). This can be stated as a heuristic basic working principle of transcription:

Principle One
Segment the sequence of speech into well-formed units of the language that is being spoken.

There appears to be, however, a second heuristic principle, operating unconsciously:

Principle Two
Refer to a higher level of linguistic structure only when absolutely necessary.

By "higher level of linguistic structure" I mean the kind of spatial hierarchy, shown below, in which phonetic features are "the lowest level" (Linell 1982).

pragmatic
semantic
syntactic
morphological
phonological
phonetic

Let us assume, for the purposes of this model (regardless of any psycholinguistic plausibility or the reverse), that reference to a higher level is in some sense likely to be more "costly" in processing the signal for the person trying to decode the acoustic signal on the tape. Thus, while it may be easy enough to identify a voiceless alveolar fricative [s] at the phonetic level, the identification of a voiceless stop [p] as /p/ or /b/ may require reference to a "higher" level of phonotactic rules, and an unreleased voiceless stop may be "heard" only by reference to the morphological or syntactic levels. According to the model, each of these identifications is progressively more "costly" in terms of processing effort. Let us also assume that for the sake of economy (or laziness) there is a tendency to stop at the first "acceptable" form recognised. This model would help to explain certain cases of mistranscription.

There is an example in a story told by a speaker in the Dundee Oral History Project that will be examined in the next chapter. The transcript reads: "your smell attracts you to people as well, in, in, in it didnae smell like him". This repetition of *in* would only make sense if the speaker had been going to say something where the preposition would have been appropriate and by self-repair changed to "it didnae smell like him". On listening to the tape all that can heard is a series of syllabic alveolar nasals which could be either unstressed *in* or unstressed *and*. Interpreting these nasals as *and* makes better sense of the sequence and that is how I chose to interpret them.

In another interview for the Dundee Oral History Project, Len M. talks about his father's attitude to religion. The transcription reads: "he called it the old theme o' the people" (DOHP 028/A/2: 10). The transcriber was apparently unfamiliar with the expression "opium of the people" that can actually be heard quite clearly on the tape. Another example occurs in his sister's interview when she talks about the driver of a car that had run over the ball they were playing with on the street. The transcript reads "it was a yellow car with a lovely chauffeur" whereas what she had said was "a liveried chauffeur". Presumably the transcriber was unfamiliar with the notion of a chauffeur in livery, but the choice of "lovely" was unfortunate since the point of the story was that the chauffeur had behaved badly and had shown lack of consideration for the boy whose ball he had burst by driving over it.

The point of mentioning examples like these is not to pillory the transcribers of the project tapes (they did a remarkable job) but to make a general point: if something in the transcript does not appear to make sense, it is worth going back to the tape to make sure that there is not an alternative explanation. Even then it may be hard to hear anything other than what you first transcribed. For years I played an example in class from a conversation recorded by a student of mine more than thirty years ago in a women's dormitory at Pitzer, and transcribed by the student herself. One of the speakers is talking about cooking and the transcript reads "you put corn surgeons in the flour". I asked everybody I knew what "corn surgeons" were but nobody knew. Then one year a student in the class pointed out that what the speaker had actually said was "you put in corn starch instead of flour". Of course, immediately I could hear that quite clearly although for years neither I nor numerous other students had been able to decode it accurately.

The view that everyday speech is degenerate and ungrammatical was most forcefully stated by Chomsky (1965: 58) and challenged by Labov (1972: 203). At the present time, with greater knowledge of everyday speech and a clearer understanding of the difference between writing and speaking (Linell 1982, 1998; Miller and Weinert 1998; O'Connell 1988) few people share Chomsky's negative view. As will be apparent in the many examples given in this book, when speakers are talking about themselves and their lives, they seldom make speech errors.[3] As a general rule, people speak in such a way as to be understood, and their interlocutors usually seem to understand them. In transcribing tapes we should assume that the speaker was making sense and we should be concerned if our transcript does not make equally good sense.

---

[3] In a later chapter it will be shown how repetitions and hesitations may have a rhetorical force.

Chapter Three

A Small Soap Opera

From the midst of experience, we are always formulating tentative autobiographies that more or less make order of our lives. (Morson: 1999: 307)

This is a book about verbal art, though not the kind that is studied in literature classes or performed on stage or even for a group of listeners. This is a book about the kind of verbal art speakers often use when talking to a listener about significant events in their lives or on other topics that interest them deeply. It is hardly surprising that much of the subtlety and complexity of this verbal art largely passes unnoticed in conversation since generally listeners pay more attention to *what* is being said rather than *how* it is said, unless there are special circumstances where the latter aspect is important. There are also features of this kind of mundane verbal art that even the most acute and alert listener would be unlikely to notice at the time, though they may become apparent on analysis. The easiest way to demonstrate this is by an example.

Bella K. was interviewed as part of the community-based Dundee Oral History Project.[1] The interviewer was a younger woman from the same neighbourhood. Early in World War II, at the age of eighteen, Bella K. had become pregnant by a Dutch sailor, who left soon after. Eight years later he came back to marry her. This is how in the interview she describes their first meeting after all these years:

1.
the day that I, I went down to the station to meet him, when he was coming back, I thought I'll meet him on the station because after all these years in front of your mother and that, you know, you, you wanted to, the station was your privacy, and there I went down and no he wasnae on that train and went down on the next London train, no he wasnae on that one the one about eleven o' clock in the afternoon, in the morning, and, and in the late morning the train come in, there was a lot of pushing and shoving and people coming off the trains, and I'm looking up the the platform, could-

---

[1] The tapes and transcripts of the Dundee Oral History Project are available at the Dundee Public Library and also at the School of Scottish Studies in Edinburgh.

nae see him, em I was looking for a Dutch uniform, couldnae see him and then the next thing was this navy blue suit spoke to me, you know, he says "Is that you Bella?" I never saw his face all I saw, I only saw a navy blue suit, and he took me in his arms, and I could smell soap, Sunlight Soap. [*Interviewer laughs*] That strong washing soap, you know, and it didnae smell like him, I don't know if you know, but you, your smell attracts you to people as well, in, in, in it didnae smell like him, this strong Sunlight Soap, and as the years passed, what was love just soap, I don't know. (DOHP 022/A/2: 14)

This is from the original transcript made by the project with the punctuation retained. To make it more readable, I have, however, modified some of the spelling because the transcriber uses various spellings to indicate the local Dundee pronunciation (e.g., *Eh* for *I*) and these might have made it more difficult for many readers. In my own version below, I have interpreted the three forms transcribed as *in* in the third last line as transcription errors for *and*, since the unstressed forms are almost impossible to distinguish on the tape.

Set out as in (1), this is a well-told account of the event and clearly an effective one, since the interviewer indicates her enjoyment, most notably through her laughter. But such a transcript does not help to bring out the full rhetorical force of the telling. Presenting the story in what looks like prose form makes it seem artless, partly because of the absence of the kind of devices that contribute to a successful prose style (e.g., subordination, compound noun phrases), and partly because the rhythm of speech is different from that of written prose. To bring out the difference of transcribed speech from prose, many scholars of oral performances of this kind have argued for the benefits of presenting such narratives in **lines**, though the definition of a line has varied (Labov and Waletzky 1967; Labov 1972; Hymes 1981, 1996; Tedlock 1978, 1983; Chafe 1995; Gee 1990; Fabb 2002). If, in this case, we follow Fabb's example (2002: 204) in identifying lines by finite verbs (with two exceptions), we have thirty lines. Fabb also suggests a formula for grouping these lines into what he calls "line-groups" (2002: 206). When lines form a line-group, "then they are a distinct unit of meaning" (2002: 207). Fabb's mechanical procedure will not work for this text but we can use a similar notion of grouping the lines into units that contain a separate section of the narrative. This gives the division in (2) indicated by capital letters.

2.

A) the day that I– I went down to the station to meet him	1
when he was coming back	2
B) I thought	3
I'll meet him on the station	4
C) because after all these years in front of your mother and that you know you–	
you wanted to–	5
the station was your privacy	6
D) and there I went down	7
and no he wasnae on that train	8
E) and went down on the next London train	9
no he wasnae on that one the one about eleven o' clock in the afternoon–	
in the morning	10
F) and– and in the late morning the train come in	11
there was a lot of pushing and shoving and people coming off the trains	12
G) and I'm looking up the– the platform	13
couldnae see him	14
H) em I was looking for a Dutch uniform	15
couldnae see him	16
I) and then the next thing was this navy blue suit spoke to me you know	17
he says "Is that you Bella?"	18
J) I never saw his face	19
all I saw– I only saw a navy blue suit	20
K) and he took me in his arms	21
L) and I could smell soap Sunlight Soap that strong washing soap you know	22
and it didnae smell like him	23
M) I don't know if you know	24
but you– your smell attracts you to people as well	25
N) and– and– and it didnae smell like him this strong Sunlight Soap	26
O) and as the years passed	27
what was love?	28
just soap?	29
I don't know	30

The story in this format consists of 30 lines grouped into 15 line-groups. All but three of the line-groups consist of two lines. This creates a regular pattern of two-line units leading up to the climax of the story (K) in line 21 "and he took me in his arms" which is a unit by itself. It is only at this point that we know that her husband-to-be, Dirk, has actually arrived. Prior to this line, "the navy blue suit" that spoke to Bella could simply have been an acquaintance greeting her. As listeners/readers we do not yet know whether Bella is going to be disappointed yet again. The suit and the voice have not been identified, but when Bella says "and he took me in his arms", we can have no doubt about the reference of *he*.

The other single-line unit (N), line 26, "and it didnae smell like him this strong Sunlight Soap" is the culmination of the story. We are taken into Bella's mind at this stage in the sequence of events. She has not recognised the man she came to meet. She can only assume that he is the one who has taken her in his arms, but "it didnae smell like him", so how can she be sure she is right? She then confirms that it was her long-missing sailor not by saying so explicitly but by referring to the passage of years since that day, concluding with the question "What was love?" and the unresolved answer. Thus, setting out the narrative as in (2) makes it easier to identify a structure that is less obvious in the kind of transcription given in (1). It should be pointed out, however, that there may be other structural analyses that are equally effective or more revealing, as Hymes (1996) has shown in his re-analyses of stories discussed by Gee (1991) and Labov (1972a). The essential point is that looking at the structure of narratives in this way may bring out both skill in the telling and the meaning of the story.

What can we learn from looking at the structure of this extract? What makes it a successful narrative? A narrative is not simply an account of a succession of events or actions (Quastoff and Nikolaus 1982: 22). There must be something more. Herman (2002) gives the following definition: "a sequence of actions, states, and events qualifies as a narrative by virtue of how it situates remarkable or tellable occurrences against a backdrop of stereotypical expectations about the world" (Herman 2002: 85). Herman, following some of the work in Artificial Intelligence (e.g., Mandler 1984; Schank and Abelson 1977), emphasises the amount of knowledge in the form of scripts, frames, and schemata we bring to understanding stories. For example, when Bella says that she first went down to meet Dirk and "he wasnae on that train", Bella's interviewer would have known what it is like to go to meet someone at the train station. How one stands about watching the crowd streaming off the train and sometimes waiting till everyone has got off the train, still hoping that somehow the person you have come to meet may still emerge. Bella does not need to explain any of this because it forms part of the "stereotypical expectations" the listener would bring to the story. Instead, Bella can concentrate on other parts of the story.

An important aspect of narration is the creation of suspense and Bella does this throughout the story. Until almost the end, we do not know whether her attempt to have a "private" meeting with her husband has succeeded. She begins her story by twice recounting a series of two failures followed by success, though in neither case does she immediately realise that success was finally at hand. She went down to the station twice and he did not come, but on the third he had arrived even though she did not see him. On that third occasion she looks for him twice but "couldnae see him" and then he speaks to her. Even then she "never saw his face", only "a navy blue suit". This pattern of two unsuccessful attempts followed by success at the third is common in European folklore (Hymes 1996). The suspense at this point is created through the repetition of negatives "no he wasnae on that train" (8), "no he wasnae on that one" (10); "couldnae see him" (14/16), "I never saw his face" (19). Labov (1972a: 380–387) points out the importance of negatives as evaluative devices[2]. After all, if you think of a narrative as simply telling you what happened, why would anyone want to tell you what did not happen? The negatives here help to create a sense of concern and doubt on the part of the listener: Will Bella succeed in meeting her husband at the station or will there be some other outcome?

There are other repetitions that contribute to the effective telling of the story. In line 12, there are the forms *pushing* and *shoving*, followed by *people coming off the trains*, verbs emphasising movement and providing an explanation for her failure to see him. The *navy blue suit* in line 17 is repeated in line 20, making clear by this reference that she has not yet identified the wearer of the suit. Then there are the several references to soap:

I could smell soap	(l.22)
Sunlight Soap	(l.22)
that strong washing soap	(l.22)
this strong Sunlight Soap	(l.26)
just soap?	(l.29)

---

[2] The notion of *evaluation* will be explained below.

The repetitions reinforce the change of sensation from sight to smell. When Bella goes to meet her husband she emphasises the visual: *looking* (13/15), *couldnae see* (14/16), *I never saw* (19), *I only saw* (20), then the auditory takes over when he speaks to her, and finally when he took her in his arms the sense changes to smell (22, 23, 26).

There is also a change of tense at line 13 *and I'm looking up the – the platform*. Until this point all the verbs have been in the past tense, which is the most common tense for narrative clauses. Schiffrin (1981) and Johnstone (1990: 82–83) have argued that there is an evaluative function to the use of a historical present in a narrative, while Wolfson (1982) argues that the switch between past tense and present often serves to indicate significant parts of the story. In this case, line 13 serves as the transition between the first section of the story in which her husband does not arrive and the second section in which he has arrived even though Bella does not see him. Line 15 gives an anticipatory explanation of why she did not see him *I was looking for a Dutch uniform*. The reason she did not recognise him was because he was not wearing a Dutch uniform but a navy blue suit.

What might have seemed at first glance to be an artless story turns out to be a very skilfully told tale. On the surface, it tells how Bella met Dirk, her husband-to-be, at the station after a long separation but the way of telling brings out the significance of the event. Bella had not known Dirk for long when he was stationed in Dundee early in the war. She had become pregnant with his child, who was born after Dirk had left. They had corresponded during the war and now that the war was over he told her he was coming back to marry her. Bella had endured the stigma of having an illegitimate child for eight years, and now Dirk was coming back to marry her. It is not difficult to imagine her anxieties as the day approached. Would he actually come? Would she recognise him? Would he still want to marry her when he saw her? Would she still want to marry him? On top of all this, she was living at home. She went down to the station to meet him so that she could see him alone ("the station was your privacy"). When she goes there the first two times, he is not on the train. Has he changed his mind and decided not to come? On the third occasion, he arrives but she cannot see him. When she finally gets to meet Dirk again she does not see his face at first and it does not smell like him.

After eight years, she can still remember how he used to smell. The negatives create suspense for the listener but they also reflect Bella's anxieties. She had waited a long time to find out whether this was love.

William Blake wrote of seeing the world in a grain of sand. This narrative is only a brief moment in a long interview, taking up only a paragraph in the 72-page transcript of the Dundee Oral History Project interview, only 270 words in a transcript of over 35,000 words. The story is not something that either Bella or the interviewer treats as being remarkable. It is simply part of the story of her life that Bella is recounting and she goes straight on to describe the actual wedding ceremony in comic terms. Yet this story of meeting Dirk again after eight years encapsulates in its tiny form one of the most important aspects of Bella's life. There is no indication in her account of her wartime experiences with Dirk that they contemplated getting married, though they wrote to each other during the war. Bella made jokes to interviewer about his "broken English" in the letters, and it is not clear how successful the correspondence can have been. The story in (2) is almost like a microcosm of Bella's life. Her repeated visits to the station are paralleled by her repeated unsuccessful efforts to get a job as a welder after the war. She was frustrated again and again but in the end she managed to get back to working as a welder in the shipyard.

So there she is at the station, waiting for a man she had not seen for long eight years. She will marry him and go to live in Holland in a situation that was not easy for her, since they were poor, she was unable to get a decent job, and the prevailing attitude was that the women should wait on the men. When they came back to Dundee later she was unable to get a job as a welder, although she had done well in that position in the shipyard during the war. How different would her life have been if Dirk had not come back or if she had not married him? The story in (2) ends on a question, but it is not just a question about love, it is also about Bella's life.

There is no reason to think that Bella was aware of the structure of the story in anything like the way in which I have analysed it. On the other hand, Bella is a good storyteller and she knows it. As will be apparent in later chapters, she is able to use a wide range of rhetorical devices to express herself. She would not recognise the names for these devices or analyse her own utterances in the way that I do, but she is sufficiently self-aware to know that there are ways of expressing herself effectively and that she is good at doing so.

Bella's story is an example of the kind of narratives that can occur in the genre known as **interviews** (Macaulay 2001). Perhaps because Labov has been so influential in the analysis of oral narratives, there has arisen a view that narratives in interviews are "elicited". In his specifications for what he calls the Sociolinguistic Interview (Labov 1981) sets out the procedure for eliciting what he calls Danger-of-Death narratives. His examples show how very successful he was in eliciting such narratives. Other investigators (e.g., Trudgill 1974, Macaulay 1977, and L. Milroy 1980) have found this technique to be less effective, but the general impression seems to persist that narratives in an interview have somehow been "elicited", that is, a response to the explicit instruction "tell me about it". In fact, most of the narratives that will be examined in this book arose spontaneously, much as Bella's story "emerged" as part of the account of her life. There is no need to stigmatise them as "elicited" because such stories are simply one of the ways in which people try to make sense of their lives to other people. As Linde (1993: 60) observes: "The interview is part of real life, too".

The first major sociolinguistic work on discourse was Labov's analysis of oral narratives of personal experience (Labov and Waletzky 1967), a work that continues to dominate the field. A volume celebrating the thirtieth anniversary of the paper's publication (Bamberg 1997) showed that the more than fifty celebrants had benefited from Labov and Waletzky's model but few had much to offer in the way of additions or improvements, though Labov himself has continued to refine his approach (Labov 1972a, 1984, 1997, 2003). Labov and Waletzky showed that oral narratives of personal experience had a structure that followed a similar pattern even though there were variations in the ways that speakers followed the pattern.

In the Labov/Waletzky model a narrative consists of clauses presenting some unstable situation, known as the **Complicating Action**, and clauses presenting something that happens to change this unstable situation, known as the **Result** or **Resolution**. The basic element in all narratives is the **narrative clause**. A narrative clause is one that advances the action and is normally in the past simple (or conversational present) tense, as in lines 1, 7, 8, 9, 10, 11, 14, 16, 17, 18, and 21 in (2) above. A minimal narrative consists of two clauses that are temporarily ordered, as in the child's example discussed at length by Sacks (1992):

3.
the baby cried
the mommy picked it up

As Sacks pointed out, the order of the clauses is crucial because this is a very different story from that in which the order of the clauses is reversed:

4.
the mommy picked it up
the baby cried

In Labov and Waletzky's terms, *the baby cried* in (3) is the Complicating Action and *the mommy picked it up* is the Result or Resolution. In (4) *the mommy picked it up* is the Complicating Action and *the baby cried* is the Result or Resolution. In most narratives, tension is increased by intervening material that delays the result or resolution. We bring "stereotypical expectations" (Herman 2002) even to as simple an example as (3). Sacks pointed out that we tend to assume that it is the baby's mommy that picked it up and that she did so because it had cried.

The example in (3) could only function as a complete narrative in a situation where the hearer was already in possession of a great deal of information about the participants, the location, and the time when the event occurred. Usually the narrator provides this in the course of telling the story. Labov and Waletzky label such background information **Orientation**, and clauses providing this kind of information can occur at any point in the story: at the beginning, in the middle, or (less frequently) at the end (e.g., lines 3–6 in (2) above). By providing this kind of information in an appropriate place the narrator anticipates the listener's needs and eliminates questions asking for clarification. The amount of orientation provided will of course depend upon the extent of common knowledge shared by the narrator and the recipient. For this reason, orientation clauses are likely to be more prominent in narratives told to strangers than in those told to close friends or family members.

Labov and Waletzky also stress the importance for a good narrative of what they call **Evaluation**, though a better term might be **Justification** or **Validation**. In telling a story, the speaker is placing a burden on the listener, who is obliged to pay attention until the end. In most circumstances, it would be extremely rude to walk away when someone was in the middle of a story. The reward for being a patient listener should be that the story is sufficiently interesting to justify the time spent listening to it. The notion of Evaluation is that the story should contain its own justification. If this is a story in which, for example, the narrator felt he was in a really dangerous situation, then the listener should be convinced that this was the case. One way in which to convey this information is for the narrator to say it explicitly *I thought I was going to die.* A more effective way is to have someone else in the story say *You could easily have died.* Labov and Waletzky call the first **External Evaluation** since the comment is not an integral part of the story but a comment on it; the latter they call **Internal Evaluation**, since the quoted comment comes from a participant in the story and is therefore embedded in the narrative. Another way of looking at the distinction is that External Evaluation is stated openly by the narrator, while the significance of Internal Evaluation must be inferred from the story itself. There are many other ways in which a narrator can provide Internal Evaluation in the course of telling the story by emphasising certain aspects, and these will be frequently illustrated in the examples examined in later chapters. In (2) above the evaluation is very complex but at least part of it is contained in the line "and it didnae smell like him this strong Sunlight Soap", as discussed above.

Labov and Waletzky also mention two other aspects of oral narratives that are particularly important in multi-party conversations. The first is what Labov and Waletzky call the **Abstract**. This is when a speaker announces something like *I had the strangest experience yesterday* or *the oddest thing happened to me last night*. In such cases, the listener(s) may say *tell me* and the speaker then has permission to speak for the time it takes to tell the story. In complementary fashion, the speaker has a responsibility to let the listener(s) know when the story is finished, and this is what Labov and Waletzky call the **Coda**: for example, *so I won't try that again*. After telling the story in (2) Bella's next remark is "but em that, that's the way that em" and she then goes on to talk about the wedding itself without saying anything more about the meeting at the station. I omitted this coda from (2) because it detracts from the elegance of Bella's narrative but in this remark she makes it quite clear to the interviewer that she has finished this story and is ready to go on to another.

My comment on the omission of Bella's coda from the narrative in (2) is an example of how all cited examples are in some sense "edited". Unless, the total context in which the session was recorded is given, there has to be some decision as to where to begin the extract and where to end it. Since it would be impractical to include in any text the totality of all the material recorded, any selection requires judgments as to what to include and what to leave out. Justifying these choices would often take even longer than including the complete texts, so implicit in any discourse analysis of this kind is the trust which the reader must place in the analyst to have chosen the examples as honestly as is humanly possible and not to have biased the picture too much. It is a trust which most scholars try to justify, while allowing that it may be impossible to earn that trust fully.

In the chapters that follow dealing with narratives, reference will be made to aspects of Labov and Waletzky's model, particularly the notion of evaluation, but no attempt will be made to analyse each story strictly according to their framework. One reason is that longer stories often contain episodes that need to be considered separately (Ochs and Capps 2001) or have a more complex event structure (Labov 2001b). Consequently, a more eclectic approach has advantages, but the influence of Labov and Waletzky's model and Labov's later work will be obvious throughout.

Chapter Four

The Uses of Dialogue

My concern here is the way in which discourse representations in stories typically involve coordinated exchanges between two or more participants. (Herman 2002: 173)

Interest in the structure of oral narrative (e.g., Labov 1972b; Johnstone 1990) has focused attention on situations where a speaker in telling a story reproduces the actual words someone (including the speaker) allegedly said or thought at the time. Traditionally known as *oratio recta* (in contrast to *oratio obliqua* or "reported speech"), this form of reporting "an utterance belonging to *someone else*" (Voloshinov 1986: 116, emphasis in original) has been examined as "direct speech" (Coulmas 1986), "quoted direct speech" (Macaulay 1987), and "constructed dialogue" (Tannen 1989). Li claims that "direct speech is universal; indirect speech is not" (1986: 39) and that "direct quote is the most common expression at the peak of oral narratives in many languages" (1986: 40). Tannen points that "many researchers (for example, Labov 1972b, Chafe 1982, Ochs 1979, Tannen 1982, Schiffrin 1981) have observed that narration is more vivid when speech is presented as first-person dialogue ("direct quotation") rather than third-person report ("indirect quotation") (Tannen 1986: 311).

By presenting parts of the story in a dramatic form reproducing what are purported to be the exact words used by the participants, the narrator not only makes the story more vivid but allows the listener to interpret the situation without overt direction (Voloshinov 1986; Wertsch 1991). Quoted direct speech can also convey information implicitly that it might be more awkward to express explicitly. As Goffman observes, by repeating the words said by someone else, the speaker "means to stand in a relation of reduced responsibility for what he is saying" (1974: 512). This can be important even when the narrator is quoting his or her own words. In narratives that present the teller in a favourable light where the teller may not want to give the impression of boasting, because of what Pomerantz (1978: 88–92) has called the constraint on self-praise.

Here is an example from a Glasgow working-class woman talking to another working-class woman about a conversation with her daughter.

1. (13 R, Glasgow)

That's what Diane was saying the other day	1
we were talking about it	2
she says to me "When er Susan's fifteen I'll only be thirty-two"	3
thirty-four or something like that	4
and I went "Aye and you'll be watching o'er her weans" [*children*]	5
and I said "It's the granny that watches not the great-granny"	6
she went "I'm not watching them	7
I'm not watching the weans"	8
I says "How not?	9
I'm watching her"	10
"Ah but that's different" she says	11
"I'll be that and I'll be oot and I'll be enjoying myself"	12
I says "Ah well she has a wean you'll be watching them"	13
I says "I've done my bit as granny"	14

Examples of this kind of reported conversational exchange do not normally occur with any overt indication to serve as quotation marks, like the use of expressions such as *quote/unquote* or finger gestures of the kind that sometimes occur in lectures (Goffman 1981: 161). In (1) all the examples are introduced by quotative verb such as *says*, *said*, or *went* which acts to bracket the quoted utterances, except in line 11, where the quotative verb comes in the middle of Diane's response. Thus there is never any doubt at any point in (1) as to when someone's speech is being quoted, the identity of the speaker, or the referent of the deictic *you*.

In some cases it is difficult to decide whether a sequence of words should be treated as an example of *oratio recta* or as a less direct form. Anyone who has transcribed a number of oral narratives knows that there are ambiguous utterances whose attribution to a speaker is problematic. In most cases, however, the direct speech is signalled not only by intonation but usually also by some "overt introducer" (Ferrara and Bell 1995: 265), "dialogue introducer" (Johnstone 1987), or "quotative" (Tagliamonte and Hudson 1999). The most common introducer is one of the *verba dicendi*, such as *say* though in some cases there is no introducer. The absence of an overt introducer has been termed a "zero quotative" (Mathis and Yule 1994). This can happen when one of the remarks is the second part of an "adjacency pair" (Sacks, Schegloff and Jefferson 1974) in which the asking of a question assumes that an answer (or some response) will normally follow. When one speaker is reported as saying "Can I use the phone?" it is natural to assume that the following "Yes" was uttered by the person to whom the question was asked. Quoted direct speech in this way (and many others) is consistent with what the conversation analysts have identified as normal behaviour in conversation.

The use of exophoric pronouns (i.e., a pronoun that takes its referent from the situation rather than referring back to an earlier noun phrase) is also more common in conversation than in writing. In line 10 "I'm watching her" the speaker is presumably referring to her daughter's child, Susan, present during the exchange. In line 13 the speaker produces a form that is more common in spoken than written language: "Ah well she has a wean you'll be watching them". This is a paratactic construction, equivalent to a conditional clause *if/when she has a wean*.

There is no action in this story. The speaker and her daughter are simply talking about baby-sitting. The speaker uses dialogue to reveal that her daughter does not appear to be sufficiently grateful for her mother's contribution. She could have reported this explicitly but that might have been perceived as negative criticism of her daughter. By dramatising the exchange to show the difference of attitude between her and her daughter she allows the listener to draw her own conclusion. The speaker shows herself as having been helpful to her daughter but there is a limit to her willingness to do it for her great-grandchildren: "I've done my bit as granny". By presenting it in dialogue form the narrator not only gives this information but also shows the way in which she and her daughter interact.

The narrative also shows the cultural norms that the speaker takes for granted "it's the granny that watches [the children]". There are several references in this set of conversations to the grandmother helping to look after children and the speaker expects her listener to share this knowledge. However, since her daughter is young (probably about eighteen), she does not see herself in a grandmother's role in her early thirties, though she assumes that her daughter will have a child at as young an age as she did. When that happens, she will still be young enough to "be oot and […] enjoying [her]self". Her mother, however, does not see any likelihood of cultural change coming: "she has a wean you'll be watching them". There is no suggestion in this story that looking after the grandchildren might be a pleasure and something that the grandmother would like to do, whether needed or not. *Watching the weans* is presented only as a duty to be fulfilled. There is no indication that (grand)children can be interesting or amusing. There is also no suggestion that males might be involved in looking after children.

The example in (1) thus reveals quite a lot about the speaker's values and attitudes, and by implication also her listener's, since there is no indication that the speaker believes she is saying anything unusual. Nor does the listener express surprise or disbelief at what the speaker says. Since the two participants are from the same community and similar backgrounds, it is not surprising that that they should hold similar views and this shared set of attitudes can be taken for granted. In speaking to an outsider, however, there may be a need to be more explicit.

Most performed narratives have examples of dialogue, as will be seen in many of the examples given in later chapters. Here I simply want to illustrate some of the ways in which dialogue can be used effectively. Bella K. told the interviewer how her father had responded to the news that she was pregnant by the Dutch sailor who had since left (see Chapter Three):

2. (Bella K.)
when my mother discovered that I was pregnant in the morning
at teatime when I sat down to tea where father was
and put my hand across for the jug for the milk
my father said to me "You'll be entitled to free milk now"
(*Int: Your mother had told him yeah?*)
my mother had told him you see

The gentleness with which her father referred to her unexpected pregnancy contrasts with the blunt unhelpfulness of the doctor she had gone to see who simply said "Well I think you'd better get married". On the other hand, Bella and her brother told a number of stories in which their father had been quite outspoken.

Bella also makes effective use of dialogue for a different purpose to describe her moment of triumph when, because of anti-discrimination legislation, she at last gets an opportunity to apply for a job back in the shipyard:

3. (Bella K.)
so I got the ticket from them from the bureau from the job shop
and I marched up to the shipyard
and I put in this request for work
and I'll never forget the lodgekeeper's face
he says "Is this a ticket for a job hen?"
I says "Aye"
he says "Is it for the cleaner's joab?"
I says "No no it's for the welder's joab"
and there was a slight pause and cough
"Oh well eh just just wait a meenit" see
and he goes away back
around comes the personnel officer
he didn't recognise me any more
but I recognised him from years back and
"Here's a form
you've got to fill it up
Were you a member of the boilers makers union?"

It had taken Bella many years of frustration and inferior jobs until this moment when she could apply for the kind of work she was qualified to do. "I had had to have a lower standard of living because I wasn't allowed to use the skill that they had given me. It suited them in war-time. It didn't suit them in peacetime". Now at last she could not be turned down because she was a woman. So she can savour the "slight pause and cough" as the lodgekeeper takes in the situation. The lodgekeeper's patronising attitude, addressing her as "hen" and assuming that she would only be eligible for the cleaner's job exemplifies the kind of sexism that Willis (1977/1979) found characteristic of working-class attitudes towards manual labour as uniquely male territory. This attitude is made even clearer in the situation Bella reports when she actually started work again in the shipyard.

When Bella returned to the shipyard, she was put to work in the construction shed and the man who had been doing that work was sent up to work on the boat, where the other tradesmen teased him:

4. (Bella K.)
so this man went– goes away up on the boat
and they bothered the life oot of him
"I telt you it was a lassie's joab you were on
it was a lassie's joab
a lassie was daeing your joab"
and so there was great rivalry between the different trades
"Och aye aye a bloody lassie'd dae that
a welder's joab it's aw just cissies that's on the welding"
as well you know there was a lot of banter

The welder could not have been doing "a man's job", since a woman was able to replace him.

There are many other examples that show different aspects of the working-class man's world of work. One of Willie Lang's stories describes a scene in which he had to go to help a miner who had been injured in a fall of coal.

5. (Willie Lang)
and there were another wee one doon there at Dailly
and this seam of coal it would be– oh it would be as high as this hoose here
it would be aboot nine feet
and this– he was a wee chap –eh– oh what was his name?
Jackie Tait I think you caw'd him Jackie Tait
and I think he'd been having problems at hame
his wife wasnae peying the weys sort of thing
and he'd ta'en ower the purse
so my neeghbour come
and he says "You'll have to come Willie
Jackie Tait is hurt"
so of coorse I'm away again up to this end
I'll never forget the look on his face when I went up
he was lying you see
so I row'd up his– his troosers   [*rolled up*]
"Oh" I says "Jackie, your leg's broken"
"Oh no, Willie it cannae be
it cannae be broken "
says I "Jackie your leg's broken
make no mistake aboot that"

"Oh" he says "it cannae be"
he says "this is the end of the quarter"
this was the Cooperative
"The end of the quarter as sure as I never move"
that's the words that wee man said
and I could see you know the hunted look on his face
it just couldnae be
because he'd to pey this Cooperative there at the quarter
that was a fact

This is indeed a pathetic story. The Cooperative was usually the major form of credit available to people like Jackie Tait (note how his name is repeated) and it was paid every three months. In working-class households normally the wife handled the finances but Jackie had had to take over the purse because his wife had not been paying her bills. His broken leg meant that his income would be drastically reduced and he would not be able to pay the Cooperative bill. Lang does not hesitate to tell Jackie straight out the bad news about his leg: "Jackie your leg's broken make no mistake about that". Instead of trying to comfort Jackie with false reassurances, Lang tells him the truth. As in other stories he told me, Lang says straight out what he believes to be important. In presenting the story in dramatic form with dialogue Lang manages to portray "the wee chap" whose wife "wasnae peying the weys" as someone who is not making a success of his life and who tries, even in this situation, to deny the reality "it cannae be". Implicit in this story is the notion that a man's wife should be able to deal with "the purse", that is, manage the family budget. It is the man's responsibility to bring his wages home and give them to his wife. Her role is to make the best use of this money to keep the family clothed. Jackie Tait's wife apparently could not manage this. Willie Lang implies in his story that he himself did not have this problem with his wife.

Willie Rae told a story that illustrated the expectation that a man should be able to do hard physical work to support his family.

6. (Willie Rae)

I landed at the corner and this aul yin –	[*old one*] 1
he wasnae sae auld	2
he retirt with a sore back you know a bit of a fly man	[*smart operator*] 3
just ken here this guy that was generally looking for work had been unemployed	4
and this was him starting work again	5

and the aul yin says to him "Whaur are you going?"	6
he says "I'm going to my work"	7
"Oh you got a job?"	8
"Aye"	9
"Whit are ye daeing?"	10
says "I'm labouring tae a bricklayer in the town"	11
"Oh very good away and get your bus" he says	12
he goes away for his bus	13
and – eh – this yin says to the rest of the men	14
"Imagine that yin labouring	15
he couldnae labour to a watchmaker" he says [*laughs*]	16
he wasnae much of a worker	17

Here we can see that the "aul yin", although he was "a bit of a fly man" himself, knows what the standards are for physical labour. It is, of course, Rae who is telling the story, and the standards are his, but by putting most of the story in other people's words he can convey this without having to state it openly.

The narrative in (6) is a good example of the control of dialogue by different means. Lines 6, 7, and 11 signal the direct speech by the verb *says*, but lines 8, 9, 10, and 12, each of which indicates a change of speaker, have no such introducer. As pointed out earlier, the absence of an overt introducer has been termed a "zero quotative" (Mathis and Yule 1994). However, lines 8 and 12 are signalled as change of speaker by the discourse marker *oh*, line 9 is an answer to a question, and line 10 the follow-up to the original question. The discourse marker *oh* is well-known as a turn-taking signal (Schiffrin 1987: 73–101). (There are 60 examples of *oh* in quoted dialogue in the interviews I recorded in Ayr and they all mark a change of speaker.) There is never any doubt in (6) about who is speaking and where the quoted speech begins and ends.

Andrew Sinclair told a story that concerns the times when the miners would get together in a pub and have a singsong:

7. (Andrew Sinclair)
but anyway at this time John used to be the kind of chairman in the pub room
and he was getting a singsong up
and there were a wee soldier sitting this night
and he asked the wee soldier to favour the company
and the soldier says "Oh no sir"
he says "I'm the worst singer you ever heard in your life"

well John says "Oh no sir"
he says "you're no that"
the soldier says "I am"
John says "No you are not"
he says "because you cannae be worse than I am"
and he wasnae telling a lie I can assure you
so they argued and argued a wee while like that
till at the finish up John says "I'll bet you a pint sir"
he says "you're no a worse singer than I am"
so the soldier agreed
and they tossed up a coin to see who was to sing first
so the coin turned out that John Rennie was to sing first
and John got up
and he started singing
and he'd about six words out of his mouth
and the wee soldier shouted "For Christ sake give him a pint"
well that was right you know
John knew every song that was to be sung
but he had one tune for everything

Unlike some of Sinclair's narratives, this is an economically as well as effectively told story. There is none of the long-windedness of some of Sinclair's descriptions of life down the mine. After the initial lines providing the background orientation, all the verbs are in narrative tenses. The dialogue is particularly effective with the authentic-sounding formality of the repeated remark "Oh no sir" and the soldier's conceding shout "For Christ sake give him a pint". The use of a "graphic verb" (Labov 1972b; Tannen 1986) such as *shout* as an introducer is rare in the narratives in the present collection of narratives. Also rare is the use of reported speech, as in the initiating remark "he asked the wee soldier to favour the company". *Favour the company* was a traditional formula for requesting someone to sing in such settings, but we are not told explicitly how John Rennie made the request.

Johnstone says that stories often reveal the "social and sociolinguistic norms for how to live and how to talk in the local world" (1990: 11). Sinclair's story shows how the soldier's violation of etiquette (you are supposed to agree "to favour the company" if you are sitting in on a singsong) is resolved by the wager and its outcome. It also shows how the men addressed each other. As will be seen also in later examples, the address term *sir* is used quite frequently by working-class men addressing each other. In the present example, it presumably indicates lack of familiarity rather than any attempt to express respect. Since John Rennie and the soldier reciprocate in using the term, it cannot indicate a power differential. In examples that will occur in other stories it will become apparent that *sir* can be used in a situation where the utterance indicates the reverse of respect for the addressee.

Dialogue is often used by a speaker for the purposes of self-revelation. In this way, a speaker can give an example of how he or she behaves in a particular situation leaving the hearer to draw any inferences about the speaker. Duncan Nicoll had been at one time a hotel keeper. He gave me an example of how he talked to his guests.

8. (Duncan Nicoll)
and uh this morning I was in a chatty mood
and I said "Oh hello Mr So-and-so
I forgot to mention to you that since you were here last year
we're charging extra for sunshine"
it was a beautiful morning
so he was a man of about my own build
and he looked me straight in the eye
and said "Well that's unusual and you might have mentioned it to begin with
but if it's a fair question what do you charge for the sunshine?"
and that was back to me
I had to think quickly you see
so I thought "Five pound a day"
[*pause*]
so he looked me straight in the eye
he said "That's not unreasonable Mr Nicoll
I've had twelve bloody wet days
you owe me sixty pounds" [*laughs*]
and of course what's good to give is good to g–
see this– th– this– this was the sort of bonhomie– the feeling
this is people

On the surface, this is a story about how Duncan Nicoll was beaten in an attempt at banter by "a man of about my own build". But it is really a story about how good Duncan was at talking to a wide range of people. As he said about his visits as a church elder, "you've got to be able to talk bookie, you've got to be able to talk pub, to talk everything". The example in (8) shows his pleasure in doing this even when he might appear to have lost the banter battle.

In using dialogue, narrators often dramatise the situations and act out the part of the speakers whose utterances they purport to be reproducing verbatim. This is done through intonation and other linguistic features implied to be faithful to those of the original speaker. While all examples of *oratio recta* have some features of this kind of imitation in them, there are cases where the speaker is not just trying to report what someone said but also clearly wishes to send another message by imitating the original speaker as closely as possible (*cf.* Polanyi 1982: 163).

One of the middle-class men interviewed in Ayr, Wallace Gibson, was a theatrical producer and an amateur actor, so it is not surprising that much of his use of quoted direct speech was apparently to show off his skill as an actor in directly imitating others. In relating how his teachers at school were surprised at his success as Malvolio in the school production of *Twelfth Night*, he reports them as saying "Gibson, we didn't know you had it in you". His intonation and tone of voice caught the Scottish teacher's patronising and sarcastic manner very effectively. This is polyphonic speech (Bakhtin 1973) at its richest. Gibson has managed to convey both the attitude of the teachers to the boy and the boy's (and the adult's) reaction to them. There is no need for explicit comment on either.

Gibson also uses mimicry to represent different varieties of language. In (9) he describes a visit to the house of the parents of a member of the amateur theatrical company.

9. (Wallace Gibson)

his parents– are– ah– are– em– sort of [*coughs*]	1
at least his father is a self-raised man	2
who's now very wealthy	3
his mother is a very– uh– brilliant char– mind and	4
but the father– still– speaks– sort of–	5
I was up at the house recently in Troon	6
and– eh– we were wanting to use his recording gear for something	7
and he was "<u>Oh just a minute noo</u>	8
<u>I can get the plug</u>" and so on	9
"<u>Here we are now boys</u>"	10
quite a wealthy man but he speaks like that	11

but mother *talks like that*	12
"*You know Mr Gibson*"	13
and Douglas said "**Oh it irritates me**	14
she's a nice person mother	15
but she puts on this voice"	16
he says "**I like my father better**	17
because he doesn't cover up"	18

In this passage Gibson uses four voices. (1) his own (not underlined); (2) the father's (the underlined parts of lines 8–10); the mother's (the italicised parts of lines 12–13); and (4) Douglas's (the parts of lines 14–18 in bold). Gibson's imitations of the father's and mother's speech is similar to the use of parodied sociolects found in Scottish comedians (Macaulay 1987a). It is clear that Gibson identifies with the form of speech he uses for Douglas, which lies between the affected form used by the mother and the lower status form used by the father. Later in the interview he tells of an English curate's wife visiting a miner's family in a village nearby, and he mimics both her speech and that of the family. His mimicry of Douglas's father's and the miner's speech is quite effective, but his mimicry of Douglas's mother's affected speech and the Englishwoman's is closer to parody than a realistic imitation. This use of dialogue to indicate different varieties of language would be hard to do in any other way, but it requires skill in mimicry. Few of speakers in this set of recordings employ mimicry for any purpose. There is instead, an interesting example of what might be called reversed mimicry.

Hugh Gemmill described to me his first visit to London with his daughter. They had arrived without any idea of where to stay.

10. (Hugh Gemmill)
eventually we come to a corner
and here there's addresses in this
so we're stauning looking at this   [*standing*]
when this woman came along
and said what were we looking for
and we're looking for somewhere to stay the night
"Where do you come fae?"   [*from*]
"Scotland"
"You're no feart of coming here without somewhere to stay"   [*afraid*]
so she gi'en us half a dozen addresses.   [*gave*]

It is highly unlikely that the woman whose speech is quoted was herself Scots. If she had been, the exchange would probably have included some reference to that or questions about which part of Scotland Gemmill and his daughter were from. If the woman had been Scots, that would have been a reportable fact, since it would have been a remarkable coincidence that the first person who spoke to them in London was herself Scots. It is even more unlikely that anyone not from Scotland would say *Where do you come fae* and *you're no feart*. In this case it seems obvious that Gemmill is reporting informal speech in the form that is normal for him and not for the speaker to whom the remarks are attributed. This is the mirror image of mimicry. For Gemmill to present the speech of the London woman in an appropriate form he would have to abandon his normal form of speech. Since this was the first time he had been in England it is not clear how successful he would have been if he had tried to imitate her. One possible reason is that, unlike the cases of mimicry, the woman's form of speech is not integral to the story. On the contrary, it is her friendly behaviour to two strangers that is important. An attempt by Gemmill to imitate her form of speech might have implied a critical attitude to that kind of speech or appeared to mock her. Instead, Gemmill employs the most neutral form of speech, his own, regardless of the realism of the quoted speech. It is interesting that in the fifth line Gemmill uses a form of free indirect speech in reporting the woman's first question *what were we looking for*, as this avoids the problem of the woman's own voice.

Finally, as everyone knows, dialogue is often employed in telling jokes. Leslie Simpson told a story about someone he knew travelling in a tramcar. When the woman sitting next to him got up her umbrella was caught in the loop of the belt on his coat and pulled it off. Simpson reports the following exchange between them:

11. (Leslie Simpson)
she says "I'm frightfully sorry
have I done any damage?"
he looks at [...]
"No no" he says "it's quite all right
you've only broke the loup [laup]"

The point of the story is to poke fun at his friend's hypercorrection of *loop* [lup] to *loup* [laup] (Macaulay 1987a), presumably on the analogy of "correcting" pronunciations such as *doon* and *oot* to *down* and *out* when speaking to a certain class of person. The woman's "superior" status is indicated by her use of the adverb *frightfully*. This adverb is frequently used in working-class parodies of upper-class speech. Thus Simpson does not have to say anything about the social class of the woman; her remark reveals it.

The examples in this chapter have shown various ways in which speakers use dialogue: to convey information indirectly, to illustrate someone's personality, to dramatise a significant event, to exemplify cultural values, to report an amusing incident, to reveal one's own personality, to parody the speech of others, and as a feature of joke-telling. Examples in later chapters will give additional evidence of these uses, but the important point is that the use of dialogue in conversation is extremely common and is not restricted to accounts of highly dramatic events. Dialogue is one of the economical devices that speakers make use of that preclude the need for lengthy descriptions or explanations.

Chapter Five

The Significance of Stories

Narration, as the unity of story, story-teller, audience, and protagonist, is what constitutes the community, its activities, and its coherence in the first place. (Carr 1986: 128)

People tell stories for a variety of reasons, depending upon the situation and those who are present. Many accounts of story-telling examine stories that arise in conversation among friends or family. In such cases, the motivation for telling the story may be that it is part of the day's news (Blum-Kulka 1997; Ochs and Capps 2001) or as an anecdote to illustrate a point (Eggins and Slade 1997). The stories that I will examine in this chapter come from interviews that I recorded in Ayr (Macaulay 1991a). Stories told to a stranger are likely to differ from those told to acquaintances or family because less background knowledge can be taken for granted. As a result, stories told to strangers tend to be longer and include more background information. This creates a problem in presenting an analysis of the structure of the stories, as Tabakowska (1999) points out:

It involves a dilemma only too well-known to text linguists: discussing a text in its entirety (which is the only methodologically sound procedure) carries the risk of making the discussion so long as to reduce the audience to tears of boredom. On the other hand, cutting the illustrative material to reasonable proportions necessarily involves tampering with the text, which in turn must mean distortion. (Tabakowska 1999: 411)

The stories that I will deal with here are presented uncut despite their length, but I hope this will not produce too many tears of boredom.

The events that can be reported in good narratives need not be particularly dramatic or exciting in themselves. What is important is that it should be an occasion that remains memorable for some reason. One of the important aspects of life for most people is working and many people have a clear recollection of their first entry into the world of work (Linde 1993, 1996). Often stories about a first job would appear banal and even trivial in summary but in their narrated form take on a dramatic character that brings out the significance for the speaker. This dramatic character does not inhere in the story itself but is a consequence of the linguistic devices used to create those effects.

Barbara Johnstone in her account of "narratives from Middle America" points out that "we use narrative to structure our experience of the past and give it meaning" (1990: 5). In telling about some important part of our past life we do not simply relate what happened; we also present the event in such a way that its wider significance is brought out.

I interviewed Andrew Sinclair, an ex-coal miner, in 1978 as part of the Ayr study (Macaulay 1985, 1991a). He had warned me when I was setting up the interview that he would not "sound as broad" talking to me as he would talking to other people (Macaulay 1991a: 249) and his interview confirmed this because of the direct comparison with the language used in interviews with two men from very similar backgrounds and with similar experience as coal miners (Macaulay 1991a: 250). Sinclair, however, had spent several years in the Merchant Navy as a young man during World War II and this would have given him the experience of talking with a wide range of people speaking different varieties of English.

Sinclair was an ex-coal miner when I interviewed him in Ayr, but it was clear from his account that he was proud to have been a miner. The story that follows deals with his first job and came in response to my question: "What did you do when you left school – you'd be fourteen when you left?"

1. (Andrew Sinclair, Ayr)

yes eh fourteen when I left school	1
in fact I was–	2
I left school–	3
you know how school closes down in June– the end of June	4
well I wasnae fourteen until the August	5
and the same day as I left school	6
we used to go up to a farm	7
it's still there yet on the other side of the by-pass	8
but at that time eh you used to go to the farm for milk et cetera and that	9
I mean as one of thirteen of a family eh	10
and I'm one of the oldest ones	11
well there were four– two boys and two girls older than me	12
but eh I mean things was pretty tight and that	13

and eh it used to be a regular thing	14
you were sent up to the farm many a time for a pennysworth and tuppenceworth of skimmed milk	15
I mean you got the skimmed milk cheaper than the ordinary milk and one thing and another	16
and the same day as the school closed	17
I went up to the farm that night for– to get milk	18
and eh we often got what they caw'd the buttermilk	19
eh for baking et cetera and that there	20
and eh when I was waiting on the milk eh	21
the farmer came oot	22
and he says "That you left the school noo Andrew?"	23
says I "It is"	24
he says "You'll be lucking for a job"	25
says I "Aye"	26
he says "How would like to stert here?"	27
well I would have liked to have started at the farm	28
I did like farm work	29
because as a boy for years before that I used to run aboot the farms	30
there was Thornyflat there	31
there was Fulshawwood and the Sanquars	32
that was aw just roond aboot here	33
used to be an awful lot of potatoes et cetera and everything grown in this area at that time	34
and at the harvest time and that you went aboot them all periodically	35
I mean you knew most of the farmers' sons	36
them that had sons and that	37
that were at school with you and all that	38
and the cotmen's sons and that	39
and you run aboot with them aw	40
and we used to run aboot the farms	41
and it was great you know	42
you'd sit up in the cairt driving the horse	43
going to the station with the tatties et cetera	44
and then sitting on the tap of the long cairt	45
when they were cairting in the hervest	46
and aw these different things eh and that	47
I mean I liked farm work and that	48
and eh I said I would like it fine anyway and	49
"Well" he says "think and ask your mother" you see eh	50
"see what they say at it and tell her" he says "you've fifteen shillings a week"	51
so I went hame with the milk	52
and I told my mother and faither what was said and that	53
and they said "Well if you want to start there you can start"	54
so I sterted work on the farm the next day eh and that	55

that was me	56
I enjoyed it	57
I worked there for quite a while	58
to I got my hand poisoned here [*shows hand*] at the harvest time	59
and eh as I say I didnae really know much aboot it at the time	60
but there was a wee bit kinda dispute between–	61
for compensation et cetera between the farmer and that you know	62
and whatever happened I never ever was back working at the farm	63

It is clear that in response to my question Sinclair could have answered simply that he had worked on a farm for a time as a boy before he went into the mine. However, he provides a great deal more information about his background: In fact, the actual narrative itself is contained in only a quarter of the lines, as can be seen in (2).

2.

and the same day as the school closed	17
I went up to the farm that night for– to get milk	18
and eh when I was waiting on the milk eh	21
the farmer came oot	22
and he says "That you left the school noo Andrew?"	23
says I "It is"	24
he says "You'll be lucking for a job"	25
says I "Aye"	26
he says "How would like to stert here?"	27
and eh I said I would like it fine anyway and	49
"Well" he says "think and ask your mother" you see eh	50
"see what they say at it and tell her" he says "you've fifteen shillings a week"	51
so I went hame with the milk	52
and I told my mother and faither what was said and that	53
and they said "Well if you want to start there you can start"	54
so I sterted work on the farm the next day eh and that	55

Even in its stripped down form this is still a tellable story and contains the essential events: (1) Sinclair goes up to the farm; (2) the farmer asks him if he would like a job; (3) Sinclair says he would; (4) his parents give their approval; (5) he starts work at the farm. If this was all Sinclair wanted to tell me, he could have summarised it much more succinctly, but he includes many more details, and rather than detracting from the narrative they add significance.

Many of the details are background information, some of which he might have expected me to be familiar with since I had grown up only about twenty miles away and was about the same age as Sinclair. Nevertheless, he makes sure that I understand the setting clearly. It will be obvious that he likes to get things exactly right. When I said that he would be fourteen when he left school, he corrected me to make sure that I understood he was not quite fourteen when he left. The importance of this becomes apparent as the story unfolds. He also is at pains to tell me his position in the family, fifth eldest of thirteen, the ways in which a poor family managed when things were "pretty tight" by getting cheaper, skimmed milk direct from the farm, and the names of the farms nearby. People do not tell stories for no reason at all. As Fleischman (2001) observes:

Narratologists who have studied (nonfictional) narrative are keenly aware that what storytellers provide is not a verbal icon of a pre-existing structure of real-world experience. Rather, they cull from, and configure, the experiential database from which the story is constructed, notably in ways that support "the point" they wish to make in telling the story. (Fleischman 2001: 480)

Sinclair could easily have answered my question by saying something like "I worked on a farm for a while before going into the pits", so there was presumably some "point" in giving such a long and detailed account of his first job. It became clear later in the interview that, by his own account, Sinclair had had a reputation as a good worker as a miner. This story of his first job shows that even as boy of less than fourteen the farmer recognised his ability and offered him a job before he even asked. The conclusion to the story shows that he lost the job, not through any fault of his own but because of a dispute between his parents and the farmer over compensation for his injury.

When he says that he was not even fourteen when he left school, he is drawing attention to something that makes it seem even more remarkable that he was offered the job, although in fact a few weeks' difference in age would not have been important. When he says that it was "the very same day" that he left school, he is emphasising how he did not even have time to think about looking for a job and suggests that the farmer was anxious to get in first with his offer. He makes it clear that he was one of a large family by mentioning the number of children so it is understandable that money was scarce. This meant that getting a job was important for his family.

Sinclair reinforces the notion of his worth as a boy by the dialogue he uses to report the farmer's offer. There is no reason to believe that, more than forty years after the event, he remembers the exact words the farmer used. Tannen (1987) has pointed out that all quoted dialogue is "constructed", in the sense that the narrator has chosen to report it in this way. The important point here is that Sinclair reports the farmer treating him with respect, more or less as an adult.

In speaking to Sinclair, the farmer does not use the tone of an adult speaking to a child but a form of speech closer to the polite way one adult might enquire of another ("You'll be looking for a job", "How would you like to start here?"). Indirection of this kind is an example of "positive politeness" (Brown and Levinson 1987). The rest of the farmer's remarks are equally designed to preserve the boy's face. By suggesting that Sinclair should "think and ask your mother" the farmer is recognising the boy's right to consider the offer before telling his parents. It is, of course, Sinclair's mother who would get the fifteen shillings so she is the one who has to be told how much he will get. Sinclair's parents also speak very politely to their son: "Well if you want to start there you can start".

Sinclair tells his story with deliberate "slow disclosure", delaying the response to the farmer's question by the long aside about farm work. Between the farmer's question in line 27 and Sinclair's response ("I said I would like it fine") in line 49 there is a long "suspension of the action" (Labov 1972: 374) but Sinclair does not lose the place and continues the dramatic action as if there had been no interruption. The section that constitutes the long aside also includes the liveliest part of the narrative in which Sinclair explains why he liked farm work:

3.

and it was great you know	42
you'd sit up in the cairt driving the horse	43
going to the station with the tatties et cetera	44
and then sitting on the tap of the long cairt	45
when they were cairting in the harvest	46
and aw these different things eh and that	47

In his tone of enthusiasm Sinclair is at his "broadest" in this passage with forms such as *cairt, tap*, and *hervest*, in contrast to, for example, *harvest* in lines 35 and 59. This section is also marked by greater speed and more variation in the tone of voice. Dramatically, this is Sinclair "thinking it over" even before instructed to do so. This is the strongest example in the story of what Waletzky and Labov call Internal Evaluation. Sinclair is showing that he did not want the job simply because it was a way of making money or because he had to find a job when he left school; he wanted this job because he liked the idea of farm work. This is a theme that recurs in many of the recorded materials, as will be demonstrated in later chapters. Almost regardless of the money earned, the important thing for a worker is to have some kind of job satisfaction. Sinclair would have been happy to continue working on the farm, but he had to leave because of "wee bit kinda dispute" over compensation for an injury. He later found great satisfaction and pride in being a coal miner.

Sinclair's narrative is not a piece of imaginative fiction but (purportedly) a true story. The details of his family background help to make clear the necessity for him to find work as soon as he left school. Later in the interview Sinclair was to make it clear to me that he had had a good reputation as a coal miner. This story, told right at the beginning of the interview, brings out very clearly that even before he had reached the official minimum school-leaving age ("I wasnae fourteen until the August") the farmer recognised his potential as a worker by offering him a job before he had to ask. Sinclair's story about his first job is a success story. He got offered the kind of job he wanted without having to go out and look for one, he enjoyed it, and he did not lose it through any fault of his own.

It is remarkable that Sinclair should have produced such an effective narrative since the plot is so simple. What makes it "tellable" is the message it conveys that he was the kind of boy who at an early age showed the kind of promise that Sinclair was later to achieve in his work as a miner. Part of the success of the narrative lies in the self-effacing way in which Sinclair allows this impression to emerge. Many narratives about early experiences of this kind contain more dramatic episodes illustrating a significant event in the speaker's life.

Ella Laidlaw's story of her first job is a very different kind of narrative from Sinclair's. It is a long story so I have divided the transcript into five sections for ease of reference.

4. (Ella Laidlaw, Ayr)

A

oh I went to the carpet works	1
oh I forgot aboot that wee bit – three weeks	2
I went into the carpet works	3
my mother had been in it aw her days	4
and she got me a job to start in Gray's factory	5
oh I thought this was great	6
I was going to get money among my fingers	7
I was going to get my pay	8
and I went	9
and she got me into one of the nicest	10
what she termed the nicest parts of the carpet works Gray's	11
it's closed noo	12
the finishing room	13
so– in the other places	14
the weft shed	15
the kiddering department	16
the dyehoose	17
and aw these places	18
they were wild	19
the women were	20
they werenae wild	21
they were workers	22
but they worked like men	24
and they swore like men	24
so she got me into the place	25
she thought I'd be safe in	26
the finishing room	27

B

I goes in	28
and a wee woman with the name of old Maggie Jamieson took me to	
this machine	29
and she showed me what to dae	30
well these two young women –	31
they're baith living yet	32
they had pointed nails	33
well I never had seen pointed nails and painted nails	34
my mother didn't alloo these things	35
oh and I fair admired their nails and their make-up you see	36

·

and what they did was they finished a carpet off   37
they rolled it over the table   38
and there were a thread ran up the middle   39
coming off the loom you know   40
and they had that to pick oot   41
so they sent me to help them   42
wee Maggie Jamieson says to me   43
"When you're no busy on your wee machine   44
you go and help them to pick oot this white thread"   45

C
well I went   46
Dorothy Mackenzie   47
that was one of their names and Jean Quinlan   48
Dorothy Mackenzie says "Come on wee yin   49
get your skates on   50
you're too slow"   51
I says "I'm just learning"   52
"Don't cheek us back" she says   53
"or I'll break your neck"   54
so that was the first threat   55
so I pu'd this carpet   56
and in pulling this carpet   57
she must have had her hands on the roller   58
and I pulled the carpet   59
and it bent her nail back   60
well the oaths – was a guinea a box   61
I couldnae repeat them   62
and I just stood and looked at her   63
"Get yourself to hell" she says   64
"oot of my road" she says   65
"before I–"   66
oh and of coorse one word borrowt another   67
I went to the wee machine where I was fringing the rugs   68
putting the –   69
see these rugs?   70
well we were putting fringes on some of them   71

D
I stuck it for a fortnight   72
and here this day   73
oh Dorothy Mackenzie had really been   74
I think they'd been oot the night before   75
and had a night oot   76
and had a hangover   77
and she really went to town on me   78

she caw'd me for everything	79
I was everything but a human being that day	80
and I went up to my mother	81
my mother worked in the dyehoose then	82
and I says–	83
on the drying machine–	84
and I says to her "I'm no going back in there"	85
she says "How are you no going back in ?"	86
I says "I'm no going back in	87
You should hear the swears of them in there"	88
she says "They don't swear in the finishing room"	89
I says "Do they no?	90
You want to come and hear them"	91
so there were a big wuman worked with her	92
she was an Italian girl – Ina Solotti	93
and Ina Solotti says "Who said the feenishing room didnae swear Mary?"	94
my mother says "Me"	95
"Well" she says "we've nothing on them	96
away you go and listen to them at their door" she says	97
"and you'll get the shock of your life	98
Who was swearing at you hen?" she says	99
and she was a great big wuman	100
she was aboot eighteen stone	101
I says "Dorothy Mackenzie and Jean Quinlan"	102
"Ah well" she says "I'll go oot to them"	103
so on goes the cap again	104
and away she crosses the yaird	105
and what she gied these two lasses was naebody's business	106

E	
but I went out that Friday	107
and then I wouldnae go back	108
that was my first job	109

There are five episodes (Ochs and Capps 2001) in this story. In the first section (A), Ella carefully sets the scene, particularly the reference to the actual place where she would be working. The second section (B) introduces the setting for the action and the principal characters. The third section (C) describes the problems Ella had with her fellow workers. The fourth section (D) provides the resolution, and the final section (E) the conclusion.

In telling her story, Ella prepares the way for later events by making reference to elements that might appear to be irrelevant at the time but later they will turn out to be important, a technique known as *foreshadowing* (Ochs and Capps 2001). In section (A) she explains how her mother got her a job in the carpet factory, but having worked at the factory for a long time and knowing that the women could be coarse and ill-spoken, had chosen the finishing room as the safest place for her daughter. In section (B) she mentions the "pointed nails" of the two young women she would be working with. The third section (C) presents the refutation of Ella's mother's view that this was "one of the nicest parts" of the carpet factory and an illustration of Ella's statement that the women "swore like men" since "the oaths was a guinea a box" and "one word borrowt another". Ella goes back to her "wee machine" which was her primary responsibility.

The fourth section (D) provides the resolution and the main point of the story in the form of Ina Solotti's remarks:

5.

"Who said the feenishing room didnae swear Mary?"	94
my mother says "Me"	95
"Well" she says "we've nothing on them	96
away you go and listen to them at their door" she says	96
"and you'll get the shock of your life"	98

Not only do the women in the finishing room swear but they would give Ella's mother "the shock of [her] life" even though Ina Solotti confirms, as Ella had indicated earlier, that some swearing occurred in the dyehouse ("we've nothing on them"). Ina Solotti is introduced as "a big wuman" (line 92) but later referred to as "a great big wuman" (line 100), so she is a formidable person to give "these two lasses" a suitable reprimand.

The final section (E) marks the end of the story but it also contains the important statement "I wouldnae go back". Implicit in the "wouldnae" is the implication that her mother wanted her to continue despite the swearing but Ella in this case asserts her independence of her mother. It is clear that it is not just the swearing but the way she is spoken to that upsets Ella. The style of the narrative is very direct. Once she has set the scene and prepared for the climax she goes through the story with very little qualification.

Almost all the clauses in sections (C) and (D) are action clauses or quoted dialogue. She does not need to amplify her description because she has provided in advance the information that is needed: her mother's view that the finishing room was the best place in the factory for Ella, the attitude of the young women to Ella, and the important feature of their pointed and painted nails. The drama is allowed to unfold without interruption.

As was illustrated by some of the speakers in the previous chapter, Ella creates the dramatic effect mainly through extensive use of quoted dialogue (Tannen 1989; Macaulay 1987; 1991a: 177–203). Johnstone (1990: 78) points out that dialogue of this kind is the way narrators manipulate what Goffman (1981) calls "footing" in relation to the other characters in the story and also in relation to the audience. By reporting what they say, Ella conveys the different characters and their attitude to her and to each other. First there is wee Maggie Jamieson who showed Ella "what to dae".

6.

"When you're no busy on your wee machine   44
you go and help them to pick oot this white thread"   45

The tone is gentle and friendly, ("wee machine", "go and help them") unlike that of Dorothy Mackenzie:

7.

"Come on wee yin   49
get your skates on   50
you're too slow"   51

The epithet "wee yin" is not affectionate in this case but derogatory, "get your skates on" is always used as a complaint about unnecessary delay, and this is made explicit in "you're too slow". This is the kind of unmitigated face-threatening speech that Brown and Levinson (1987) call "bald-on-record". Ella's response although accurate enough is not deemed to be conciliatory enough and is treated as impudence by Dorothy Mackenzie:

8.

I says "I'm just learning"   52

"Don't cheek us back" she says   53
"or I'll break your neck"   54

Although she does not swear on this occasion, Dorothy Mackenzie's threat can hardly be considered "nice". However, when "the oaths was a guinea a box" (and unrepeatable, at least in the context of the interview) Ella did not attempt to respond, though her silence was probably just as provocative:

9.
and I just stood and looked at her   63
"Get yourself to hell" she says   64
"oot of my road" she says   65
"before I–"   66
oh and of coorse one word borrowt another   67

Ella again does not attempt to repeat any of the profane language used and at the climax simply summarises the content:

10.
she caw'd me for everything   79
I was everything but a human being that day   80

Here is why swearing is not "nice". As Hughes 1991 has pointed out in his historical account of profanity, there has been a progression from swearing BY and swearing THAT to swearing AT. Ella makes it clear that she felt being sworn at meant that she was being treated as less than human.

Swearing is not the only use of language that is important in this story. The exchange between Ella and her mother suggests the kind of relationship they had:

11.
and I says to her "I'm no going back in there"   85
she says "How are you no going back in ?"   86
I says "I'm no going back in   87
You should hear the swears of them in there"   88
she says "They don't swear in the finishing room"   89
I says "Do they no?   90
You want to come and hear them"   91

Instead of sympathizing with her daughter, Ella's mother simply challenges the claim. However, Ella's mother does not attempt to contradict Ina Solotti, the "great big wuman":

12.

and Ina Solotti says "Who said the feenishing room didnae swear Mary?"	94
my mother says "Me"	95
"Well" she says "we've nothing on them	96
away you go and listen to them at their door" she says	97
"and you'll get the shock of your life	98

It is Ina Solotti who shows sympathy, addressing Ella as "hen", a term of affection here, and it is Ina Solotti not Ella's mother who "goes oot to them".

13.

Who was swearing at you hen?" she says	99
and she was a great big wuman	100
she was aboot eighteen stone	101
I says "Dorothy Mackenzie and Jean Quinlan"	102
"Ah well" she says "I'll go oot to them"	103

Once again the major invective is not quoted but only summarised: "what she gied these two lasses was naebody's business". By the use of dialogue Ella has not only brought out the differences in character of Maggie Jamieson, Dorothy Mackenzie, Jean Quinlan, Ina Solotti, and her mother, she has also made a point about the proper use of language. In particular it shows Ella's view of how her mother ought to behave by showing what Ina Solotti actually does.

Although the story is about Ella's first job, the "point" of the story is about how her mother was not always right. At the very beginning of the interview Ella had told me that she was illegitimate, because her father had been a French-Canadian and Roman Catholic and as Ella remarked "mixed marriages didn't take place then". It was probably important for Ella to tell me this right at the beginning because she believed that her illegitimacy had made her mother much more strict with her than she might otherwise have been. Elsewhere in the interview Ella told me several stories about how she had got into trouble as a child but in the story about her first job she makes it clear that, in spite of her independent character, her mother wanted to protect her from the wild women of the carpet works. Ella first starts to say that her mother had got her into "one of the nicest" places in the factory, then qualifies it by saying it was what her mother "*termed* the nicest" (cancelling the presupposition that it *was* the nicest). Ella marks the end of section (A) by the use of the connective *so*. She has described the wildness of the women elsewhere in the factory to explain that her mother's choice was a deliberate decision, not an accidental or arbitrary result:

14.

so she got me into the place	25
she thought I'd be safe in	26
the finishing room	27

Whatever happened was thus going to be Ella's mother's responsibility.

Ella's story is not about some event in her life that she immediately recalls as being remarkable ("I forgot aboot that wee bit – three weeks") but in telling it she creates a dramatic performance that makes a tellable story out of it. She also conveys not only a vivid sense of her relationship with her mother but also the kind of values that prevail in the community. As Johnstone observes the plot of a story "is a conventional way of organizing memories so that culturally relevant lessons or illustrations can be learned from them" (1990: 34). In this story Ella shows that she did not want to be subjected to abusive and offensive language at work. In Johnstone's words: "Men and women tell stories that show how men and women act, in terms of how men and women ought to act" (1990: 89). As will be shown in Chapter Ten, Ella Laidlaw is not the only worker who objects to being spoken to in disrespectful terms.

The world of the carpet factory was a harsh one and even in the finishing room that Ella's mother thought was "one of the nicest parts" the women swore "like men". The young women see nothing wrong in swearing at Ella when they are not pleased with what she has done. Like men, the young women also go out drinking and suffer from the after effects. It is the older women, "old Maggie Jamieson" and the Italian Ina Solotti, who treat the young girl more considerately. Ella's mother, however, despite her concern to get Ella into "one of the nicest parts" does not seem to think there was much wrong with the situation, since she presumably wanted Ella to continue ("but I wouldnae go back"). This event was clearly what Bruner (2001) calls "a turning point" in Ella Laidlaw's life. She had been brought up strictly (perhaps harshly) by her mother, but she told me "I never kicked against the traces". This episode in the carpet factory may have been the first time that she actually stood up to her mother and went against her wishes.

Ella Laidlaw's and Andrew Sinclair's stories are on the same topic, first job, but they also have a similar theme, how to speak to young people. Ella Laidlaw "wouldnae go back" because of the way the wild women spoke to her; Andrew Sinclair, who was treated with respect, "enjoyed it" and left only because of the dispute between the farmer and his parents over compensation for an injury. Both stories illustrate the importance of "voice" in the community (Bakhtin 1981), Andrew's a positive example and Ella's a negative one.

As will be shown repeatedly in Chapter Ten, many people report situations in which they felt that they had been spoken to in inappropriate terms, and in some cases they reacted strongly to the perceived lack of respect. Ella Laidlaw's story is an example. Based on the account Ella gives, the young women had not treated her badly other than to call her names, and Ella admitted that they had legitimate cause for complaint since she was not as quick as they wanted her to be. Another girl of Ella's age might just have ignored the abuse and carried on. However, Ella, perhaps because of her strict upbringing, finds the situation unbearable. Rather than accept a situation where women worked like men and swore like men, Ella preferred to go "into domestic service".

It is not only the working-class speakers who tell stories about being spoken to inappropriately. Here is a middle-class speaker telling me about a job interview, though it was not a first job. When I was interviewing him in Ayr (Macaulay 1991), Duncan Nicoll told me how he had been interviewed for a position at a small local museum. He had already been told by a mutual friend that he was the leading candidate ("Now the job's yours if you would like it"), so this may have affected his attitude during the interview. He had been told to bring his wife and explained that "we were interviewed by the Lord Lieutenant, who is the Queen's representative in the district you see, he's the chairman of the Trustees". Elsewhere Nicoll makes it quite clear that the chairman was a member of the upper classes. After some preliminary questions, the chairman asks the question in line 1:

15. (Duncan Nicoll)

"What do you know about manuscripts?"	1
and I says "Nothing"	2
he says "Well you've got to have a knowledge of manuscripts"	3
I says "Well I don't know"	4
he says "But possibly Mr Hamilton"	5
that's my boss-man – my English boss	6
"He could maybe help you"	7
I says "Oh"	8
I says "We'll find out that all right"	9
he says "The other thing is that when you've an assistant"	10
whom you've seen wandering about this morning	11
"when he's off you've got to do the toilets"	12
and I said "Well that wouldn't worry me one bit	13
I've done toilets in the hotel business	14
when somebody didn't come in	15
somebody was sick or something	16
and you go and clean them up"	17
I says "That wouldn't worry me"	18
but I said to myself I says "Now chum if you're wanting a man	19
what does toilets and the car park and a man what does manuscripts you want two men"	20
now I'm just– I didn't say it to him– but I said "I'm big enough to be the two men"	21
it was a two-man job you see	22
tha– tha– that a librarian who's knowledgeable in manuscripts is not going to do toilets you know	23
and I'll come to the toilet story in a minute	24
however the outcome was we got appointed	25
and we've been here two and a half years	26

This is a story told almost completely in dialogue, as is fitting for an account of an interview. There was no suspense for me as the listener since I knew that Nicoll had been appointed to the job, but the way that he tells it brings out his concern that he might not meet the chairman's expectations. He admits that he knows nothing about manuscripts and that might have been a disqualification, but he has no problem in showing that he is prepared to deal with the toilets when necessary. It is interesting, however, in a narrative presented mainly in dialogue, that the key clauses for evaluation (19–20) report something that Nicoll did *not* say.

At the time that I interviewed him, Nicoll was 67. At that age he probably felt that he should have been able to live comfortably in retirement, but for variety of reasons his earlier life had been less successful than it might have been and he was apparently still working because he needed the money. There was absolutely no doubt that he enjoyed his work but at the same time he gave many signals that he felt the job was a little below what he should have been doing. This was clear when he explained that he might have to interrupt the session suddenly because of his "boss-man". (I was interviewing him at the museum on a Sunday morning.)

16.

and this is the man that's coming for his money at twenty minutes to ten	1
and he'll not come in	2
he just stops the car there	3
and I have to run out like helter-skelter	4
but it's all right	5
I don't mind	6
he's going to church	7
and he wants it in the bank first	8
and it's always the last minute	9
so if I suddenly rise and leave you	10
that's the reason	11

Of course, it is not true that he does not mind. Why does the boss-man have to come "always the last minute" so that Nicoll has "to run out like helter-skelter"? Nicoll has been in positions where he has been the "boss-man" and it is hard that he should now be subjected to this kind of inconsiderate treatment at his age. His account of his job interview in (15) gives a very good indication of his attitude towards those who consider themselves to be his superior.

The chairman is willing to brush off Nicoll's admission that he knows "nothing" about manuscripts although "you've got to have a knowledge of manuscripts" because "possibly" Mr Hamilton could help him. Equally crucial seems to be the problem that when the assistant is off "you've got to do the toilets". This juxtaposing of the two tasks suggests that for the chairman they were of equal importance (and that both were beneath the kind of activities that the chairman considered worthy of his attention). Nicoll's internal response to this is very revealing. He says to himself:

17.

"Now chum if you're wanting a man   19
what does toilets and the car park and a man what does manuscripts you want two
    men"   20

There are two very interesting features in this unvoiced remark. The first is the address term *chum*. Nicoll would not have used this word in addressing the chairman and if he had used it, the interview would probably have terminated immediately and Nicoll would not have been appointed[1]. It is also probably not a term Nicoll would have used at any time talking to an actual interlocutor. It is used here as a deliberate mental insult to someone Nicoll felt (probably justifiably) was patronising him. The other feature is the use of the relative marker *what*. This is not a form that Nicoll uses as part of his normal speech. He is using it as a class-based form that if he *had* used it in his interview would probably have led to the chairman downgrading him as someone who used nonstandard language. Nicoll is not a nonstandard speaker, though he has been in contact enough with nonstandard speakers to be able to mimic their speech for dramatic purposes. He reports his thoughts in this form as a way of indicating that he was not overawed by the presence of the chairman with his (no doubt) RP accent and commanding tone of voice.

At the same time, Nicoll makes it clear that he is not intimidated by the challenge either: "I'm big enough to be the two men". Since he "got appointed" and had "been here two and a half years", presumably

---

[1] Elsewhere he remarks of the chairman:
whom I know as "Good morning sir" or "Good afternoon sir"
he calls me Duncan
but that's neither here nor there
I wouldn't dare call him by his Christian name
I feel he's somebody above me
maybe not

he was big enough. He was also big enough to put up with the demands of his "boss-man – my English boss". This is the only reference Nicoll makes to the fact that his boss-man is English but it is not an irrelevant piece of information. The museum that Nicoll is employed by is a symbol of Scottish culture but neither the chairman nor the boss-man is identified with that culture, and by implication neither values it very highly. This is a good example of how complex social and cultural values can be expressed in what seems like a simple narrative about being interviewed for a job.

The three examples in this chapter show how ordinary events can be the basis for highly effective narratives. All three speakers were simply telling me about experiences that they recalled as significant in their lives. None of the stories is about an event that would be worth my retelling to a third party. These are not tales of danger or adventure, but they are tellable because these events were salient in the lives of their narrators (Linde 1993). The stories are not primarily about the events but about the tellers themselves. While the narrator says "This is what happened", the important message is "This is the kind of person I am". That is why the stories contain so many details.

Andrew Sinclair makes it very clear that, despite coming from a poor family, with many siblings, he had the kind of qualities that impressed the farmer. His enthusiasm for farm work suggests an eager, willing boy. He portrays himself as mature for his age and treated as such by the farmer and by his parents. The picture he presents of himself as a young boy is consistent with the impression he gives of himself as an adult. Ella Laidlaw told me several stories about getting into trouble as a child and how her mother would punish her severely, but Ella said that she "never kicked against the traces". In this story she shows that now she has left school she can successfully assert her independence and resist her mother's wishes. Although she does not say so explicitly, this episode marks a transitional stage in her life. Duncan Nicoll's fortunes had fluctuated during his working life but he manifested a positive attitude throughout the interview, presenting himself as both flexible and optimistic. In the story in this chapter he shows how he was able to retain his self-respect in the potentially humiliating situation of the interview by mentally criticising his interviewer and feeling "big enough" to do the jobs of two men. An example given in Chapter Ten shows him taking a positive attitude in even more trying circumstances. Thus the significance of the stories does not lie in the events themselves but in what the speakers tell me about themselves by telling the story in a particular way. Among other things, all three speakers tell me in very different ways how important it is to be respected. This is a common theme in many episodes reported by a wide range of speakers (see Chapter Ten).

Chapter Six

Third Person Narratives

They were superbly qualified for the task, both in terms of their life histories and in terms of their gifts for recreating their lives verbally on tape. Both Sutherlands showed marked strength as speakers. Mrs. Sutherland had a wonderful capacity for vivid narrative, and Mr. Sutherland a special clarity and exactitude in recalling matters of detail. (Dorian 1985: 101–2)

When someone tells a story about something that happened to them, we tend to assume that the narrator is presenting an accurate account of the event. As Labov observes "credibility is as essential as reportability for the success of a novel" (1982: 228). That is, when Ella Laidlaw tells about the women in the carpet factory with their painted and pointed nails swearing at her, we have no reason to believe that this did not happen or to think that it happened very differently from the way that she tells it. Similarly, we have no reason to disbelieve Andrew Sinclair's account of how the farmer offered him a job without Andrew even asking about one. As Lewis observes: "In the world of story, the act of story telling is truth-telling about matters whereof the teller has knowledge" (1978: 40).

There are, of course, stories that are not designed to receive this response. Bauman, for example, cites examples of "tall tales" that range from stretching the truth to outright lying. Bauman observes that "considerations of truth and belief will vary and be subject to negotiation within communities and storytelling situations" (1996: 161). Ella Laidlaw and Andrew Sinclair were telling me about their lives and it would have been very odd if I had expressed any doubts about the accuracy of their accounts. Like the tellers Labov has studied, I assume that they "did not manufacture events" (Labov 1997: 397) but were attempting to convey an important experience in their own lives. In their stories they themselves necessarily appear as one of the main protagonists.

However, sometimes narrators will tell a story in which they are not one of the actors. Third person narratives are less common because, as Linde (1993) observes: "at a conscious level everyone believes that he or she has privileged access to his or her plans, motivations, and intentions, whereas these can only be inferred for others" (Linde 1993: 121). Consequently, third person narratives are more problematic in terms of their credibility. As Ochs and Capps point out "credibility depends in part upon the plausibility of a chain of objective events and whether they can be corroborated" (1997: 83). We assume in narratives of personal experience that narrators have unchallengeable authority over the events that are related because they were present and are able to recall them. In telling about what happened to a third party when the narrator was not there to witness the event the narrator has reduced authority. Usually, however, the only way in which the narrator's account can be challenged is if there is some internal inconsistency in the story that makes it less likely to be accepted, or if there is another way to interpret the sequence of events that differs from the way the narrator presents them (Labov 1986).

Labov (2004) reanalyses a narrative that was first discussed in Macaulay (1987) and later in Macaulay (1991a). In her interview with me, Ella Laidlaw told a story about how her stepfather had died suddenly: "He just lay down on the settee and turned over and that was him gone". She went on to tell me how her mother had left him sitting in the garden while she took the bus into town to buy groceries:

1. (Ella Laidlaw)
well she walked away and left him sitting in the garden in a basket chair
and he was aw right
he knew everybody in the street
everybody knew him
he was well liked
and when they went past his gate they used to stop and speak to him
well that passed his day for him
and it was an exceptionally good afternoon
and she put him out in a basket chair
sitting at the window ootside in the garden
she went in one the one bus
and came back on the same bus
because the conductress says to her
"Thought you said you were going for messages"   [*shopping*]
she says "So I was"
"Well" she says "I'm awful glad I'm no waiting on you" she says

"You couldnae have got much because you've got the same bus back"
"Ach well" she says "I don't like the idea of leaving him too long"
and she went up the road
she noticed his basket chair was there
but he wasnae there
she never thought anything aboot it
because it was too warm
she thought he'd naturally gone inside
and when she went in he was lying on the settee
and she's auld-fashioned very tidy very smart
everything had to go in its place
she took off her coat
hung it up
put away her shopping bag
and she says "It's rather early for wer tea– wer dinner
so I'll go and ask him if he wants a coffee"
and she made the coffee
and she through and shook him to ask him if he wanted tea
and he dropped off the settee in front of her
and she just– her mind just broke
and she's never known what it is since.

There are only two pieces of information in this narrative for which Ella herself is the authority. The first is the comment that her mother was old-fashioned and tidy. The second is the conclusion about her mother's mind breaking. Otherwise, Ella tells the story in a transformed version of how her mother might have told it: "I went in on the bus and the conductress said to me", etc. The dialogic exchange between Ella's mother and the conductress, however, is totally convincing, including the use of the discourse features *well* and *ach well*. The conductress's comment makes it clear that Ella's mother did not waste time doing her shopping. The remark "I don't like the idea of leaving him too long" is crucial in the story because it foreshadows (Ochs and Capps 2001) the central event. (Morson says that foreshadowing is "the first of all literary devices to be taught in high school" (1999: 285).) Whatever the origin of the dialogue, it is an essential part of the narrative.

At no point in the narrative does Ella suggest any uncertainty about what actually happened. She does not hedge her narrative with expressions such as *I think*, *maybe*, and *from what I heard*. As Lewis has observed about story-telling in general "the story is told as known fact" (Lewis 1978: 40), although in this case Ella did not know what happened through being a witness of the events she relates.

In addition to the dialogue, Ella relates her mother's thoughts, both indirectly and directly. Examples of the first are "she noticed his basket chair was there" and "she never thought anything aboot it". As Margolin (1999) observes "claims about situations that could occur but did not can be as factive and certain in this context as claims about what did and did not happen" (1999: 148). Labov (to appear) claims that because she *could* have thought something was wrong, Ella's mother felt guilty. There is also an example of the direct reporting of her mother's thought: "It's rather early for wer tea– wer dinner". As I pointed out (Macaulay 1991a: 192), the repair in the latter reported thought is unlikely to have been Ella's mother's. As it was afternoon, Ella's parents presumably would have had their dinner in the middle of the day and their later meal would be tea, but Ella may have thought that coming from a middle-class situation I would misunderstand the reference to tea as being to afternoon tea.

In addition to the dialogue there are many details that Ella did not observe herself, so she must have heard them from her mother. She gives examples of how her mother was tidy: she took off her coat, she hung it up, and she put away her shopping bag, before she made coffee. As Labov points out, these are ordinary events:

As in other effective narratives of personal experience, these are simple events and they revolve around basic objects. Laidlaw's mother did not hang up a "light spring coat with a belt in the back"; she hung up her coat. She did not make a "steaming pot of good strong Java"; she made coffee. This is the warp and woof of experience, free of literary devices. Indeed, it is the very objectivity of these objects and events that adds to the credibility of the story and intensifies the emotional content. (Labov forthcoming: 17)

Ella Laidlaw's mother is a prominent figure in Ella's interview. In addition to the story of Ella's first job (Chapter Five), there are several stories showing how severely Ella was brought up by her mother. Despite the harshness of the punishments she had received, Ella reveals little resentment. The story she tells in (1) is sympathetically told and Labov is probably correct in suggesting that the central point is the guilt that Ella's mother felt at not having immediately checked to see whether her husband was all right. If Labov is correct, this might account for Ella's ability to include details that only her mother could have known, e.g., what the conductress said. Ella's mother because of feeling guilty may have told the story over and over again so that the details became as familiar to Ella as the main events. Ella's story may be the result of her mother trying to come to terms with the reality of her husband's death.

Although this is really her mother's story Ella's is the only version that we have. In rare cases, however, more than one narrator will give an account of the same event and then the different versions can be compared in an attempt to uncover what Labov (2001) calls the "event structure". In my corpus of materials there is one useful example of the same event described by a brother and sister.

In 1985 Len M. was interviewed as part of the Dundee Oral History Project. He described an incident during the General Strike in 1926 in which his father was arrested.

2. (Len M.)
and eh he was unemployed eh during the General Strike
he was em at the bottom at the bottom of eh Hunter Street
that was eh just across the road from Blinshall Street
during the General Strike he jumped up one dinner time on a lorry
on an empty lorry– a a cart lorry– a horse and cart
the cart– they used to tip the carts up against the side of the road
and take the horse maybe away for its–
down to the stable for a– its dinner or that you know
and he jumped up there
and held a meeting
and he was arrested
and he was given fourteen days for eh for political
cause they werena allowed to have an unofficial meeting sort of stuff

In my interview with his sister, Bella K., she gave a rather different account of the same event:

3. (Bella K.)
and during the General Strike nobody stopped anything from going to the hospitals
and my father had been coming home
and my– my brother who was about four or something with him
and there was a crowd rushed out of the mills

and there was a lorry– a big lorry full of coal going to the D.R.I. the Dundee Royal
    Infirmary
and the crowd wanted to knock over the cart
and my father had said to the carter "Whar are ye gaeing laddie?"
and he said "I'm going up to the hospital"
"Oh" my father said "this has go to go through
you stop this
you let this go through"
and with that the police lifted him
and my– the– the first my mother knew of it
she'd been in the washhouse
was my brother coming down the stair with an axe
and my mother said "Where are you going with that?"
and he said "I'm going away to chap aff the Bobbie's legs
because he's taken my father away"
[*laughs*]
and then my father got fourteen days in Perth

The accounts differ and there is no outside evidence to say which of
them is more accurate, but the important point here is less what the
facts were than how each narrator chooses to report the events.

There are several elements that are common to both stories. (1)
the time is during the General Strike; (2) there was an incident that
involved a cart in some way; (3) it happened not far from where they
lived; (4) their father was arrested; and (5) he was sentenced to fourteen days in prison. There are also many differences. The most striking is that Bella's account puts her brother at the centre of the story,
while Len does not report it as an event he had witnessed but simply
as something that had happened to his father. Contrary to what Bella
says, Len would have been seven rather than four at the time; it was
Bella who was four in 1926. This is the one piece of factual information that can be verified, since the birth dates of both Len and Bella
are known and the date given for the General Strike is accurate. If Len
had been only four, it might have been easier to explain why he did
not report it as an actual witness. On the other hand, Bella's inaccu-
racy in reporting the one fact that can be verified might raise questions
about the accuracy of her statement about her brother's involvement.

The stories illustrate very different narrative styles. In his version
of the story, Len concentrates on the physical setting, the exact location "at the bottom of Hunter Street" that was "just across the road

from Blinshall Street" (where the family lived). Like many male speakers (Macaulay, to appear), Len mentions many places by name in his interview and makes frequent reference to spatial organisation. He also reports his father's action "he jumped up [...] on a lorry". He mentions that it was "an empty lorry" and is very concerned to explain the kind of lorry (it was "a cart lorry"), and then possibly because he was worried that his young interviewer still would not understand he adds "a horse and cart". He then goes on to explain why the cart was there. It was left at the side of the street while the horse was taken away to the stable for "its dinner or that". He wants to make sure that the interviewer gets these details right. He repeats the information that his father "jumped up" and then reports that his father held "a meeting". There is no reference to what his father said or why he did it. He was arrested because "they werena allowed to have an unofficial meeting sort of stuff". Len does not mention his own role in telling his mother (assuming Bella's version is correct on this point). Len's account concentrates on visual details and does not report any remarks. Len does not explain what his father was doing by holding "a meeting", only that it was illegal.

Bella's narrative style is very different. She presents many more details than Len. She states that it was "a big lorry full of coal" and that it was going to the Dundee Royal Infirmary. She reports that "the crowd wanted to knock over the cart" and that her father had argued that the lorry should be allowed to go through because "during the General Strike nobody stopped anything from going to the hospitals". It was at this point that the police "lifted" (i.e., arrested) him. Bella also includes a report of how their mother heard from Len that her husband had been arrested.

Labov (2003) sets out a recursive rule of narrative construction to account for the way in which credibility is established: "Given an event r_i, that is unaccounted for, locate an event r_{i-1} for which the statement "r_n happened because r_{i-1}" is true" (Labov 2003: 11). What this means is that if you start from the event that is the culmination of the story and work backwards, you may be able to identify a causal chain that will explain why the event happened. The aim is to produce a narrative chain of events linked by their causal relations. In (2) and

(3) the event that needs to be accounted for is the arrest of Len and Bella's father. Len's narrative chain is shown in (4).

4.
1. Father was on the street
2. Father jumped up on a cart
3. Father held a meeting
4. Father was arrested

What is unsatisfying about this account is that the causal chain does not go back far enough or include enough details. We do not know from this sequence why their father jumped up on the cart or why he held a meeting. Labov argues that the narrative chain "is terminated when the event is not 'unaccounted for'" (2003: 11), in other words, when we understand why the event happened. Len's narrative leaves his father's arrest unaccounted for.

Bella's narrative chain in given in (5):

5.
1. Father was coming home
2. A crowd rushed out of the mills
3. The crowd wanted to knock over a lorry carrying coal
4. Father asked the carter where he was going
5. The carter said he was going to the hospital
6. Father told the crowd to let the lorry through
7. Father was arrested

Bella makes it clear that their father was not responsible for the attempt to stop the cart. Bella's causal chain shows that their father was not the instigator of the event, since he was simply on his way home when the crowd rushed out of the mills. He happened to be there when the disruption started and his intervention did not appear to be premeditated. Bella's version shows their father to be interceding on humanitarian grounds to let the coal cart through to the hospital. The police arrested him presumably on the grounds that he was a leader of "the crowd" that wanted to knock over the cart. The implication is that the police should have recognised that he was, as it were, acting on their side, but instead they "lifted" him. On the other hand, the fact that he assumed the authority to tell the crowd to let the lorry through helps to explain why the police took him to be their leader. Bella's version thus provides a more plausible sequence for their father's arrest than Len's account of "a meeting".

Unlike Len, Bella presents much of the story in dialogue, although she was not present at the first event (the arrest), nor presumably at the second (her brother telling their mother), since if she had been present then she might have been expected to report it in the first person. She dramatises the exchanges between her father and the carter, her father and the crowd from the mills, and between her brother and their mother. She reports these exchanges in dialogue that sounds quite convincing, particularly her brother's determination "to chap aff the Bobbie's legs". What possible source can there be for the dialogue? The most likely source is that this was a story that was part of family lore and had been told more than once in Bella's presence. Her father was well-known as a political activist and this may have been one of the stories told to illustrate his career.

Bella's account is not simply a report of what happened but a dramatic recreation of an episode of family history. As Langellier and Peterson observe: "Family stories are the basic way in which the lived-experience of doing family is organized and legitimized" (1993: 56). It was an important event for both Len and Bella because their father lost his job as a result and the whole family suffered. In many places in the oral history interview and in my interview with her, Bella paints a very strong picture of her father as a man of great integrity who was passionate about the socialist cause. (In 1919, he named his son Lenin, and remained a true believer throughout his life.) Bella's dramatised version of this episode encapsulates some of this spirit. Len's version does not bring this out.

Is there anything that might help to explain the difference between the two versions? If this is such an important part of family history, the story may have been retold many times. What made it a more vivid story for Bella than for Len? There are a number of possible contributing factors and one of them is suggested by their differing responses to a question from the oral history interviewer about talking with their parents.

6. (Len M.)
(*When grownups were talking can you remember were you allowed to join in?*)
eh I couldna tell you offhand
no well we wouldna
if the conversation involved me I suppose I would be involved then
but I wasna if it wasna me

7. (Bella K.)
our table was a conversation piece
where em all the political– all the news items were analysed discussed
and eh oh great discussions
and you were encouraged to– to voice what your opinions were

The striking difference in these two recollections may help to explain the difference between the two versions of the story as well as elsewhere in the interviews. Bella believed that as a child she had been encouraged to voice her opinions but Len has no such memory from his childhood. It seems plausible that Bella was more interested in the family discussions and therefore she may have paid more attention to the details about her father's arrest. Len, in contrast, remembers the fact that their father was arrested rather than the details, though he does recall exactly where it happened.

There are many other ways in which the interviews with the brother and sister differ (Macaulay 1996). One difference is that Bella tends to give more specific details. This can be seen in their responses to one question.

8. (Len M.)
Were there any books kept in the house?
oh yes there was always a lot of books
Can you tell me what sort of books?
eh we never had any comics

Instead of providing any information on the kind of books, Len tells the interviewer what was not there. Bella's response is much more informative.

9. (Bella K.)
Did you have books in the house?
yes my father had a bookcase full of books– full of books
mostly political but an awful lot of Wordsworth em Dickens

The Ragged Trouser Philanthropist
dictionaries
em about eight volumes of em bakery– baking– about bakers
em encyclopaedias
and an awful lot on astronomy
my brother was very keen on astronomy
but eh there was such books as *Forty Years of an Agitator's Life*
and eh that sort of thing

This is a good example of the kind of listing behaviour that Schiffrin (1994) has found to bear some similarity to story-telling. Bella is an excellent story-teller, as we have seen in Chapter Three, and she is good at lists. Interestingly enough, Bella reports herself as not being very interested in reading when she was young, something she attributes to her father's uncompromising attitude ("You don't read rubbish, you read good books") and his refusal to allow imaginative literature as well as comics. Bella says that her brother and elder sister were the ones who read, but she is the one who remembers which books were in the house. Len, who according to Bella was interested in astronomy, does not mention this to the interviewer.

The greatest difference between the two interviews, however, is in their narratives. Len remembers lots of details from his wartime experiences, but he says less about his feelings. Here is an example from his first trip overseas as a soldier in World War II. He was one of the last to go on board the ship because he had been detailed to work in the baggage party, and he had expected his friends to keep a bunk for him:

10. (Len M.)
and when we come through
expecting some of my mates to come out the cabins you know
and say "Oh in here Willie"
and "In here Jock" you know and that
right through
right through the cabin area
right through
out the deck and doon into the hold
we were in the hold
we were in the hold
and there was no places for my hammock
I was the last one there

there was no place for my hammock
and eh I had to tie my hammock from the–
the gangway come down
the hold was there sort of style
and the pipes were here
and the banister was going down to the– below– right underneath
whar there was another load of fellas under there
and I'd to hang my hammock from here to the pipes across there
and I think it helped to stop me getting seasick
because the boat was going up
and all your hammocks were laid that way
whar I was across the opposite way
and eh I think it stopped me from being sick
cause of the way the action would be

The account is clear both in detail and moral, but it lacks any personal details of how he felt or description of his mates. What Len concentrates on are spatial details: "right through the cabin area", "out the deck and doon into the hold", "we were in the hold". Len carefully explains how his hammock was arranged, no doubt with gestures, "the gangway come down", "the hold was there sort of style", "and the pipes were here" "and I'd to hang my hammock from here to the pipes across there". Note that his use of quoted dialogue in this passage is not of an actual exchange but of what he expected his mates to say. There are, in fact, no examples of dialogic exchange with his mates in his total account. This is typical of the contrast in style throughout the interviews. Len's responses tend to be factual and impersonal whereas Bella's usually reveal her own feelings and values, often in dramatised situations, as in (11).

Bella's interview is mainly a story of success but also in some ways one of frustration. The peak of her success was to become a welder in the shipyard during World War II, but after the war there was no place for women in the shipyard, or as welders anywhere. Then after years of being denied the possibility of using her demonstrated skills, when equality of opportunity for women arrived, she was able to go back to work in the shipyard, although at the last moment she had doubts:

11. (Bella K.)
so on that first morning that I started

though I– I really– I was on the shipyard bus with aw these men
and coming down the brae
I'm quite sure some of them were saying to theirsel
"What the hell is that woman coming down this brae for"
and I stopped halfway
and thought "Christ will I turn back"
or "Oh no what the hell am I doing here"
and then I pulled myself up
and I said "I'm here to prove women have it"
I didn't have to prove myself
I had proved myself during the war
"I am now here to reap the benefit of my war experiences"
so in I marched

Here Bella dramatises her feelings very vividly, showing her doubts and anxiety but ultimately her confidence.

It is impossible to know whether the contrast between the two interviews is typical of the two individuals in their use of language in other situations. I interviewed Bella myself at a later date and she was just as involved, as entertaining, and as animated as in the oral history interview, so I have some confidence that her oral history interview is a good example of one of her ways of speaking. I was not able to interview Len, so I have no idea whether this is his usual style. The contrast between the two interviews is clear even from this limited comparison. The differences are even more obvious when listening to the tapes.

The main differences between the two oral history interviews are not of the kind that Coupland (1996) has called "dialect style", namely, the kind of features that are usually counted in quantitative studies of stylistic variation. So perhaps the other differences don't matter much but we cannot be sure how these differences affect the occurrence of "dialect" features. Moreover, the differences between the interviews cannot be easily explained in terms of attention to speech, formality, role, social position, audience design, topic, or genre (see Chapter Seven). That two individuals from such similar backgrounds, interviewed by the same interviewer, under equivalent conditions, should differ might raise questions about the weight to be attached to relatively minor kinds of stylistic variation. The kind of differences that Bella and Len display might easily affect the occurrence of sociolinguistic variables in an interview.

There are numerous factors that could affect the nature of the language in these interviews. First, there is an age difference. Len is only three years older than Bella but his memory may be less good on some kinds of details. Second, the relationship between the interviewer and each respondent is different. The interviewer clearly got on very well with Bella. There is a lot of mutual laughter. The relationship between the interviewer and Len is much more restrained. Third, there is the gender difference. Len admitted to being shy about women as a young man and while he seems to be relatively at ease with the interviewer, it is possible that he might have reacted differently to a male interviewer. Bella clearly enjoyed talking with other women and she shows it in the interview. Fourth, there is the interviewer's own interests. She prompts many of Bella's stories by her (apparently genuine) interest in topics such as childbirth, weddings, household arrangements, and the situation of a woman working in a man's world.

In contrast, the interviewer makes little response to Len's extended narrative about his wartime experiences in North Africa. She allows him to tell his story at great length and he provides a great deal of information but she does not probe with helpful questions when his narrative meanders. Nor does she seem excited when Len tells her about his visit to Russia (see Appendix A). As a boy he had been a member of the Young Communists' League and when he was twelve he was chosen as one of two young Scots on a delegation to Russia. Len has a really interesting story to tell: going to Russia at the age of twelve, seeing Stalin, and meeting Lenin's widow. Yet he fails to make it effective. It is a story that calls out for greater detail than Len gives but the interviewer does not intervene to elicit more details. Finally, there is the question of temperament. Bella told me that her brother was very like her father and she told the interviewer "my father was a factual man" and his encouragement to his children was to be factual: "you werenae allowed anything for your imagination". In this respect, as with her response to much of the rest of her schooling, Bella was not a good learner since she often displays imagination in her comments.

There is one example in which Len gives a fuller account of a story given by both. (The stories are given in Appendix A.) This is not a story of which they had any first-hand experience that was relevant. It is a story they have heard from older members of the family and neither can recall all the details. The interest in the comparison of the two versions lies in what they report as being essential parts of the narrative. The story concerns a family belief that a song entitled *The road and the miles to Dundee* was based on their grandmother's experience. According to family history their grandmother had walked from Aberdeen to Dundee as a young girl. Bella tells how her grandmother had set out with her sister but that the sister stopped at Montrose, a town between Aberdeen and Dundee. Later someone had given her grandmother a brooch as in the song. Bella gives details such as what the brooch was like and brings the story to a dramatic climax with her grandmother fainting on the doorstep of the first house she came to.

Len's version is longer, gives different details and is much fuller. He is concerned to get the approximate date right. He explains the conditions that led to the two sisters setting out for Dundee. He mentions his grandmother's sister getting pregnant by a soldier in Montrose, which explains why his grandmother set out from there on her own. Once again, Len is concerned about location. There is a lot of detail about the roads and what interests him is how she got lost. He does not reveal how his grandmother arrived in Dundee. He also makes it clear that he does not know the story exactly. Bella's version is vague on the route but contains two details that Len does not mention: the gift of the brooch, which is apparently mentioned in the song, and the dramatic way in which her grandmother arrived in Dundee. Even with scanty materials Bella dramatises the event; Len concentrates on the factual details. The examples of different accounts of events given by Bella and Len underline the risks of taking any narrative at face value, but they also present revealing differences in narrative style. Sociolinguistic investigation has not yet solved the problem of how to deal with stylistic differences (Eckert and Rickford 2001). This topic will be explored in the next chapter dealing with a more complex example of narrative style.

As with first person narratives, the important point is not how accurately third person stories represent what actually happened. The stories create their own reality. Ella Laidlaw's story is about her parents. She had earlier told me how her stepfather used to come home on a Saturday after drinking heavily and make his own dinner of "sliced sausage and one black pudding". Ella's mother would be angry with him and refuse to help him, but Ella said he showed no resentment: "nothing upset him". Since she also had said of her stepfather "everybody liked him", it seems obvious that he was easy-going, in strong contrast to his wife, for whom "everything had to go in its place". So it is fitting that "he lay down on the settee and turned over and that was him gone". No fuss. It was a very different situation with her mother whose mind "just snapped", and ended up in hospital. When Ella would go to visit her, her mother usually did not even recognise her:

12. (Ella Laidlaw)
I go oot to see her every Saturday
some Saturdays she'll say "Whit are you wanting?"
she doesnae know us
last week she says "Oh I'm gled to see you"
I says "Oh for once in my life I've got a welcome"
then she forgets aw aboot you

The story in (1) is not just about her stepfather's death but about both parents and the differences between them.

The difference between Bella's and Len's stories about their father's arrest reflects many contrasts between the complete interviews. Both talk a lot about their father, but Len tends to focus on factual details. Bella's stories about her father are more personal and show her great affection for him. Bella's stories support her claim: "I had an unusual father – yeah a great wee guy" (see Appendix C).

In telling third person narratives the speakers are not just reporting events. They are telling *their* stories, and they can choose what to include or emphasise. Their choices can be as revealing as when they are reporting on their own situations. Brockmeier and Harré (2001) warn against what they call "the ontological fallacy" and "the representation fallacy", that is, of assuming that narratives exist independently of the telling, but they also claim that narrative is valuable "because it works as an open and malleable frame that enables us to come to terms with an ever-changing, ever reconstructed reality" (Brockmeier and Harré 2001: 53).

Chapter Seven

A Stylistic Anomaly

The living utterances, having taken meaning and shape at a particular historical moment in a socially specific environment, cannot fail to brush up against thousands of living dialogic threads, woven by socio-ideological consciousness around the given object of an utterance; it cannot fail to become an active participant in social dialogue. (Bakhtin 1981: 276)

Ever since Labov 1966a introduced an operational method of dealing with stylistic variation, the notion of style has been problematic in sociolinguistics. Extralinguistic factors, such as attention to speech (Labov 1966a), audience design (Bell 1984), topic choice (Rickford and McNair-Knox 1994), participant role (Brown and Fraser 1979), social position (Keenan 1989; Irvine 1990) and involvement (Tannen 1989) have been selected as critical influences affecting (and even determining) the choice of linguistic variants. Most of these different approaches share the hope that stylistic variation can be reduced to a single dimension, a goal that some have found unrealistic (Macaulay 1999; Coupland 2001; Finegan and Biber 2001).

In 1996 at Stanford University there was a workshop on style to discuss the different approaches to style in sociolinguistic investigation (Eckert and Rickford 2001). Much of the discussion focused on three models that were presented: (1) Attention to speech (Labov); (2) Audience design (Bell); and (3) Register variation (Finegan and Biber). All three models were presented in forms somewhat modified from earlier versions.

Attention to speech.

Labov's focus on the attention paid to speech goes back to his pioneering work in New York (Labov 1966a, b) in which he distinguished a range of styles from "casual speech" to the reading aloud of a list of minimal pairs. One of the theoretical problems with this approach comes from the use of materials to be read out loud as representing increasing attention to speech. Several investigators (e.g., Milroy 1980; Romaine, 1980; Macaulay 1997) have pointed out that there are problems in treating speech and reading aloud as a continuum. However, at the Stanford conference, Labov's main concern was how to distinguish "casual" speech from "careful" speech in the context of the sociolinguistic interview (Labov 1966, 1981):

the goal of stylistic analysis is to disengage those sections [of the interview] where the effects of observation and audio-monitoring are most clearly diminished, which come as close as possible to the vernacular speech that is used when the interviewer is absent. (Labov 2001: 88)

This follows from his notion of the *vernacular*, which he had earlier defined as "that mode of speech that is acquired in pre-adolescent years", in which "the minimum attention is paid to speech", and which he claimed "provides the most systematic data for linguistic analysis" (Labov 1981: 3). As has often been pointed out, there are problems with this definition of the vernacular (Macaulay, 1988a; Reah 1982; Romaine 1984), but Labov remains committed to the goal of identifying this level of speech. Labov's major innovation introduced at the conference was to replace his earlier use of channel cues (e.g., changes in volume, pitch, tempo, etc.) to identify casual speech by what he calls a **Decision Tree** in which sections of the interview are identified as Casual Speech or Careful Speech by topic or genre (Labov 2001: 94). Casual Speech is to be found in narrative, speech addressed to persons other than the interviewer, talk about childhood games and experiences, and **tangents**. Tangents are defined as "an extended body of speech that deviates plainly from the last topic introduced by the interviewer, and represents the strong interest of the speakers" (Labov 2001: 92). Assigned to the category of Careful Speech are immediate responses to the interviewer's questions, talk about language, and what Labov calls **soapbox**. Soapbox is "characterized as an extended expression of generalized opinions, not spoken directly to the interviewer, but enunciated as if for a more general audience" (Labov 2001: 91). Any speech that does not fall into one of the identified categories is also assigned to Careful Speech. The Decision Tree is designed for structured sociolinguistic interviews (Labov 1966a, 1981) in which specific questions are asked in a certain order.

Audience design.

At the Stanford conference Bell put forward the three basic tenets of his theory of style-shifting:

1. Style is what an individual speaker does with a language in relation to other people.
2. Style derives its meaning from the association of linguistic features with particular groups.
3. Speakers design their style primarily for and in response to their audience. (Bell 2001: 141–143)

The third tenet is "the heart of audience design" (Bell 2001: 143). It corresponds to the notion of "convergence" in Accommodation Theory (Giles and Powesland 1975). Bell's modification to his earlier model was to place more emphasis on what he calls *Referee Design* which is "the linguistic representation of our identities, particularly in relation to those others we are interacting with or who are salient to us" (Bell 2001: 165).

Register variation.

Finegan and Biber presented their functional model of register (or style) variation and introduced as the basis of style-shifting what they call a **Register Axiom**:

If a linguistic feature is distributed across social groups and communicative situations or registers, then the social groups with greater access to the situations and registers in which the features occur more frequently will exhibit more frequent use of those features in their social dialects. (Finegan and Biber 2001: 265)

Finegan and Biber identify items that they characterise as "economy" (or "ease") features in contrast to "elaboration" (or "clarity") features. Economy features are those that reflect ease of production, while elaboration features are those that reflect a desire to be as clear as possible. They find that these features distinguish different genres of language (e.g., conversations vs public speeches) and also social status groups (higher vs lower).

The three models of Attention-to-speech, Audience Design, and Register Variation all received critical attention at the Stanford conference and many of their assumptions were challenged (Eckert and Rickford 2001) but I do not propose to examine those issues closely here. (Some of my critical evaluation of Labov's and Bell's earlier models can be found in Macaulay 1999). Here instead I want to use the three models to examine the style of one exceptional speaker.

Johnstone (1990, 1996) places the emphasis on individual style and choice. She claims that researchers have tended to "see individuals as governed, in the main, by rules external to them, rules which in theory (notwithstanding minor glitches from time to time) determine everything people do" (1990: 38), while she prefers to look not only "at what people do because they have to, in order to be understood, [but also] at what people do *because they choose to*, in order to create and express their individualities" (1990: 5, emphasis added). She observes that "storytellers capitalize on their own strengths and weaknesses, their own stylistic tendencies" (1990: 63), and she shows how "a teller who uses nonverbal cues to signal chunks at the beginning of a story is likely to use nonverbal cues throughout, and a speaker who uses preposed temporal clauses will continue to do so throughout"(1990: 63) and "how slow, hesitant speakers use pauses to indicate shifts from one episode to another in their stories, while other speakers use words or rhythms" (1990: 5–6). The example in this chapter is from a speaker whose individual style reflects an interesting sociolinguistic phenomenon.

I interviewed John Wilson in 1973 as part of the survey of Glasgow speech (Macaulay and Trevelyan 1973; Macaulay 1977). His was by far the longest of the Glasgow interviews and the only one that produced a lengthy narrative. The whole interview gives the impression of someone who is trying hard to be on his best behaviour and this was his manner during the interview. He knew that the interview was in connection with education since I had earlier interviewed his

15-year-old daughter at school, as part of the survey of language, education, and social class (Macaulay and Trevelyan 1973). She was doing well, and her older brother had also done well at school. Wilson obviously took the interview very seriously. He was dressed in a suit and the interview took place in what was the Wilsons' "best room". Mrs Wilson was present throughout but made only a few comments, and she was not consulted by her husband. The interview lasted two and a quarter hours but there were no diversions and I was not offered a cup of tea or any other hospitality. This was serious business and John Wilson made a great effort to answer my questions fully. In terms of Attention-to-speech, it would be accurate to say that Wilson was monitoring himself fairly carefully throughout the session. He did, however, respond to a version of the Danger-of-Death question (Labov 1966a, 1981) with an interesting narrative, although it was not focused on the danger.

In 1940, in the second year of World War II, Wilson, who was born and grew up in central Glasgow, was working as an office boy for a shipping company when he heard that one of the ships was going to take on a galley boy. He describes the situation as follows:

1. (John Wilson)

I was designated as a junior clerk	1
which I think was just a posh name for an office boy	2
but we had the task at times of taking messages down aboard the ships	3
and one even– one afternoon we were in this– this small wooden hut	4
and a message came through from Liverpool by phone you know	5
and it came through	6
and it said "Will you take a message down to the S.S. Norwegian	7
and tell Captain Morris"	8
who was the shore superintendent	9
"that Captain Reid had decided	10
to go ahead and employ a galley boy for the Norwegian?"	11
so I was told to take this message down	12
I went aboard the Norwegian	13
and I ferreted out Captain Morris	14
and I said to him	15
as I say I was only fourteen at the time too	16
I said to him	17
"The word has just come through on the phone Captain Morris	18
that you've to– Captain Reid says you've to employ a galley boy for the S.S. Norwegian	19

and can I get the job?"   20
all in one breath you know   21
And he just smiled the way you're smiling now you know   22
he thought it was very funny you know   23

This short narrative contains many features that will be apparent in the longer story that follows. There is a concern for precision, shown in the self-repairs in lines 4 and 19 and in details "this small wooden hut". He also uses rather pedantic phraseology "I was designated", "we had the task", and "a message came through". His report of his own speech "The word has just come through on the phone", if it corresponds at all closely to what Wilson may have said at the time, would indicate that he developed his particular style of speech at an early age. Put another way, this is how he represents himself as talking at the age of fourteen. His characterisation of the job of "junior clerk" being "just a posh name for an office boy" may show an awareness of different styles of speech at this age. He also uses an interesting metaphor in telling how he "ferreted out Captain Morris".

Wilson first had to get his parents' permission but he succeeded in getting the job. The narrative in which he describes his first trip across the north Atlantic is the best example of his polyphonic discourse style. As with Ella Laidlaw's account of her first job (Chapter Five), this is a long story and it is told without any prompting from the listener. This is a story that Wilson chose to tell and he was in no doubt about how he wanted to tell it.

2. (John Wilson)
oh this– this– this is really funny you know   1
in as much as that I didn't see it the fear this fear   2
that you're talking about   3
this is strange   4
I was on that first journey across the north Atlantic   5
we sailed on January the ninth   6
eh and eh the weather at time was pretty rough in the north Atlantic   7
and then convoys it's eh things get built up you know   8
but eh I think that what was uppermost in my mind was two things   9
first would I be seasick   0
and was it as antagonizing as most people were telling me it was you know   11
I was very afraid of this seasickness   12
because everybody said that it was pretty gruelling   13

and eh the second point that was– that was uppermost in my mind was seeing

    the New World   14

and eh as far as I was concerned that what   15

wunst again what people were telling me   16

it was an Aladdin's Cave   17

because we were right in the middle of a war   18

and we could get nothing here   19

everything was on ration   20

and there was no luxuries at all   21

but over there there was everything you know   22

and I was dying to see this   23

and eh the seasickness wasnae too bad first time   24

when we were sailing from Glasgow here   25

some of the lads said to me   26

"There's two other first trippers on the ship forbye yourself"   27

well looking for some sort of companions as it were you know   28

somebody in the same predicament as myself   29

I sought them out   30

the first one was a– a cadet first tripper   31

oh typical English upper crust you know   32

and I said to him   33

I said eh "Do you think you'll be seasick?" you know   34

just like that you know   35

and he sort of looked down his nose at me you know   36

gave me a glower   37

and he said to me "I've been to sea on destroyers" he says   38

"Oh" I says "me I've never been anywhere"   39

[*laughs*]

"I've been here in Glasgow   40

that's it   41

never been further than that   42

except wunst again the Ayrshire coast   43

never been on a boat before except the ferry the local ferry"   44

so I says to myself "Oh well I've no got much of a companion there"   45

so I went and sought out the second character   46

and he was Highland   47

he came from Skye   48

and very nice lad   49

much more amiable than the– the cadet officer   50

so eh I had a longer talk to him   51

he wasnae near as snooty   52

he was only an ordinary seaman right enough   53

but he said to me   54

he says "Well" he says "I– I– living in Skye" he says   55

"we come in contact with the water quite a lot   56

been out a lot in rowing boats and things like that"   57

he says "I think I'll be okay" 58
[*laughs*]
so I felt very alone 59
but eh the cooks on the ship they said to me 60
"You're– when the seasickness hits you you're no lying up" 61
because first and foremost they were thinking 62
that if I was going to lay up they would have my work to do 63
and they werenae going to fall for that 64
they had fought to get a galley boy 65
they never had one prior to me 66
they had fought to get a galley boy employed on the ship 67
and they werenae going to re– give up 68
concede the duties that I was going get 69
so– and eh– but they didn't– they didn't put it that way 70
it was for my benefit they were going to keep me working 71
ostensibly you know 72
but it proved that it was right enough 73
eh so they kept me working 74
well the first couple of days off the north coast of Ireland oh I was going
    through purgatory 75
but they were pulling me along to the– the saloon up to where we got fed 76
and they were making me eat 77
well this as bo– was borne out 78
this was the right thing to do 79
even if it meant that 80
you see this was a coal-burner 81
and the– the ashes used to come up from the– the stoke-hole in a chute– in a lift
    sort of thing 82
come out in small canvas bags 83
and the– the trimmer would take them to this chute down the side of the– the ship 84
where he poured these ashes out 85
well it– it was quite handy to the– the galley where I worked 86
and I'd be standing there scrubbing or cleaning pots 87
and every now and again I'd make a beeline for this chute 88
and be sick there you know 89
but wunst I got by the first day 90
keeping working 91
and keeping being sick and that 92
and eating 93
being made to eat 94
I definitely got by the first day quite well 95
but eh I was the first to be sick 96
but I think I was the first to get over it too 97
the cadet officer 98
him that had been to sea in destroyers 99
when he got hit with this off the north coast of Ireland 100

he– he didn't know what had hit him	101
actually the story was related	102
that they were all seated at the table in the saloon	103
and the skipper was at the head of the table	104
when he took one of his bilious bouts	105
[*laughs*]	
and spewed all over the table	106
the skipper picked himself off– off his seat	107
and said to the– the chief steward	108
"Give me my meals up in my room from now on"	109
he says "I wouldn't eat amongst these people"	110
[*laughs*]	
and as for the Highland ordinary seaman oh he had the worst time	111
actually I think we were out about a week from Scotland	112
and he was still going through Purgatory	113
he laid up	114
the bosun allowed him to lie up	115
And because he was lying up and being sick into this pail	116
he didnae get over it very quick you know	117
but one of the days the cook said to me	118
"You think you were bad" he says	119
"go up the stair and take a look	120
go up that accommodation ladder"	121
so I went up this accommodation ladder	122
and here's this Highland sea– ordinary seaman	123
he's got his arm round about a guy rope from the funnel	124
and he's got– clad in his oilskins seaboots leggings the coat and the souwester	125
and the– the spray's coming right over the boat deck where he is	126
with his– his arm linked in this– this guy rope	127
and he's still looking not well	128
and this is him after being about a week laid up in his bed	129
he was– he was overcoming it by this time	130
but it was– it was a struggle	131
so I think I got by it best of all	132

Although the story was elicited by Labov's Danger-of-Death question (Labov 1972) it is not primarily about danger. The background to the story is the naval war in the north Atlantic and the risk of being torpedoed. Wilson because of his age and innocence did not think of the danger. As he said elsewhere in the interview:

3. (John Wilson)	
but danger it's only a word	1
so eh my first trip at sea eh I peeled off	2

the first nights there	3
stripped off all my clothes	4
got into my pyjamas to go to bed	5
and I appalled everybody completely appalled them	6
some of the old sea lags who had been torpedoed three or four times saw fit	7
they were so frightened so afraid	8
that they were sleeping underneath the boats on the boat deck	9
so that if anything happened they would be right there	10

However, he does not mention this danger in the story presented in (2).

The story in (2) is an unusual type of narrative. Labov defines narrative as "one method of recapitulating past experience by matching a verbal sequence of clauses to the sequence of events which (it is inferred) actually occurred" (Labov 1972a: 359–360). As Fleischman (1990: 994–100) points out, the notion of "event" is problematic. She cites, among others, Bauman:

Events are action structures, organized by relationships of causality, temporality, and other such linkages; narratives are verbal structures, organized by rules of discourse. Most commonly narratives are seen as verbal icons of the events they represent. (Bauman 1986: 5)

But what are the "events" in (2)?

a. The seamen told Wilson that there were two other "first trippers".
b. Wilson asked the cadet if he thought he would be seasick.
c. The cadet haughtily rejected the notion.
d. Wilson asked the Highland seaman the same question.
e. The seaman said that he did not expect to be seasick.
f. Wilson became seasick.
g. Wilson recovered quickly.
h. The cadet vomited at the dinner table.
i. The Highland seaman was seasick and did not recover quickly.

None of these is a typical "action structure". The sequence (a–e) consists of speech acts. In the sequence (f–i) none of the protagonists is an agent. Yet this is clearly an effective story. When I have played the tape to audiences they have reacted appropriately, including laughing at the climax when the cadet is humiliated, and nobody has ever given "the withering rejoinder 'So what?'" (Labov 1972a: 366). This is not a "pointless" story and it is eminently tellable. The difference between this narrative and most others is that the important events in this story are not actions but mental states.

After providing the vital background information about the weather being rough in the north Atlantic at the time of his first trip, Wilson proceeds to explain his state of mind at the time. He focusses first on the immediate anxiety of seasickness, because he had been told that it was "pretty gruelling". He then explains why he "was dying" to see the New World, because "over there there was everything". (He later mentioned "candy" and "comic books" as examples of the "goodies" that he found in the U.S.) Thus, both things that "were uppermost" in his mind are reflections of his youth and lack of experience.

This is followed by the introduction of the principal characters, the other two "first trippers" in addition to himself, the English cadet officer and the Highland Ordinary Seaman, who are not named but are always referred to by their titles. The repeated references to them by their titles keeps them as anonymous, impersonal figures. This contrasts with the careful naming of the captains in example (1). Wilson presents himself as the innocent compared with the others (presumably both older than he was) who do not share his anxiety. He makes two good-natured approaches and is rebuffed in each case. The point of the story is his vindication. As it turns out, Wilson was right to be concerned about seasickness and the confidence of the others is shown to have been misplaced.

Perhaps even more than in other narratives, the language of the quoted dialogue is important, not just for the information it conveys directly but also because of the attitudes revealed. Wilson's approach to the cadet is direct and innocent "Do you think you'll be seasick?" but the cadet "looked down his nose" at him and gave him "a glower" and ("typical English upper crust") responded with a face-threatening-act (Brown and Levinson 1987) "I've been to sea in destroyers". This is clearly a deliberate attempt to intimidate Wilson and make him feel inadequate. Although having been to sea in destroyers need not be (and was not) a guarantee against seasickness, the pragmatic force of the remark is to imply that experience of this kind is of crucial importance. Wilson is trapped into accepting this implication and admitting that he has not had this type of experience ("me I've never been any-where"). It is not clear whether Wilson said this to the cadet or only thought it. It is unlikely that the expansion in lines 40–44 were uttered at the time. They either represent Wilson's thoughts or they are an elaboration for my benefit. The reference to "wunst again the Ayrshire coast" refers back to a remark he had made to me earlier in the inter-view about his mother not having travelled further than some of the local holiday resorts on the Ayrshire coast, so the latter interpretation is more likely.

Wilson's realisation that he has not got "much of a companion there" again shows his innocence. He had apparently expected that the fact of their being "first trippers" would have provided the basis for some kind of friendly relationship. He had not anticipated the strength of the barrier that social class erected between them. The cadet, by his manner and his speech, rejects any possibility of breaching the barrier. Although Wilson does not make any attempt to imitate the cadet's accent, it can safely be assumed that it was very different from his own, possibly RP or close to it, and this would have increased the so-cial distance. It is also quite possible that this was the first time that Wilson had directly encountered this kind of accent and use of lan-guage in someone close to his own age. There is no reason to believe that he would ever before have met "a typical English upper crust" person of his own age. The satisfaction with which he tells the story suggests that the episode made a strong impression on him.

The Highland seaman from Skye was "a very nice lad" and "much more amiable" than the cadet. Wilson "had a longer talk with him" since "he wasnae near as snooty". The Highland seaman's form of speech would also be very different from Wilson's, being a form of Highland English, but the differences would be regional only, not di-rectly related to social class, and much less face-threatening. The fact that he had "been out a lot in rowing boats and things like that", even in form, is much more friendly than "been to sea in destroyers". Al-though "been to sea" could be true even if the cadet had only made a short trip it could also refer to an extended naval career. "Been out a lot" does not have this ambiguity. Similarly, "destroyers" carries the implication of access to power, while the reference to "rowing boats and things like that" presents a much less threatening association. The cadet's tone and manner do not encourage Wilson to ask the kind of questions that might make the nature of the experience more explicit: "How often? For how long? In what capacity?" Unlike the cadet, who does not deign to answer Wilson's question directly, the seaman says "I think I'll be OK". The tentativeness of this reply is not much solace to Wilson and he "felt very alone".

However, the cooks on board provided the right guidance: "when the seasickness hits you you're no lying up". This is the kind of voice that Wilson would find much more familiar, using the kind of forms common in his community. "You're no lying up" contains the contracted auxiliary and the common lowland Scots negative *no* (instead of *not*) that Wilson himself uses. Neither the English cadet nor the Highland seaman would use this form. So it is only fitting that the response that is given by Wilson's own type of people should prove "right enough".

The climax provides dramatic irony and sweet revenge. While Wilson had been working in the galley scrubbing pots, the cadet officer, "him that had been to sea in destroyers" (and with what pleasurable sarcasm Wilson utters the words) had been sitting in the saloon ready to eat the food prepared in the galley. Wilson enjoys the story "that was related" (a story within a story, as it were) about how the cadet "took one of his bilious bouts" and "spewed all over the table". Wilson's revenge comes when the captain says "I wouldn't eat amongst these people" putting the ("typical English") cadet into a rejected category. Note that the captain is quoted as saying *wouldn't* and not *wouldnae*. The implication is that it is someone from the cadet's own background (and who might also have been to sea in destroyers) that makes the judgment on him. This is internal evaluation in Labov's sense (Labov 1972a).

Meanwhile, the poor Highland Ordinary Seaman "was still going through Purgatory" after a week at sea. The use of the phrase "going through Purgatory" which Wilson had employed to describe his own "gruelling" experience suggests a sympathy for the Highland seaman that is totally lacking in his account of the cadet's humiliation. Since the other thing that "was uppermost" in Wilson's mind was "seeing the New World" (that "Aladdin's Cave"), we can expect Purgatory to be followed by Paradise. As is appropriate in a divine comedy, there is a mixture of high style and low style in Wilson's narrative.

Wilson's interview is full of what Bakhtin calls "hybrid constructions". A hybrid construction is

an utterance that belongs, by its grammatical (syntactic) and compositional markers, to a single speaker, but that actually contains mixed within it two utterances, two speech manners, two styles, two "languages", two semantic and axiological belief systems" (Bakhtin 1981: 304–5, cited by Wertsch 1991: 59).

In Finegan and Biber's terms, Wilson exhibits an unusual combination of "elaboration" and "economy" features. A clear example is the contrast between the elaborated form "took one of his bilious bouts" (1.105) and the more economical "be sick" (1.89). Other obvious examples of elaborated forms are "prior to" (1.66) rather than "before" and "amiable" (1.50) rather than "friendly".

It is, however, not only in the story in (2) that Wilson uses a mixture of economy and elaborated forms. Throughout the interview Wilson uses many examples of elaborated features that give his speech a remarkable style, and it is worth presenting them in some detail. In each section the clear examples from the narrative in (2) are given first, with line references in parentheses:

1. Elaborated phrasing

What was uppermost in my mind (9), was it as antagonizing (11), pretty gruelling (13), in the same predicament (29), much more amiable (50), prior to me (66), concede the duties (69), for my benefit [...] ostensibly (71–72), was borne out (78), took one of his bilious bouts (105).

Earlier when I had asked Wilson if anyone in his family other than his father had worked when he was young, he replied: "No, he was the sole source of contribution", a rather elaborate way of saying that his father was the only wage-earner. Other examples of elaborated versions of simple statements are: "we realize the benefits to be accrued from it", "marbles were a great source of fun at that time", "[TV] made a major inroad into social life", "to acquire just a few comic books was quite a masterful thing", "it's the type of snow you can frolic in", "he'd been friendly with my dad on occasions", "the company contracted", "these sorts of things are instantaneous success", "he's been very fortunate in that respect", "it had to be catered for", "you could probably find a social community which was more amiable than the harshness of Glasgow", "they were all apprehensive of it", "that was she– her designation", "the only action we took was one of averting a collision", "[if] we were geographically situated the way the English are".

These examples are distributed throughout the interview, on a variety of topics, and the choice of words does not seem to be triggered by any internal context. Words such as *accrued, amiable, antagonizing, averting, bilious, concede, designation, frolic, instantaneous, ostensibly,* and *predicament* seem more likely to have been learned out of a dictionary rather than from other people. This is the obverse of Bakhtin's view that we learn words from the ways in which other people use them (Bakhtin 1981). They are the kind of words that Finegan and Biber would include in the elaborated register, and which they would probably consider part of a "literate" register, affected by written language but not restricted to the written form. They point out: "'Literate' cannot be altogether equated with 'written' nor 'oral' with 'spoken'" (Finegan and Biber 2001: 267) and they cite a passage from an earlier paper:

a variety can be called *literate* to the extent that it has the situational and linguistic characteristics associated with stereotypical writing; a variety can be called *oral* to the extent that it has the situational and linguistic characteristics stereotypically associated with speech. (Finegan and Biber 1994: 326, emphasis in original)

Wilson's style in the interview has linguistic characteristics stereotypical of both writing and speech. (In this it bears a resemblance to the "hybridization" that Wales (1988: 181–82) finds in some of Philip Larkin's poetry.) But it is not just that the words are unusual in this kind of discourse; the situations Wilson describes with them belong to domains in which more economical features would appear to be more appropriate. When Wilson says that the cooks were not going "to concede the duties" that he had, he might have said that they were not going to let him off his work. When he says "to acquire just a few comic books was quite a masterful thing" it would have been more usual to say that boys were popular if they had some comic books. This elaborated style is pervasive throughout the interview.

2. Metaphors

it was an Aladdin's Cave (17), I was dying to see this (23), going through Purgatory (75, 113), make a beeline for this chute (88).

Wilson used quite a few metaphors in the course of the interview. When I asked him about his schooling, he responded: "I thought that schooling and all education was just *a shackle* imposed upon you". Other examples of metaphors are "[I] *ferreted out* Captain Morris", "so of course I went home that night all quite *wound up*", "I *clung on* to an excuse", "it became *a sort of mania* the pictures", "things were *mushrooming*", (on the reduction of the work force at the factory where he worked) "it's like *pruning a rose*, they're back to *live tissue*, all the *dead wood*'s gone", (on social life in New York) "this *cut and thrust*", (on the value of education) "you'll have the–the *passport* as it were to this level where we all strive to get", "take the *hard slog* through the educational system", "this makes *a great platform* for a child". When I asked him where he put himself in social class terms, he replied: "Right at *the bottom of the heap*". Drink, Bingo, and smoking are "the *opium* that [the working class] manage to get through this harsh life with".

Such a high frequency of metaphors is rare among the people I have interviewed in Scotland, whatever their education or social class. As will be shown in Chapter Eleven, speakers make use of a variety of rhetorical features, but metaphor is not common. Wilson's metaphors are not simply clichés; they are appropriate for the meaning he wishes to convey. Like his elaborated vocabulary, Wilson's metaphors often have a foregrounding effect, because they are unexpected in the context. It is not common in everyday conversation to equate bingo with *opium* or to envisage education as a *passport* to new opportunities.

3. Nominalisations

the seasickness wasnae too bad first time (24), somebody in the same predicament as myself (29), when the seasickness hits you (61).

Wilson quotes the cooks as saying "when the seasickness hits you" rather than the more economical "when you feel sick" that would seem more likely to precede "you're no lying up". When I asked Wilson about the kind of schooling he had received, his answer was: "I daresay the– the schooling at that time was– was adequate but eh my own approach towards it because of the environment that I came from was one of sheer apathy and indifference". His use of nouns such as *apathy* and *indifference* rather than adjectives or verbs to express his attitude provides a kind of depersonalizing effect that contrasts strongly with the directness of statements like "so I felt very alone" (l.76) in the narrative in (2). Other examples of nouns used in this way are: "the war gave us a golden opportunity to get out earlier", "no doubt all these things are contributory factors to the whole", "then the seriousness of the situation crept in", "the task was unsurmountable", "these sort of things are instantaneous success", "this nostalgia tends to creep in", "marbles were a great source of fun", all these things are contributory factors to the whole", "parents who have a great insight into the educational system", "having had the upbringing that I had", "me in my youngness" (i.e., when I was young).

These are examples of a very nominal style (Brown and Fraser 1979) and there is a tendency to use longer words ("opportunity", "youngness") rather than shorter ones ("chance", "youth"). It would be hard to claim, however, in Finegan and Biber's terms that these more elaborated forms add clarity to what Wilson is saying. Instead, there is again an unexpectedness about the language Wilson uses to make what would generally be fairly simple statements, e.g., "having had the upbringing that I had" rather than "the way I was brought up". The avoidance of the latter is not because of any reluctance to use the passive voice.

4. Passive voice

things get built up (8), where we got fed (76), was borne out (78), being made to eat (94), he got hit with this (100), the story was related (102), they were all seated (103), after being about a week laid up in his bed (129).

Other examples include: "it was never brought home to us by wer own parents", "releevoh [a children's chasing game] it was called then", "the ones that were captured", "these were all types of games that they were enjoyed at that particular time", "I was designated as a junior clerk", "it was brought home to me by my wife", "all the waste has been cut back", "because he's been shoved aside", "everybody being emptied out", "nobody else in the convoy was allowed to stop", "if it was turned round the other way".

Wilson uses verbs in the passive voice with a fairly high frequency, higher than any of the working-class speakers in the Ayr interviews (Macaulay 1991a), or the more recent Glasgow conversations (Macaulay, to appear). Many of the passives are appropriately used but examples such as "it was brought home to me by my wife" are less economical than something like "my wife pointed out to me", and consequently draw attention to the form.

The above types of language use are features of Wilson's elaborated style but he also uses many expressions that are much more colloquial or even slang. Whether or not Finegan and Biber would consider these forms to be economy features, they are certainly in contrast with the highly elaborated forms.

5. Colloquialisms

typical English upper crust (32), looked down his nose at me (36), gave me a glower (37), he wasnae near as snooty (52), make a beeline for this chute (88), spewed all over the table (106).

Some similar examples from the rest of the interview are: "the schooling sort of *went for a burton*", "this is *a crying need*", "which I think was just *a posh name* for an office boy", "Captain Morris *done the needful*", "she *put the– the peter on* that right away" (i.e., rejected the idea), "so that sort of *called my bluff*", "you don't meet this New York *honky-tonk* thing", "my first trip to sea eh I *peeled off* the first few nights", "I'm *an oddball* in this respect".

It is to a great extent the incongruity of these expressions with the elaborated, straight-out-of-the-dictionary vocabulary that gives the language of Wilson's interview its individual flavour. Wilson also makes effective use of certain other discourse features that are more common in informal conversation styles

6. Self-repairs

they weren't going to re– give up– concede the duties that I was going to get (68–69), the ashes used to come up from the– the stoke-hole in a chute– in a lift sort of thing (82), and here's this Highland sea– ordinary seaman (123).

Other examples include "I've been abroad in the Merchant Navy– Merchant Marines", "our attitude– both my wife's and myself's attitude", my father was a– a burner– oxyacetylene burner", "my mother used to give us thruppence– three pence old money". Sometimes, like Andrew Sinclair (Chapter Five), he shows great concern for precision regarding his age: "I was about fourteen– no it was thirteen coming up on fourteen". This concern includes quoted dialogue. In his response to the captain's comment that he would need his parents' permission to go to sea, he quotes himself: "'Oh I'll get that Mr Morris' you know– 'I'll get that Captain Morris' you know". Realizing that as a boy he would have been careful to address the captain by his title, he corrects himself. A more extended example is when he quotes one of the seamen on his birthday: "he says to me 'You realize' he says 'that at fifteen years of age you've seen most of the world– more of the world' that was what it was 'more of the world than what most people at home have– have seen in all the days of their life'".

Like his use of elaborated vocabulary and metaphors, Wilson's use of repair indicates his total seriousness about what he is saying.

7. Discourse markers

this is really funny you know (1), things get built up you know (8), but over there there was everything you know (22), I said "Do you think you'll be seasick?" you know just like that you know and he sort of looked down his nose at me you know (34–36).

The principal discourse marker (Schiffrin 1987) in Wilson's interview is *you know* which he uses with a very high frequency (12.89 per 1,000 words). Sequences of a particular discourse marker, as in the example in lines 34–36, are not uncommon (Macaulay 2002). Like many speakers, Wilson tends to use *you know* in three ways, and most frequently in final position. The first is as a bracketting feature, as in "and he sort of looked down his nose at me *you know*". The second use is following a remark that gives supplementary background information, e.g., "everything was in a chaotic turmoil at that time *you know*", "which was unofficial by the way *you know*", and "and a message came through from Liverpool– by phone *you know*". The third use is in response to the interviewer's questions. After the initial sequence of family background questions, Wilson uses *you know* about a third of the time in response to my questions, e.g., "What kind of things did you do when you weren't in school?" "Oh gosh things have changed *you know*", "How did you decide who was 'het' (i.e., 'it' in a chasing game)?" "We used to eh wet one hand *you know* behind your back eh *you know*", "Have you seen much change in the working conditions?" "Eh the– the shop's got bigger *you know*". The high frequency with which Wilson uses *you know* is an indication of fluent, impromptu speech (Östman 1982, Macaulay 2002b) and this would be in line with Finegan and Biber's notion of "Be quick and easy" as characteristic of economical expression.

   To what extent are the three models presented at the beginning of this chapter, Attention-to-speech, Audience Design, and Register Variation, helpful in explaining Wilson's style? As stated earlier, it is obvious that Wilson is very conscious of the interview situation and that his speech is affected by the fact that he is being interviewed by a middle-class, academic interviewer. This can be seen in a number of features. First of all in pronunciation. Four vowel variables were investigated in the Glasgow study (Macaulay 1977) from which Wilson's interview comes. The details of the variation need not be presented here, but a composite scale for the vowel variables was constructed showing how the individual ranked. On that scale Wilson is much closer to the middle-class speaker immediately above him than he is to the next ranked working-class man who is from a very similar background but had spent all his life in Glasgow (Macaulay 1977: 58). Wilson also uses fewer glottal stops before a following vowel or pause than any of the other working-class men in the 1973 Glasgow sample. Secondly, in morphology. Wilson uses the negative clitic *-nae* much less frequently than any of the working-class speakers in the Ayr study (the comparative figures were not tabulated for either Glasgow study). Wilson uses *no* for *not* only half as frequently as the working-class speakers in the Ayr interviews. There are only rare examples of forms such as *done* as a finite past tense, *went* as a past participle, *wer* for "our", and *wunst* and *twicest* [twaɪst] for *once* and *twice*.

The small number of these phonological and morphological features suggests that Wilson was accommodating to me to some extent and monitoring his form of speech. Without other evidence there is no way of knowing how close the recording comes to showing Wilson's "vernacular speech that is used when the interviewer is absent" (Labov 2001: 88), but it is highly unlikely that it represents "that mode of speech that is acquired in pre-adolescent years" (Labov 1981: 3). The young Wilson would not have known many of the words he uses in the interview.

Turning next to Bell's Audience Design model, his second tenet is repeated below:

Style derives its meaning from the association of linguistic features with particular groups. (Bell 2001: 142)

What particular group would be relevant for Wilson's style? When I asked Wilson what kind of schooling he had received, he said that he assumed it was "adequate":

4. (John Wilson)
but eh my approach to it
because of the environment that I came from
was one of sheer apathy and indifference

I thought that schooling and all education was just a shackle
imposed upon you
something that you had to do because you had no option

Since then, Wilson said that he and his wife had learned "the benefits of education" and "we realise the benefits to be accrued from it". When I asked him what it took to get ahead in life, he mentioned either having a natural athletic or artistic "flair" that would lead to success or "you take the hard slog through the educational system". He said how when he was younger he did not recognise the importance of parents in bringing up children: "but it's been brought home to me now that you've got to be feeding kids more than one way when they're young".

5. (John Wilson)
I realise now that parents who have a great insight into the educational system know
that you don't talk down to a child
you speak to it as an adult
you try to nurture and bring it along
and this makes a great platform for a child when it goes to school
and when it starts to circulate in other social groups
then it's– it's got this start that the working-class child hasn't got
because he's been shoved aside all the time
he's had to make his own experiments
and draw his own conclusions
they havenae been passed on from parents

This is Wilson's version of Finegan and Biber's Register Axiom and it also gives the answer to the question regarding Bell's second tenet. Wilson is keenly aware of the significance of language well beyond the kind of "dialect features" (Coupland, 2001) that his speech contains. When I asked Wilson if he could always tell a Glasgow speaker by his accent, he said he was not sure but his wife intervened to say that she always could. This was one of her rare contributions to the interview. Wilson knows that "the great platform" that middle-class parents provide is not only accent but also access to wider knowledge.

So how successfully do the three models of stylistic variation explain Wilson's remarkable style? Labov's Attention-to-Speech model does not help much. Given Wilson's emotional involvement in telling the story in (2), Labov's Decision Tree would predict a closer resemblance to Wilson's basic form of speech, because it is a fully performed narrative and ought to come into the category of Casual Speech. Although we have no evidence of how he speaks outside of the interview situation, it would be unwise to take (2) as an example of his everyday use of language. Presumably, Wilson had told this story about his "first trip" on various occasions before. One can only speculate whether in other versions he used such words as *predicament* and *antagonizing*.

Bell's Audience Design model is obviously relevant here. In his appearance, in the setting, and in his language, Wilson sends signals that he considers the interview a serious matter. Unlike some of those I interviewed as part of the survey, he has no doubts that his responses will be an important contribution to the research project. He knows that I am an academic and it would not be surprising if he chose his words carefully, having some conception of how academics think and write and even speak. He is quite aware of my reaction. In (1) above he spoke of the captain's response to his request for the job as a galley boy: "and he just smiled the way you're smiling now you know". He was obviously monitoring my responses. So his speech is to some extent consistent with Bell's third tenet "Speakers design their style primarily for and in response to their audience".

However, there is a difficulty in interpreting Wilson's speech in the interview as "primarily" designed for my benefit. It is unlikely that Wilson would have been able to "design" the kind of style he manifests in the interview solely "in response to" my role as hearer. There are too many examples of "elaborated" features for them to have been created anew in the interview. This brings us to Finegan and Biber's Register Axiom. Finegan and Biber present their axiom as a general principle for social differences in language.

Finegan and Biber's **Register Axiom** refers to the notion of access to certain forms of speech as a predictor of style:

If a linguistic feature is distributed across social groups and communicative situations or registers, then the social groups *with greater access* to the situations and registers in which the features occur more frequently *will exhibit more frequent use* of those features in their social dialects. (Finegan and Biber 2001: 265, emphasis in original)

Wilson left school at the age of fourteen and had not been formally educated at a later age. His parents would have had no greater formal education. Yet, in his interview, Wilson manifests frequent use of the kind of elaborated features that Finegan and Biber associate with higher status. None of the higher-status speakers interviewed in the Glasgow survey (Macaulay and Trevelyan 1973) uses elaborated language to the extent that Wilson does. Of course, Finegan and Biber's model was designed to deal with large numbers of speakers not individual cases, but Wilson's style is a clear, if idiosyncratic, counter-example to their register axiom.

The problem with defining styles in terms of registers was pointed out by Bakhtin (1981):

The word in language is half someone else's. It becomes "one's own" only when the speaker populates it with his own intention, his own accent, when he appropriates the word, adapting it to his own semantic and expressive intention. (Bakhtin 1981: 293)

Wilson has adapted quite a few words and expressions from different registers and "populated" them with his own distinctive accent, presumably "for his own semantic and expressive intention".

In his paper from the Stanford workshop on style, Coupland (2001) criticises Labov, Bell, and Finegan and Biber for taking a unidimensional approach arguing that style variation is inherently multidimensional. He quotes (2001: 200) a statement by Erving Goffman: "When an individual appears before others, he knowingly and unwittingly projects a definition of a situation, of which a conception of himself is an important part" (Goffman 1959: 242). Coupland glosses this by saying that "we can think of our speech-style choices as being oriented to our own self-evaluation" (Coupland 2001: 200). This suggests a way in which to interpret Wilson's style in the interview.

Rather than an attempt to accommodate to me, his style is a way of presenting himself to me. My own speech in the interview is much less elaborated than his, but he knows that I am an academic and he may wish to show that he can talk to someone like me in a form that he considers appropriate. When I asked him about social class in Glasgow, he replied "the working-class, the middle-class, and the upper crust, more or less the same as it's always been". When I asked him where he would put himself, he replied "right at the bottom of the heap". I pointed out to him that he lived in a nice house and that his children were doing well, and he said that was because he and his wife were careful with their money and did not squander it on drink, bingo, smoking, "the opium that the working-class manage to get through this harsh life with". Later he commented on the fragility of life:

6. (John Wilson)
every now and again it comes home to us
if you happen to be unfortunate enough
to be made redundant by a harsh economical system
then you experience then just what a harsh society it is

Wolfowitz (1991), in a study of stylistic choice in Suriname Javanese, observes that "at some level the *style* of performance serves to set apart [...] one category of practitioner from another" (Wolfowitz 1991: 246, emphasis in original). John Wilson's style in the interview sets him apart from the others who "squander" their money and are interested in football. It is also an affirmation of the qualities he wishes to display in the interview: seriousness, honesty, and formality.

The models of Labov, Bell, and Finegan and Biber are designed for the quantitative analysis of stylistic variables. They are not well suited to the task of accounting for individual styles such as Wilson's, which depend on a complex set of features. While it is possible to investigate variation in some discourse features by using quantitative methods (Macaulay 1991a, 1995, 2002c, to appear) more complex aspects of style are harder to quantify. Does this mean that sociolinguists are justified in ignoring such stylistic variation? The answer is both yes and no. Obviously, those who are looking at stylistic differences in the use of phonological and morphological variables may need to take a more limited and general approach to stylistic variation since they cannot deal with the complexity and subtleties of language such as Wilson's. On the other hand, if the sociolinguistic investigation of style is going to be limited to such features as vowel height or consonant cluster reduction, then much of the linguistic variety in the community will be ignored.

Chapter Eight

Family Stories

For storytelling is a primary way that families are produced, maintained, and perhaps transformed. (Langellier and Peterson. 1993: 50)

The previous chapters have focused on situations where the speaker has a privileged position in that there is no competition for the floor and the listener is attentive and sympathetic. This does not mean that the examples do not constitute examples of dialogue. Since all language is dialogic, the listener, even when silent and apparently passive, plays an important role. The stories that Andrew Sinclair, Ella Laidlaw, John Wilson, and others told me would have been told differently to a close friend, a member of the family, or someone who had not grown up in Scotland. Bella K. spoke to me differently from the way in which she spoke to the young woman from her community who interviewed her for the Dundee Oral History Project. But the interviewer's role is different from that of a ratified participant in a conversation.

Wilson suggests that conversations can be distinguished from other kinds of speech events "by an equal distribution of speaker rights" (Wilson 1989: 20). In other words, in a conversation all the participants have equal rights to initiate topics or to respond to the remarks of others. This distinguishes conversations from, say, classroom exchanges, patient/doctor consultations, service encounters, and so on. It also indicates an essential difference between conversation and the kind of interviews I have been dealing with up to this point. It is generally assumed that in the interview situation the interviewer is in total control of the topics and the progress of the speech event. This may be true in the case of formal interviews, but in the case of the interviews I carried out in Ayr my tactic was to allow the speakers to follow their own interests as much as possible. In this respect, those I was interviewing had great freedom to introduce topics or speak at length on any of them. The degree to which they took advantage of this opportunity is described in Macaulay (1991a). Some of the speakers reversed the roles by asking me to tell them about myself. In many ways, the interviews came close to conversations but it would not be true to say that we had equal speaking rights. There were, however, two occasions, both in Aberdeen, when what I had expected to be an interview with a single individual turned into a group session. The different dynamic in the two sessions makes for an interesting comparison.

The session with the Dalgleish family took place in their home one evening. All the participants had been born in Aberdeen and had always lived there. I had gone there to interview Nan Dalgleish who at the time was working as a cleaner at the local college of education. Her husband, Bill Dalgleish, had worked on the railway as a conductor for forty-three years. Her mother was also present but after the first few minutes when I asked her specific questions she did not say much. Shortly afterwards, their daughter Pat came in, and a little later Jim Dyce, Pat's husband arrived. Although I continued to ask questions whenever the conversation lapsed for much of the time I had no control over the course of the discussion and on more than one occasion they all talked at once when the discussion became particularly animated.

The tape of the second group session was recorded in Torry, a working-class district of Aberdeen, in 1979. I had been frustrated in my attempt to locate more respondents in the area by the fact that the school was closed and driving back I saw two women talking in the street. I stopped and asked them if they would be willing to be interviewed. One of the women (Betty) immediately replied that she could not do it because her father had just gone into to hospital but she volunteered her friend Meg, who protested but apparently could not think of a good excuse. I arranged to go to the house that same afternoon.

When I got there Betty was present as well as Meg, and also Betty's brother, Bill. These are the principal speakers on the tape but Betty's daughter and three children were also in the room. I managed to have the television set turned off but there was a certain amount of extraneous noise from the children, particularly the baby. After about an hour and a half, Betty's younger brother Frank comes in, slightly drunk, with a friend. Frank participates but his remarks are difficult to transcribe, partly because of his drunkenness and partly because of his distance from the microphone. Ten minutes later Betty's uncle Leslie comes in, also from the pubs, but he speaks much more clearly and coherently though at a very rapid speed. Nobody present seems to have a job.

Both sessions began as informal interviews as I asked basic questions about family background, schooling, and children's games. Very soon the sessions took on a very different dynamic and my role was more or less reduced to that of a listener. The dynamic in each case was very different as will soon become apparent.

From the start of the Dalgleish session a family style began to emerge. It was apparent even in the early part of the session, as when I asked Nan if she had been afraid of her teachers at school:

1. (Dalgleish)
Nan: well not afraid
      but I mean I would never have talked back to them or–
Bill: you respected–
Nan: well you respected them aye
Bill: respected your teachers

As Nan hesitates apparently wondering how best to say it, Bill intervenes to suggest the notion of respect which Nan accepts by repeating it and Bill then echoes this with further specification of the object of respect. What they are carefully avoiding saying is that they were afraid of their teachers, although fear was a traditional form of maintaining order in Scottish schools. This kind of cooperative response that creates what Coates (1996) calls "a collaborative floor" occurs throughout the session with all the speakers in this session. Sometimes the cooperation consists of a simple elaboration. Nan was explaining that they had just recently had a "Hogmanay" party, although it was by now the summer. They held several celebrations over a longer period than the New Year because it was difficult for all their friends to get together at the one time.

2. (Dalgleish)
Nan: see they're all on shifts
Bill: they're all on different shifts

Bill amplifies what Nan has said in order to make sure that I understand why their friends cannot all come at the same time.

In another example, Nan was telling me about a woman in Wales where they used to go:

3. (Dalgleish)
Nan: she was a– she ended up a queer woman aye
      she was a good age
Bill: she was a goodherted woman to the bairns
Nan: she was a goodherted woman to the bairns

Bill's contribution is obviously intended to counter the rather negative effect of Nan's remark, and Nan accepts this characterisation and acknowledges it by repeating it.

Sometimes one speaker will complete a remark started by another:

4. (Dalgleish)
Nan: and just have a cup of tea and then after a=
Bill: =a drinkie
Nan: a drink and that's it

Nan is not hesitating but Bill anticipates what she is about to say and supplies it. Note that Nan does not repeat Bill's suggestion exactly but completes her remark probably the way she would have without his contribution.

There are numerous occasions when a story is told jointly. Sometimes it is rather simple as when Pat is talking about the house they used to visit in Wales:

5. (Dalgleish)
Pat: that eh the house that they had you'd to–
Nan: it was an outside toilet
Pat: it was an outside toilet
      and you'd to walk
      we– oh fen [=*when*] we went up
      I mean we aye [=*always*] got– we aye got water for Grandma Burlin
Nan: aye you'd to carry a pail
Pat: you'd to carry a pail
      and you'd to go right to the end of this road

and the water was just coming straight from the– the mountains
was it?

Nan: aye

Pat: it was that high up

Bill: spring water

Nan: spring water

Pat: oh and it was=

Bill: =beautiful

Pat: really cool

Bill: aye it was beautiful stuff

In this example Nan and Bill help Pat to tell about the cottage in Wales owned by the friend of the family. Note how when Pat hesitates in the first line, perhaps because she is not quite sure how to phrase it tactfully in order to tell me what they "had to do", Nan steps in to explain about the "outside toilet", a suggestion that Pat accepts by repeating it. Similarly Pat acknowledges Nan's elaboration about carrying a pail to fetch the water by again repeating it. Then Pat asks for confirmation that the water came directly from the mountains and Nan supplies that confirmation, which Pat acknowledges by emphasizing how high up it was. Bill then adds the information that it was spring water, confirmed by Nan's repetition. Bill completes Pat's attempt to characterise the water and probably has not correctly anticipated what she was going to say, since Pat does not repeat his *beautiful* but echoes it with a similar metre and a rhyme in *really cool*. Bill then repeats his own opinion. The family members can cooperate in telling this story because they share "ownership" of it (Goodwin 1981), that is, they share experience on which the narrative is based.

In some cases the cooperative story-telling performs several functions, as in this account of one of Jim's teachers at secondary school:

6. (Dalgleish)

Jim: later when I went to the twelve to fifteen junior secondary
there was one of the teachers there
he was a terrific fitbaa man
although he was getting near a retiring age
and unknown to us he was a terrific jazz eh piano–
played jazz in one of the local pubs in Aberdeen you see
but eh he's deid and=

Bill: =Ironsides

Jim: Tinners
Bill: aye
Pat: Tinners
        Ironsides was his name
        that was his nickname Tinners
Bill: we used to call him Tinners
        he was a great guy
Jim: oh that's what I'm saying
        I mean he's deid and beeried tae anyhow
        but ken I even read in the paper aboot– aye aboot him
        and you say "Gee ken he wasnae a bad boy"

Jim begins to describe for my benefit one of his teachers. Bill shows that he has recognised who Jim is talking about by providing the name *Ironsides*. Jim acknowledges the correctness of this identification when he responds *Tinners*. At this point Pat feels that it is necessary to explain for my benefit the connection between the two names. Jim does not acknowledge this intervention since it is addressed to me not to him, but Bill takes the opportunity to take the floor and make Jim's point that "he was a great guy". Jim confirms this and then completes the utterance he had begun earlier. Bill then goes on to tell a story about Tinners, without interruption from Jim or Pat. There are two kinds of intervention here. Bill's is to acknowledge a shared experience of a teacher with Jim; Pat's is to make sure that I can follow what is being said.

Sometimes the Dalgleishes become involved in a joint narration that is even more involved, as in the account of a trip down to Detroit from Toronto one Christmas:

7. (Dalgleish)
Pat: they liked it at Christmastime though
Nan: aye
Jim: aye it was rare at Christmas
Pat: it was an experience to see eh=
Jim: never seen so much snaa never
        couldna believe it'd be– be so cold as well
Nan: and then we went down to Detroit
        and the– the scenery aye the– the=
Bill: =the lights
Jim: the hooses– ootside the hooses
Nan: the lights outside the houses and

Bill: Christmas lights you know
Nan: oh we had a ball
        well that was an experience
        there was sixteen
        how much of us was that? no thirteen fourteen in one eh
Jim: car
Nan: mini car
Pat: oh aye we was– Shirley's
Bill: in a shooting brake
Nan: a shooting brake affair
        you know it was like a Burns Day=
Jim: =thirteen
Nan: aye
Jim: thirteen
Nan: and we were singing
All: "you cannae shove your granny aff a bus"
Bill: and that was– that was the American bairns and aa
Nan: see their mother's Scotch
        so they have
        I mean she– she's taught them all these songs
        and we were singing

Here all four speakers cooperate on telling an experience they had shared. When Nan hesitates about what had impressed them, indicating by the repeated article "the– the–" a word search (Schegloff, Jefferson, and Sacks 1977; Moerman 1988), the others join in to help. Bill supplies the notion of lights, but this would not be sufficient to identify what Nan was referring to, so Jim adds "ootside the hooses". Nan acknowledges that she meant the lights outside the houses but it is only when Bill adds the final word of explanation "Christmas lights you know" that the reference becomes totally clear. This is a good example of how the Dalgleishes co-construct a narrative.

There is a similar example when Nan hesitates over the name for the vehicle they were travelling in, probably because she is trying to recall the unfamiliar American term *station wagon*. Jim supplies the wrong item "car". Nan makes an unsuccessful attempt at repairing this with "mini car", possibly thinking of a minibus. Certainly, it would not be a mini car with thirteen or fourteen people in it. Pat apparently tries a further repair but again seems at a loss for the proper term. Then Bill comes in with the suggestion "shooting brake", the British equivalent of *station wagon*. Nan accepts this while making it clear that it is not exactly right since she calls it "a shooting brake affair".

Then Jim resolves the uncertainty about the number in the vehicle by stating unequivocally that there were thirteen in it, a figure that Nan accepts. Although Nan was the initiator of this story she is assisted in the telling by the other three. The cooperative telling reaches its apogee when all four join in a choral version of the line from the song "You cannae shove your granny aff a bus".

In this example all the speakers are interrupting each other in their eagerness to make sure that I understand the situation clearly although the event in itself is of little significance. In behaving like this they are demonstrating two aspects of their family style. One is that their interruptions are supportive of each rather than disruptive or aggressive. Secondly, they are obviously concerned that their listener should understand clearly the situation that is being described. Both are examples of positive politeness (Brown and Levinson 1987), as will be examined below.

As the evening progressed the members of the family seemed to have agreed that their role in this particular speech event was to entertain me, and they certainly succeeded. If my original aim had been to put them at their ease in the situation, it turned out that they were even more successful in making me feel at home. They did this partly by telling me the kind of stories that gave me a clear sense of their way of life and standards.

The frequency with which the Dalgleishes told stories cooperatively is so great that it was remarkable when at one point Bill was allowed to tell the longest story in the whole session without a single interruption or contribution by any of the others. This came after a pause when I asked Bill if he'd ever been in a very dangerous situation (a version of Labov's "Danger of death" question, Labov 1966a):

8. (Dalgleish)
Bill: well that was in wartime
        but eh– a boat– a port ship blew up with 500-pound bombs in it
        and the whole warehouses–
        the– the pillars that held up the warehouses just got cut right through
        and everything fell down on top of it
        fellows that we knew that was working
        and we'd to go in about and try and–

Bill described the scene on board the ship with an unexploded bomb and how frightened he was as they rescued a man trapped below decks. (The complete story is given in Appendix B.) When they had brought out the man, the Brigadier in charge told Bill and his fellow rescuer to go back and rest in order to recover, but Bill and his mate had other ideas:

9. (Dalgleish)
Bill: he said "Now you'll go back and you'll have a bath
        and you'll go right to bed"
        but we had wer shower and that
        but we says "Aw we'll go for a pint of beer"
        into the mess
        "A pint"
        I takes up the pint like that aff the table
        ]*Bill demonstrates with his teacup, showing his hand shaking badly*
        the members of the family all laugh]
        so there I was
        "Steady up with you Jock"
        I says "Lift your pint"
        [*Bill demonstrates again; the family laughs again*]
        I said "Hey come on the reaction's setting in
        let's go to bed"
        but you never felt nothing until you took a weight in your hand
        aa the beer was aall over
         you didn't know what to do with your hand
        that's the only time I was afraid
        by putting my fit on that bomb   [*foot*]
        I says "If this thing goes I'm away – away to heaven"

Apart from the laughter at the conclusion, the others do not contribute to the story, but the laughter is important, because it marks the key moment in this part of the narrative and as the recipient of the story I might have missed the point without the guidance of the overhearers. A story must be acknowledged (Moerman 1988) and the laughter cues me to pay attention to what Bill is doing, not just what he is saying. In actual fact, I had not been looking at Bill when he started to demonstrate his hands shaking and might have missed the significance of this gesture without the family's laughter.

    The others, presumably, have heard this story many times before, so they know that Bill needs no help or prompting. Moreover, it is *his* story. This is not an experience that any of them had shared, so he is allowed to tell it his way, at his pace. But I might not be a very good listener, so their laughter is there, not primarily to show appreciation to Bill, but to act as a guide to me. This is the clearest example of a monologic performance in the session and although the others could probably have supplied details or comments, they refrain from doing so, despite its length.

The examples given in this chapter are only a few of those from the complete tape showing that the Dalgleish family members practise a supportive style of conversational interaction, which does not preclude occasional disagreement on substantive issues. This is a close family. They live in separate flats in the same building. They go on holiday together. Bill Dalgleish explained part of their motivation:

10. (Dalgleish)
Bill: the mother-in-law here her chummy gave us the best advice we've ever had
       she says "When you do a thing do it together"
       see they were both widows
       but she said "When you do things do it thegether
       because if one passes away you're going to be sorry you never did it"
       and we've aye kept that

The Dalgleishes see a lot of each other and seem to enjoy being together. They do a lot of things "together" including telling stories and their conversational style reflects this. In the "dance" of conversation (Tannen 1989: 18), they seldom step on each other's toes. It is a different kind of dance with Betty Simpson and her family.

Betty Simpson is 43, her brother Bill 39, and her friend Meg 41. Betty and Meg have clearly known each other for a long time but not as children. The way in which Betty committed Meg to the interview prefigured much of what happened in the course of the afternoon. Betty, Bill, and Betty's uncle Leslie share a family sense of humour. Meg is more solemn and very determined in defence of her ideas, which are rather more conservative than Betty's and Bill's. It soon becomes clear that the family style is to tease Meg and she usually rises to the bait. The first example occurs when I asked Betty where she had gone to school:

11. (Simpson)
Betty:eh I went to eh Commerce Street School
    I went to Hanover Street School
    and I went to Frederick Street School
    all good schools
Meg: oh ho ho ho

The comment "all good schools" is an example of the kind of indirect speech act that Brown and Levinson call **off record**: "A communicative act is done off record if it is done in such a way that it is not possible to attribute only one clear communicative intention to the act" (Brown and Levinson 1987: 211). While Betty is apparently addressing me and giving me information about her schooling, her main target is Meg, to whom she is laying down a teasing challenge. It would not be obvious either from the form or the intonation that the line "all good schools" is a tease were it not for Meg's response. As Wood and Kroger observe:

The recognition or treatment by a participant of a particular utterance in a particular way (e.g., as an insult or a tease) supports the giving of that particular meaning or the treatment of the utterance that way by the analyst. (Wood and Kroger 2000: 171)

The plausibility of this interpretation of Betty's remark is reinforced by Meg's reply when I asked her the same question:

12. (Simpson)
Meg: Causewayend first then Sunnybank then Powis
    [*laughs*]
    better schools than Betty

In contrast to Betty's remark, Meg's statement "better schools than Betty" is **bald-on-record**, which means that she has uttered it "in the most direct, clear, unambiguous and concise way possible" (Brown and Levinson 1987: 69). With her laugh and comment in the last line, Meg makes it clear that she recognised Betty's comment "all good schools" as being directed to her as a tease rather than presented as information for me. In fact, Betty immediately afterwards admitted that she had hated school, so her remark was not intended to claim that the schools had been good for her. The way Betty introduces this tease so early in the session in a purely factual response sets the tone for much of what happens later. It also shows that both Betty and Meg are aware of the distinction between the addressee and a secondary audience. The comments about the quality of the schools are addressed to me but their target is someone else.

The second example shows Bill joining in when I had asked Betty and Meg about skipping-rope rhymes:

13. (Simpson)
Meg: I can mind– I can mind nane of the rhymes that we used to say
Bill: you're just feart to say it Meg
          tell the truth
Betty: P K penny packet (.......)
Meg: that's right aye (.........)
Bill: I tell you you're feart to say it
Meg: no there used to be– used to be a lot of rhymes
Bill: now nane of your (.....) now
Meg: I'm trying– I'm trying to think
          you're putting me aff it

Bill has no legitimate role in this exchange. His remark "you're just feart to say it" is an overtly face-threatening act that attacks Meg's positive self-image (Brown and Levinson 1987: 61). His bald-on-record imperative "tell the truth" is an example of what Brown and Levinson call "one of the most intrinsically face-threatening speech acts" (Brown and Levinson 1987: 191). Bill does not claim that he remembers any rhymes but he seizes the chance to put an adverse interpretation on the women's failure to supply any rhymes. Meg ignores him on the first two occasions, but on the third she responds to the interruptions by saying "you're putting me aff it". There is no particular reason why the two women should be afraid to tell me the rhymes. Bill manages to imply that there might be something shameful in the rhymes that they did not want to recall. While Bill's remarks could be true of both women, it is only Meg who is addressed and only Meg who is provoked and she is the main target of Bill's intervention. As Eggins and Slade point out "teasing targets members who are indicated in other ways as being 'different' from the group" (Eggins and Slade 1997: 158). Meg is "different" not only because she is not a family member but also because her views are much more conservative.

The teasing continues. When Meg told me that she used to go out riding her bike in the country, Betty commented:

14. (Simpson)
Betty: but you were well off
      we couldnae afford bikes
      [*laughter*]
Meg: was just a second-hand bike

The laughter that follows Betty's remark is the clue that the statement "you were well off" is intended as a tease. Betty knows that Meg and she grew up in very similar circumstances and that neither family was well off. Meg's attempt to downplay the difference does not really refute Betty's mocking accusation. The exchange also suggests a pride in being poor: to be well off would be a sign that one was not truly working-class.

Bill takes up the same theme later when Meg talks about clothes when she was younger:

15. (Simpson)
Meg: I hid my school claes   [*had, clothes*]
         and I hid my–my Sunday school claes
Bill: well you were better aff than we were
Meg: and I did
Bill: better than we are now (......)
Meg: I mean Bill dinna get me wrang
Bill: we didnae hae school claes play claes and summer claes
Meg: I got it=
Betty: =we had school claes and play clothes
Meg: ah but dinna get me wrang Betty
         I had school clothes and Sunday clothes for the simple reason
         I was the baby of the family
         I mean there was Bunty Betty Chrissie Sadie aw working
         by the time I was eh et the school Bill ken what I mean?
Bill: aye aye
Meg: that's the only way I got it
Betty: so you reaped the– you reaped the benefit really
Meg: I reaped the benefit of my mother's hard living

Here Bill's remark about Meg having been better off is not really a tease but rather a statement of fact. His later comment "better than we are now" might be taken as an attempt at a tease but Meg ignores it and goes on to explain why it was that she had so many clothes. Betty and Bill accept this as a genuine explanation and make no effort to provoke Meg further. Again Meg is greatly concerned not to be perceived as actually better off than the Simpsons. She had more clothes only because she was the youngest and her sisters were all working. However, when Betty comments that Meg "reaped the benefit", Meg is quick to claim that she reaped the benefit "of my mother's hard living". In other words, Meg wants to claim to be as firmly in the same class as Betty and Bill. The topic lapses and I go on to ask a question about jobs.

Later on Bill and Meg disagree about whether the oil business has brought a benefit to Aberdeen or not. This is a disagreement that is sustained intermittently for the rest of the session. Bill argues that the oil industry has been beneficial, while Meg sees little good and much harm that has resulted. Meg is particularly concerned about safety for women on the streets. She wants to talk about encounters with men in terms of molestation and public safety for women. Bill brings the discussion to the level of sexuality and he probably knows that she is less comfortable talking about sex. Betty has no problems on this level and joins Bill in teasing Meg:

16. (Simpson)
Meg: I'm nae joking Bill
Bill: have you ever been accosted yet on (…)
Betty:will you tell me where I could be?
      [*laughter*]
Meg: see what I mean
Betty:no eh yeh I canna think (…)
Bill: I think it happens every day
Meg: no I think Betty with this eil coming into Aiberdeen   [*oil*]
      in my opinion the eil men just come aff the rigs
      and they expect ony woman
      faever they stop in the street to have sex   [*whoever*]
Betty:well there's nobody asked me
      [*laughter*]

Meg's remark "see what I mean" is addressed to me, emphasizing that this is the way Betty and Bill treat her and her arguments. Immediately after the laughter Bill and Betty have a joking exchange presumably about sex that is impossible to decode on the tape but Meg does not join in. Instead, she repeats her position:

17. (Simpson)
Meg: no I still say the eil is changing Aiberdeen
          and naething'll change my opinion of that Bill

After some more disagreement between Bill and Meg about the state of Aberdeen Betty, perhaps noticing that Meg is getting seriously annoyed, changes the subject to the church that she attends. Meg is surprised to find that Betty attends church and this leads to a sequence in which Bill can return to teasing Meg:

18. (Simpson)
Meg: how come– how come you're a member of that Nigg Kirk?
Betty: I've always been a member of the Nigg church
          [*3 second pause*]
Meg: what a cheek
          she's my pal
          and that's the first time I've kent she's a member of the kirk
Betty: I was married in the Nigg church
Meg: aye I ken Elizabeth was married in it   [*Betty's daughter*]
Betty: so was I
Meg: sorry
Betty: eh? just because you go to the bingo and you smoke
          they– they don't think you're a churchgoer
          [*laughter*]
Meg: well I'm nae a churchgoer
          [*laughter*]
Bill: aff to Hell then
           [*laughter*]
Meg: eediot
          [*laughter*]
Meg: he's asking for a hiding
          and he's going to get it
          [*untranscribable exchange between Betty and Bill*]
Meg: I'm nae amused by you man
Bill: I know
Betty: [*laughs*]
Meg: I'm nae Betty

```
        that's my– eh my opinion
        and I'm going to stick to it
Bill:   well Mrs Spence seeing we're aw entitled to it right enough
        but I personally think oil is nothing but good
```

Meg's question "how come you're a member of that Nigg Kirk?" may be Meg's attempt to challenge Betty but if so it does not succeed, because Betty turns the tables on her. Meg's admission that she is not a churchgoer allows Bill to score off her again. Unfortunately the exchange between Betty and Bill is impossible to transcribe, partly because of the speed with which the remarks are spoken and partly because Betty is laughing while she speaks. Meg does not laugh and she is still annoyed both by the position Bill takes and the way in which Betty and Bill joke about it. Bill's comment at the end may be seriously intended but the use of the address form "Mrs Spence" can only be interpreted as an ironical honorific, like an earlier use of the full form of her first name *Margaret* when making a point. His strong statement seems designed to provoke Meg rather than to tease her. In fact, he sounds as if he has moved from teasing to arguing. Meg reiterates her view that the oil will only be good when money starts coming back to Scotland. At this point, I ask whether they think Scotland should have its own parliament. Meg is fierce in her assertion that Scotland should be independent. Betty introduces a new tease suggesting that Meg should be in politics.

Later in response to my question the talk turns to the places in Aberdeen that had a bad reputation, the water-front and a street where the farmers (according to Bill) went to find prostitutes. Meg wants to defend the view that Aberdeen was a safer place before the oil boom.

19. (Simpson)
```
Meg:    well Bill I'll you something
        I was never feart to ging doon to the harbour
        cause I used to– we used to ging doon there and fish
Bill:   oh aye I believe it an aa
        [laughter]
Meg:    aye fish for the fish that swims in the sea
Bill:   aye (and with) oil
        [laughter]
Meg:    Betty would you mind putting him oot
```

This sequence illustrates why there is so much teasing in this relation-ship. Meg begins seriously to tell Bill how she was not afraid to go down to the harbour but his intonation when he says "oh aye I believe it an aa" mocks her seriousness, and the effect is confirmed by the laughter that follows. Meg responds to Bill's ironical remark question-ing her motive not by joking back but by trying to defend herself, which makes it easy for Bill to exploit the situation. Meg simply at-tempts to defend herself seriously by repeating her reason, but Bill is able to continue the teasing by making a joke about oil. Unfortunately, on the tape it is not clear what he actually says, but the effectiveness of the remark is indicated by the laughter and Meg's response.

The next part of the tape is taken up with an argument between Bill and Meg about capital punishment and the birch, both of which she argues should be reintroduced, a view which he strongly opposes. In this argument, which Bill takes seriously, there are no attempts at joking or teasing, until Bill admits that the birch might be effective for people like himself who are afraid of pain. Meg takes this opportunity to go on the offensive by saying that men would not be able to stand the pain of childbirth. Bill responds by suggesting that then there would be no more sexual intercourse. Meg acknowledges that she is being teased but does not counter attack. When Bill tries to get back to the subject about the changes in Aberdeen that had been so fruitful earlier, Meg does not want to play any more.

Bill and Betty then go on to tell how Bill had been turned down for a job because he is considered too old, at the age of thirty-nine. This leads to a serious discussion of the problems of employment in Aberdeen and Betty's daughter Elizabeth joins in, talking about her husband. This is interrupted by the arrival of Betty's younger brother Frank and a friend, both obviously somewhat drunk. Frank's arrival disrupts the session in a number of ways. In the first place I did not understand what he was saying much of the time, and since he was often addressing me directly the interaction was anything but smooth. He also used taboo language in a way that clearly troubled Betty and she takes a more interventionist role in the discussion.

At this point Betty's uncle Leslie comes in and the tone changes to a generally joking one, which is clearly Leslie's usual style. He speaks very quickly with a throw away intonation and the others clearly expect him to be funny. Some of his remarks are regrettably impossible to understand on the tape but the laughter that greets most of them indicates that the others understood them. At this point teasing becomes a general phenomenon. Bill teases Leslie and Leslie teases Bill. Betty teases Leslie and he gets his revenge later:

20. (Simpson)
Leslie: there's nothing like the old brose and tatties and meat brose and things like that
Bill: it's all gone now
Betty: you're older than us
        you would know aboot those things (.....)
        [*laughter*]
Leslie: aye and I ken hoo to wash the dishes
Bill: that's your share
Betty: he must have his brose too
Leslie: that's right
        any word of Father?

After Betty has teased Leslie about being older, he brings the subject round to her father who had gone into hospital the day before for exploratory surgery on his stomach:

21. (Simpson)
Betty: but they're doing some exploratory work today
        to see how he's always being sick
        but I said "If they look back at his record
        and found out that he had eh-yeh this eh nervous trouble
        that they would understand it was just all through nerves"
Meg: it's all the worry
Leslie: who– who does his cooking?
Betty: I wonder who it is
        [*laughter*]
Betty: you wouldnae trust me
        [*laughter*]

Leslie's enquiry about Betty's father is perfectly serious and so is Betty's reply but Leslie's question about who does the cooking with its false start is beautifully dead-pan and Betty acknowledges it by her response. This is a different kind of conversational dance from the Dalgleishes' but it is equally well coordinated.

The conversation then turns to differences in language and the extent to which people change the way they speak in different circumstances. Meg once again leaves herself exposed by claiming that she would not change even if she went to another country. Betty turns this into a tease that Leslie takes up (to get his revenge for something Meg had said earlier):

22. (Simpson)
Meg: well I dinna think I would change
        nae matter fit part of the world I would go Betty   [*what*]
Leslie: if Rob Hudson got a haud of you you'd soon change   [*hold*]
Meg: no I wouldnae
Betty: in actual fact you=
Meg: =there's no country (.....)=
Betty: =you have changed this afternoon
Bill: that's right
Meg: uh?
Betty: in actual fact you have changed this afternoon
Meg: aw ga awaa
Leslie: I didnae ken it was you
        [*laughter*]
Betty: now Meg
Meg: they're a bunch of comedians
Leslie: I'll tell you– I'll tell you– I'll tell you
        if Frunkie was here   [*Betty's father*]
        you would have to pick him aff the flair
         I mean he just wouldnae believe it was the same lassie
Meg: ah but eh
Leslie: ah but eh

In actual fact, there are few signs that Meg has adjusted her speech to the interview situation though it is impossible to know how differently she would speak in other situations. She is the speaker who most consistently uses local forms of speech. Meg's use of the local variants is consistently higher than Betty's and Bill's. The proportion of local variants in Betty's speech increases when her brother Frank comes in, and the same happens with Bill's speech when he is talking to Leslie. Only Meg regularly uses *dinna* ('don't'), *ging* and *gaa* ('go'), *dee* or *dae* ('do'), *tak* ('take'), *mak* ('make'), *aathing* ('everything'), *ony* ('any'), *wey* ('way'), *ken* ('know'), and *bide* ('stay'). This gives her speech an overall local flavour that is much stronger than that given by Betty or Bill. The latter two are clearly accommodating to me and the interview situation to some extent but Meg rarely seems to be doing so.

It is more likely that Betty's remarks are just another tease and the quickness with which Bill and Leslie take up Betty's comment is probably because they know that Meg will rise to the tease. Leslie's exaggerations justify Meg's characterisation of him as a comedian. The only time that Leslie appears to be at a loss is when he finds out that the interaction is being tape-recorded:

23. (Simpson)
Meg: well I'll tell you he'll play it oer and he'll get a good laugh
          [*RM: oh yes that's for sure*]
Leslie: you're not recording (......) I suppose
Betty: aye
Meg: yes
Leslie: you're not
Meg: he is
Leslie: God almighty
Betty: he says none of us spoke proper
Leslie: God almighty
          [*RM: this is a rare=*]
Meg: =he can hear eh you putting on an English accent
          he wants Aberdeen slang
Leslie: slang
Meg :   slang
Bill :   twang
Meg :   he's wanting the true Aberdonians
Leslie: ah well

When Meg realises that for once she has Leslie at a disadvantage, she takes the opportunity to be the one who is teasing. Although Leslie later gets his revenge, in this sole instance Meg has demonstrated that she too can play the family game.

I had not said anything about being interested in "Aberdeen slang" but somehow Betty and Meg had deduced that my interest must be in how they spoke, since there was no other obvious reason for recording their conversation. In the section that follows (23) there is some discussion about language but such are the hazards of fieldwork that some of the comments are obscured by laughter or other people speaking and the tape runs out in the middle of it. Some of the discussion will be reported in Chapter Nine.

Betty and her family are in some ways closer to what John Wilson (see Chapter Seven) called "the bottom of the heap" than the Dalgleishes but their response is not to complain or to appear despondent. Instead, they confront the situation with humour and a show of independence. It is not necessarily the most constructive attitude but it is certainly a spirited one. Their joking style is a way of expressing this attitude to life. In their own way, they are as expert in the conversational dance as the Dalgleishes and they are probably as closely-knit a family.

The two sessions provide an opportunity to extend Brown and Levinson's (1987) model of politeness to deal with situations where the participants are not distinguished by factors of power or social distance. The participants in both sessions are intimates who interact on a reciprocal basis, but their styles of interaction are very different. The Dalgleishes go to great lengths to protect the positive face of each other in the ways in which they collaborate on telling me about their lives, as shown in (24). (The number of the example in which each item occurs is given in parenthesis.)

24. Examples of positive face protection in the Dalgleish session.

a. Clarification and amplification.
you respected (1)
respected your teachers (1)
they're all on different shifts (2)
it was an outside toilet (5)
b. Acknowledging a contribution by repetition.
well you respected them aye (1)
she was a goodherted woman to the bairns (3)
it was an outside toilet (5)
you'd to carry a pail (5)
spring water (5)
the lights outside the houses (7)
a shooting brake affair (7)
c. Adding an explanation.
it was that high up (5)
Ironsides was his name
that was his nickname Tinners (6)

d. Completing another's remark.
Nan: and just have a cup of tea and then after a=
Bill: =a drinkie (4)
Jim: but eh he's deid and=
Bill: =Ironsides (6)
[Although Bill has interrupted Jim with a piece of information that is not what Jim was about to say, Jim shows no resentment and eventually completes his remark "he's deid and beeried".]
e. Helping another's word search.
Nan: and then we went down to Detroit
          and the– the scenery aye the– the=
Bill: =the lights
Jim: the hooses– ootside the hooses
Nan: the lights outside the houses and
Bill: Christmas lights you know (7)
Nan: how much of us was that? no thirteen fourteen in one eh
Jim: car
Nan: minicar
Pat: oh aye we was– Shirley's
Bill: in a shooting brake
Nan: a shooting brake affair (7)
[The speakers show no resentment of the attempts of the others to help them.]
f. Conceding the floor for a narrative
Bill's story about the bomb (8,9)

In all these ways, the Dalgleishes are manifestly cooperative and supportive of each other. They elaborate and explain each other's stories. They work hard to achieve consensus on even quite trivial stories. In contrast, Betty and her family and Meg constantly challenge each other and take pleasure in scoring points off their interlocutors. The Simpsons indulge in a variety of face-threatening acts.

25. Examples of face-threatening acts in the Simpson session.

a. Innuendo (off record).
all good schools (11)
we couldnae afford bikes (14)
you're older than us
you would know about these things (20)
who– who does his cooking? (21)
b. Bald-on-record challenges and direct insults.
better schools than Betty (12)
you're just feart to say it Meg (13)

you're putting me aff it (13)
well you were better aff than we were (15)
aff to Hell then (17)
eediot (17)
c. Accusatory questions and statements.
how come you're a member of that Nigg church? (18)
in actual fact you have changed this afternoon (21)
he can hear you putting on an English accent (22)
d. Irony.
well there's nobody asked me (16)
well Mrs Spence seeing we're aw entitled to it right enough (18)
oh aye I believe it an aa (19)
I didnae ken it was you (22)
e. Exaggeration.
if Frunkie was here you would have to pick him aff the flair (21)
f. Insincere questions.
Will you tell me where I could be [accosted]? (16)

In addition to the differences in face-threatening acts between the two sessions, there is also a difference in their attitudes towards Grice's Cooperative Principle and maxims (Grice 1975). Grice suggested that in everyday conversation there is an unacknowledged rule that speakers try to make things easy for their listeners by neither exaggerating nor understating the situation. He stated this view as a principle and a set of maxims. One of Grice's maxims is "Make your contribution as informative as is required". The Dalgleishes show their concern that I should understand what they are telling me. They demonstrate this by their anxiety to be clear and accurate, showing that they are concerned about the truth. In contrast, in their exchanges with each other, the Simpsons are happy to violate the maxims of the cooperative principle in order to score points off each other.

The Simpsons are just as responsive to each other as the Dalgleishes are. They are able to tease each other because they know where the vulnerable points are, and they also know when to stop teasing if it gets too serious. The Dalgleishes are an example of a successful family. They all have jobs, they live comfortably, and they go on holiday regularly. Bill and Leslie Simpson are out of work and live a much more precarious existence than the Dalgleishes. Their "trips" are taken to the pub, where they can find a traditional kind of solace. It is hardly surprising that the Dalgleishes should wish to portray their lives accurately and positively since they are very comfortable in their present situation. It is also not surprising that the Simpsons should be more cynical and negative about a world they find less rewarding. Their family styles in many ways reflect these different attitudes.

Chapter Nine

The Auld Scotch Tongue

From at least the first half of the eighteenth century, Scots has been thought to be "dying out" as a spoken language. (Aitken 1985: xiii)

McCrone (1992, 2002) and Kellas (1980), along with many writers on Scottish nationalism (e.g., Harvie 1998a, b), may not see language as an important aspect of Scottish life and character but their view is not shared by many of those Scots whose speech is further removed from the standard version of southern British English. Frequently, those I interviewed would make reference to forms that they thought I might not know and offer explanations:

1. (Ella Laidlaw)
well we weren't allowed to leave the premises
the back doors as we talk aboot
the auld Scotch tongue

2. (Bella K.)
I hope you don't mind me speaking in a wee bit Scots now and again
[RM *I'm delighted*]
it's the mother tongue
and to me the Scottish language is such a rich language

When I was leaving the Dalgleishes' they expressed concern:

3. (Dalgleish)
Pat: hope you can understand the tape=
Jim: =translate it
Nan: you'll hae to get somebody to translate it

Clearly, my own form of speech and my residence in the United States gave them no confidence that I would be able to understand their variety. So these speakers were conscious of speaking a form of language different from mine.

Middle-class speakers also expressed a positive attitude regarding Scottish forms of speech. Andrew MacDougall told me:

4. (Andrew MacDougall)
certainly I think you know lowland Scots is also a very powerful medium of
    expression
well partly due to the language itself
but also partly due to the attitudes of the people
and this is one of the things that I like about this part of the world
that there is this mm kind of lack of hypocrisy or anti-hypocritical attitude

And Wallace Gibson added a common enough observation among middle-class speakers:

5. (Wallace Gibson)
there's certain things you want to say
that are best said in pithy Scots expressions

Bella K. put it even more strongly:

6. (Bella K.)
because if we lose our Scottishness
we also lose Burns
and if you canna read Burns you've lost an aafy lot

Several of the speakers showed that they were also aware of local differences in speech. I have quoted this example elsewhere (Macaulay 1987a) but it is worth repeating here. Nan Dalgleish prompted Bill to tell me a story about language differences:

7. (Dalgleish)
Nan: tell him aboot Alan Finlay though
        the night– the time you was on the– the golf–
Bill: oh he– he comes from Kilwinning this fellow
        and we were on the golf course out there
        and the rain started to come down
        I just says to him "Lucks like we'll get weet"   [*looks like we'll get wet*]
        he said "What a wey to spick man"   [*way to speak*]
        he says "you mean you'll get wat"
        [*laughter*]

Kilwinning is in Ayrshire about 150 miles from Aberdeen, with many noticeable differences in speech from Aberdonian. Bill enjoys being "corrected" not to the standard *wet* but to the Ayrshire *wat*. However, he does not attempt to mimic Alan Finlay's pronunciation otherwise. Nobody from Ayrshire would use the pronunciation *spick* for *speak*, which is confined to the northeast.

Bill also speaks about local variation nearer home:

8. (Dalgleish)
Bill: of course ootside Aberdeen you'll get a totally different speaker
 outside Aberdeen the like of Huntly and all these places
 you get the real country speaker
Jim: we canna even understand them can we?
Nan: no sometimes
 but I mean look at the folk that doesnae understand us

There is recognition here that rural dialects, spoken by "the real country speaker", are likely to be less comprehensible to outsiders, but Nan points out that even an urban variety such as Aberdonian may be difficult for others to understand.

As was shown in the previous chapter, the Simpsons also were aware of the distinct character of "the true Aberdonian". They were also aware of the kind of local variation mentioned by the Bill Dalgleish.

9. (Simpson)
Leslie: I think to get the right eh different dialects
 you must go right up as far as like of Feshie Pitsligo
Betty: aye
Leslie: and then haud oer towards– in towards Inverness   [*keep going*]
 and the nearer Inverness you get
 the more proper they talk you know
Betty: that's right aye
Leslie: whereas you talk Buchan
 and you just dinna ken
 what the hell they're spicking aboot sometimes

In addition to regional variation several speakers expressed clear awareness of social differences in language. Betty Simpson (see previous chapter) claimed that I had said none of them "spoke proper".

Since I had said nothing to indicate any such judgment, her remark could only be taken as interpreting my "proper" speech as an implicit condemnation of theirs. Jim Dyce also comments on the notion of "proper English":

10. (Jim Dyce)
and well I just spoke the wey I spoke
and I was born in Fitdee and aathing
and eh ken it was a queer thing to go to somebody's hoose
that spoke proper English
"Oh yes how are you doing?
you're the– you have come to sort– mend our roof"
and ken I associated eh I wouldnae say now
but fen I was a kid fifteen sixteen year aald
I associated somebody that spoke proper as haeing money

Jim Dyce does not make a great effort to imitate the middle-class woman's speech but there is an interesting repair. He starts to say *come to sort our roof* and then realises that she would probably not say *sort* but *mend*. It is an illustration of his clear awareness of social class differences in speech.

It would be possible to interpret the reluctance of working-class speakers to mimic or parody middle-class speech as evidence that the dominated class are not at ease in the language of the dominant class (Bisseret 1979; Bourdieu 1977, 1991), but this seems unlikely given other evidence for an independent attitude by these speakers and others that will presented in the next chapter.

In her interview Ella Laidlaw several times refers to "the auld Scotch tongue" and identifies herself as a "broad Scotch" speaker. She also referred to a meeting of the Community Centre committee where I had met her:

11. (Ella Laidlaw)
you saw us up at the Centre Council meeting
you saw how we can all sit and talk wer ain tongue
wer ain wey among werselves

But she is also aware that it may be necessary to modify her speech in certain contexts:

12. (Ella Laidlaw)
if I'm in among company the likes of Mr Bruce and them
well you talk to him ony old road
you don't blow the heid wi Jimmie
but if you go further than that highers or the cooncillors
you've got to keep your– match them sort of style
but when I'm among my ain
I just talk whatever wey that suits me

Although Ella considers herself "broad Scotch" she knows that when she is talking with people like the county councillors she has to match their style, presumably meaning that her speech would become less "broad". However, when talking with someone like Jimmie Bruce, who was the representative of Ayr County Council overseeing the operation of the Community Centre, she does not need "to blow the heid" with him, a phrase I understand to mean that she does not need to speak particularly formally with him. In her interview with me she does not "blow the heid" with me either though it was also clear that she was not completely talking "wer ain tongue wer ain wey". (See the summary in Macaulay 1991a: 241–45.) There was some accommodation to me as a middle-class speaker in Laidlaw's interview but not to the extent of Andrew Sinclair in his interview. When I was arranging to interview him he said:

13. (Andrew Sinclair)
I don't think I would sound as broad to you
as I would to other people

By this he means that he would not sound as broad talking to me as he would talking to other people. Like Laidlaw, he mentions the effect of working on community associations on his speech:

14. (Andrew Sinclair)
you begin to realise that it just doesnae do for to speak in your normal way
that you would to everybody else
you've got to try and compromise as I would say and all that

Sinclair proved accurate in his prediction because his speech during the interview was much less "broad" than that of Willie Lang and Willie Rae, his fellow miners from the same background (Macaulay

1991a: 250). Sinclair had served in the Merchant Navy during the war so he had had experience outside of his community and perhaps more importantly away from Scotland. Archie Munroe said how being in the Air Force had changed his speech. He explained why he had been chosen for a particular job after the war:

15. (Archie Munroe)
I think I was a wee bit more proper spoken than most of the boys
well for a start if you're flying
you've got to be easily understood over an intercom
if you're talking in broad Scots
there no many people can understand you

An awareness of social differences in speech need not lead to a feeling of linguistic insecurity. Nan Dalgleish told how when they go to visit friends and family in Canada, their speech will often amuse their hosts.

16. (Dalgleish)
Nan: oh yes when we go to Canada
    they just– you know they're– they're away from it
    and then we'll say something in– in real– wer own tongue you know
    and they'll kill theirsels
Jim: they'll burst out laughing
Nan: "I– I haven't heard that for years" you know

It is not clear what expression Nan Dalgleish was about to use when she referred to saying something "in real–" but possibly she was going to say "real Aberdonian". Bill Dalgleish then told how they had sent a piece out of the paper to their friends in Canada that had amused them greatly:

17. (Bill Dalgleish)
this was a lady that boarded the bus the Torry bus
she gets into the bus
and she says eh "Hello Bella"
and the other one says "Hello Beanie"
"So Bella" she says "is this your bairn?"   [*child*]
Bella "Aye"
"Whit's her name?"
"Sonia"

"Oh can she spick?"   [*speak*]
"Aye she can spick
say something to the wifie Sonia"
the– the bairn says "Awaa and shite"
so the woman says "What a rare speaker"
[*laughter*]

Giving such an example of "rare" speech is hardly a sign of linguistic insecurity. Nor is Leslie Simpson's story about the woman who had only "broken the loup" (cited in Chapter Four).

Bella K. shows confidence in her language in another respect and she explains how she dealt with the masculine world of the shipyard:

18. (Bella K.)
so I said "If anybody speaks up with me
I'm going to speak back up to them
if that's the way they speak I'll speak that way tae"

But this does not mean that she had lost her femininity:

19. (Bella K.)
and they're wrong when they say that we are coarse women
okay wer speech is coarse
we can swear
but four-letter words was left here behind with the Romans
and we– we didn't invent them
they were given to us to express werself
we're uneducated in lots of ways
and working women
what way are we going to express werself?

Bella's words bring us back to the women in the carpet factory in Laidlaw's story who worked like men and swore like men but who were not really wild (Chapter Five). As Bella says, how else could they express themselves? But Bella's interviews are irrefutable evidence against the view that those who use "coarse" language are capable only of crude thinking.

Allied to the speakers' positive attitudes towards the speech of their communities, there is a belief that change is neither necessary or desirable. Meg Spence (see Chapter Eight) was outraged at the suggestion that she had modified her speech to accommodate to my presence. She accuses Leslie Simpson of "putting on an English accent", clearly something to condemn. Bill Dalgleish told several stories about Aberdonians who had not lost their accent despite a long absence from the city. In one example he tells about serving morning tea to a passenger on the night train who tipped him with a Canadian dollar:

20. (Bill Dalgleish)
I says eh "What part of Canada you from"
he says "Alberta"
"Oh how long have you been there"
"Forty-six years"
"Gee whiz" I says
"hey man you haven't lost your tongue"

The passenger's "tongue" is not just his ability to speak but specifically his Aberdonian accent.

The speakers quoted in this section are aware of language differences. They know that their speech differs from "English", and that it does not constitute "proper" speech. But they are not embarrassed by this situation and have no desire to change. They know that in some contexts they may have to modify their speech so that others can understand and they are willing to do so when necessary, but otherwise they will speak in their own way among themselves.

The positive attitude of these speakers contrasts with the kind of negative views I recorded from some of the teachers and others I interviewed in the Glasgow survey (Macaulay 1997) and other investigators have recorded similar responses. McClure (1988: 16) observes that the practice of stigmatising the language of Scots began in the eighteenth century but still persists. Aitken (1984a) points out:

Some who profess approval of "Good Scots" for historical and patriotic reasons, and who admire its use in literature, may yet discourage in children's speech the use on any occasion of vernacular Scots forms [...] for social reasons. (Aitken 1984a: 530)

Kay (1993), Romaine (1975), and McIlvanney (1975) illustrate the prejudice of teachers against forms of Scots. Menzies (1991) found that girls were more likely to have prejudiced attitudes towards Scots.

One of the difficulties in eliciting attitudes towards Scots is that there is no agreed vocabulary for discussing such topics, as I often found when interviewing teachers and employers (Macaulay 1977). Macafee (2000) analyses the problems that were encountered by two surveys investigating the use of Scots (Murdoch 1995; Maté 1996). The responses to a question such as *Do you speak Scots?* are problematic because it is not clear to many respondents whether the question refers to a language, a dialect, or an accent. This uncertainty helps to explain why scholars such as McCrone (1992, 2001) and Kellas (1968) believe that language is not a factor in Scottish identity. However, it will be obvious from the examples given in this book and the items listed in the Glossary that most of these speakers are not using Standard English or even Standard Scottish English. The effect is, of course, much stronger when listening to the tapes. As Sheila Douglas remarked in an article on Sir James Wilson: "the miracle is that there are plenty of people who still speak a form of Scots" (1998: 21). It may be a miracle but it is a credible one because of the attitudes and abilities that are clearly displayed in the present work.

Chapter Ten

The Culture of Jock Tamson's Bairns

Stories are not merely to entertain the listeners, they may also have persuasive functions, and more generally, they may contribute to the reproduction of knowledge,
beliefs, attitudes, ideologies, norms, or values of a group or of society as a whole.
(van Dijk 1993: 125)

Giddens (1979, 1981, 1984) rejects the idea that individuals resemble
Garfinkel's (1967) "cultural dope" (i.e., someone who views norms of
interaction as inflexible rules that cannot be violated), and instead emphasises the role of agents: "An agent who has no opinions whatso-
ever is no longer an agent" (Giddens 1981: 63). How agents will act
depends on their opinions, beliefs, and attitudes, which are often
manifested in their activities. Pierre Bourdieu, in an interview, emphasised the importance of looking at language in the wider context of the
lives of the speakers:

I think that one cannot fully understand language without placing linguistic practices
within the full universe of compossible practices: eating and drinking habits, cultural
consumptions, taste in matters of arts, sports, dress, furniture, politics, etc. (Bourdieu
and Wacquant. 1992: 149)

In the kind of conversation between "intimate strangers" (Gregersen and Pedersen 1991: 97) that can evolve in what is technically
an interview situation, it is remarkable how willing people are to talk
about their lives and in so doing reveal their attitudes and values (N.
Quinn 1982: 776). In addition to giving much factual information, the
speakers often express directly or indirectly their views on many aspects of life. Thus, although my interviews were not designed for this
purpose and do not represent any kind of balanced sample, they provide an insight into the lives of the speakers. As van Dijk points out:

In everyday life, people usually formulate, reproduce, and thus socially share their
experiences through talk, and this also holds for the evaluations, norms, and attitudes
that underlie the interpretation of such experiences. (van Dijk 1987: 31)

He further explains: "Attitudes are seldom isolated. They are related to other socially relevant attitudes and many form organised clusters of attitudes, which we call *ideologies*" (van Dijk 1987: 193, emphasis in original) Therborn (1980) defines ideology as "that aspect of the human condition under which human beings live their lives as conscious actors in a world that makes sense to them to varying degrees" (1980: 2). This chapter presents some of the opinions and attitudes that contribute to what may be understood as a shared ideology in Therborn's terms. However, the limitations of this sampling must be emphasised, since many important aspects of life are not covered, and others are dealt with very briefly. Moreover, even a focused investigation on these questions (e.g., Williams 1958; Thompson 1963) may not produce a clear picture. In examining the problems of developing a theory of working-class culture, Johnson observes: "it is not possible to speak coherently about the relation between culture and other (kinds of?) practices, except continually to insist that all is part of one totality. A persistent fuzziness must result" (Johnson 1980: 218). Although the overall picture may be fuzzy, the speakers themselves are articulate and speak up clearly. In their stories they dramatise events for their listener in a way that can be seen as representing values in the community, values that the speakers assume to be shared by their listeners. In this way the stories contribute to the construction, negotiation and celebration of community values. They are allowed to speak for themselves here in the extracts from the interviews, since how they say it is as important as what they are reporting. However, since the speakers do not express an ideological position explicitly and the examples could be used to illustrate a variety of different points, I will attempt to formulate in general terms what I see as their overt or underlying significance. Collectively, these statements present a tentative common ground shared by the speakers and implicitly a possible ideology.

Three caveats are in order. One is that the wording of the general statements may be less than ideal, but I hope that they are not misleading. The second caveat is that the general statements are based on examples from individual speakers and others may not share that position, although there might be widespread agreement with many of the statements. The third caveat is that the general statements are based on my interpretation of what the speakers said and many people, including the speakers themselves, might have a different interpretation. Nevertheless, the cumulative impact of the examples suggests that the views the speakers have in common are more important than those in which they differ.

Strauss and Quinn (1999) present a theory of "cultural meaning" based on shared life experiences. They point out that what they call cultural understandings have certain basic characteristics:

Cultural understandings have five centripetal tendencies. First, they can be relatively durable in individuals. Secondly, cultural understandings can have emotional and motivational force, prompting those who hold them to act upon them. Thirdly, they can be relatively durable historically, being reproduced from generation to generation. Fourthly, they can be relatively thematic, in the sense that certain understandings may be repeatedly applied in a wide variety of contexts. Finally, they can be more or less widely shared; in fact, we do not call an understanding "cultural" unless it is shared, to some extent, in a social group. (Strauss and Quinn 1999: 85)

The examples in the present chapter cannot provide more than a brief glimpse into the cultural understandings of the speakers, but many of their remarks fit into the centripetal tendencies listed by Strauss and Quinn, and it will become apparent that many of the views and attitudes are widely shared. Many of the stories in the interviews dramatise values about equality, work, and money, and these three themes will be examined in detail first. Then some other important aspects of community values will be presented more briefly. However, it is necessary to add a further warning. Most of the interviews were recorded in the 1970s and 1980s and many were of older people, so their views cannot be taken to reflect contemporary attitudes or cultural understandings. For most working-class (and many middle-class) Scots there was a tremendous change in living conditions after World War II (Smout 1986). Many of the references to harsh conditions refer to the pre-war period.

Egalitarian beliefs

McCrone (2001) devotes considerable attention to what he calls "the Scottish myth", which he compares to the notion of the American Dream. In both, there is "the notion that hard work, coupled with ability will lead to achievement unless you are particularly unlucky" (McCrone 2001: 90). This he links to the notion of the inherent egalitarianism of the Scots: "It is as if Scots are judged to be egalitarian by dint of racial characteristics, of deep social values" (McCrone 2001: 91). As McCrone points out, this belief is symbolised by the two common expressions: "We're a' Jock Tamson's bairns" and Burns' "A man's a man for a' that". There are many examples relevant to this notion. One explicit example is what Bella K.'s father told her:

1. (Bella K.)
They may have more money than you
but they're never better than you
nobody is ever your betters bairn
you are as good as them any time

This can be rephrased as a general statement:

E1:   I am as good as anybody else.

(The other notion involving a rejection of the view that money is all-important occurs several times and will be considered in a later section.)

A second example comes from Archie Munroe. He told about one man he had on his team in the mine:

2. (Archie Munroe)
he was built like a gorilla
and he was on this team
but he was the most placid and subservient man that I've ever met
a grand man and he was a good hard worker
his name was Birl Livingston
and he lived in Ballingry
he would– he was really built like a gorilla
his neck just went straight out to the edges of his shoulders
and he had huge bulging muscles

but when we used to go into the manager
on some grievance or something or other
Birl always whipped off his cap
and when he addressed the manager
he always said "Yes maister no maister"
and this really got my goat
so when we're going in to see him about this water
I says "Birl if you take off that hat
and you call this man 'maister'
I'll shove that hat down your throat
now I'm telling you"
so Birl came in and his hand was up to take off this hat
and I'm standing looking at him
so eventually he left it on
but he's still slipping in the "maisters"
and I told Birl
I says "They were maybe your masters years ago Birl
but they're not your masters now
you're as good a master as he'll ever be"

The contrast between Birl's physical strength and his subservient attitude makes this a more powerful example than it might otherwise have been. Clearly, Birl did not need to feel intimidated by the manager, particularly since he was "a good worker". But Birl has accepted his subordinate position so deeply that even with Archie Munroe's threat his hand moves up to take his cap off.

Example (2) exemplifies a second egalitarian belief:

E2:   I do not have to accept someone as my "master".

Example (2) also illustrates a corollary:

E2a: It is no longer necessary to show respect by removing your cap

Willie Rae told a story about how the miners used to show respect for the owner and remarked that things had changed:

3. (Willie Rae)
here this day I wondered what was wrang
aw the auld yins took their caps off ken
because it was the pit owner that was going by ken
for respect ken

an auld auld man he was ken come by in a chauffeur-driven motor ken
the old yins daffing the cap   *[taking off]*
in oor days they'd be chucking stanes at that motor   *[stones]*

James MacGregor told of how a schoolboy he used to show respect by touching his cap.

4. (James MacGregor)
and they were captained at that time by a Colonel T.C. de North
who was Master of Foxhounds
and Lord Lieutenant of the county and things like that
and very definitely county but
and we always touched our caps to him when he passed
but then that was because he was the cricket captain and the great T.C.
he played for Scotland for several years you know
but –eh– we weren't conscious of a difference in class
more a difference in age-group rather than class I think

The denial of class consciousness is less convincing than the account of cap touching. It is also reasonable to guess that there might have been less frequent cap touching if the cricket captain had not been "very definitely county" (i.e., a member of the landed gentry).

Headgear had symbolic significance. Boys and working-class men wore caps, middle-class men wore hats. Archie Munroe told a story about his encounter with a manager. He had gone for a job that turned out to be different from what he had expected and he was told to do some other work while waiting for the manager to arrive. Eventually, "a little man arrives with a homburger hat and his raincoat over his arm". Archie explained that he had come on the understanding that he would be working on a particular job with his brother but the manager said he would decide where Archie was going to work. So Archie asked for his employment cards back that he had earlier put through a hatch in the manager's office:

5. (Archie Munroe)
"So you go an get those books out of there for me
because I'll no be working for you unless I'm going to this contract job"
"You'll do just as you're told"
I says "Mr Thompson either you get those books for me"
I says "or I'll jam you and your homburger hat through that hole"
so he says "You won't get paid

you won't get paid"
I says "Well that's fair enough
I'm only Archie Munroe a labourer"
and I said "but you're Mr Thompson a building contractor
and the money that I've earned this morning
you give it to charity in your name you little so-and-so"

The repeated references to the homburger hat are important in the story. Archie is only a labourer, so if he wore anything on his head it would be a cap. Archie knows at once that the "little man" is the manager because of his homburger hat and the hat symbolises his superior position. So Archie will not only jam the manager through the hole he will also add the hat as the symbol of authority[1]. Archie's rejection of the manager's assertion: "You'll do just as you're told" exemplifies another egalitarian belief:

E3:   I deserve to be treated with respect

This aspect of egalitarianism is shown in an exchange Willie Lang reported that he had had with a under-manager in the coal mines.

6. (Willie Lang)
there another wee man
he was under-manager when Kennedy was the manager
and he said to me "What aboot gieing up the stripping ken
and going to developing?"
I was developing you see making these pan runs and what-have-you
but the wee man says to me "How aboot going to any bit I send you
an honest day's work for an honest day's pay?"
but I says "What do you coont an honest day's pay?"
I says "That's the vital bit"
I says "An honest day's pay to you micht not be an honest day's pay to me"
so he suggested an amount
and I says "Oh well fair enough"
and if I went oot in the morning I didnae know where I was going

---

[1] There is another example of hat symbolism in an episode that Bella K. reports about her father's participation in a demonstration during the General Strike of 1926,wearing a navy blue serge suit and a homburg hat (see Appendix C).

As reported by Lang, the under-manager shows respect for Willie's positive face (Brown and Levinson 1987) by making his request in a non-threatening, face-saving manner: "What aboot... How aboot?" Lang does not hesitate to ask directly (bald-on-record, in Brown and Levinson's terms) how much he will be paid. He is not anxious about what might be considered "an honest day's work"; he knows he can provide that but he wants to be sure that the pay is appropriate. He is not afraid to negotiate with the under-manager as if they were equals.

In contrast, on another occasion, Willie Lang shows that he resents being spoken to as if he were on an inferior level:

7. (Willie Lang)
I was on the road home in fact when I met him the manager
and you know kenning him that weel being a local lad you see
"Where are you going?"
"Och" says I "Bobby, you ken where I'm going " says I
"I'm no trying to cheat you in any way" says I
"I'm going hame" says I
"it's stripped
there's only aboot half a dozen ledges to come" says I
"the shots are aw aff and the coal's just aboot redd up"   [*cleared*]
ken what he says to me?
"Too early"
says I "I'll no be so early the morn, Bobby
there your lamp
there your cap back
you can keep it"
[*25 lines omitted*]
it was the wrang thing to dae mind you
but still I done it

It is obvious that Lang knew from the blunt question that he was in trouble, since he begins by explaining to the manager that he was not trying to cheat him. In this case the manager makes no attempt to mitigate the face-threatening force of his question: "Where are you going?" Although Lang later admitted that the manager had a point, he was upset at having his own judgement challenged, and perhaps also by the peremptory way in which the manager said "Too early". The implication of the story is that Willie Lang did not feel that he should be addressed in this face-threatening way as if he were an inferior, particularly since he knew the manager personally.

Examples (6) and (7) exemplify another egalitarian belief:

E4:   I am entitled to speak openly, even to those in a position of power

At one point in his interview, Archie Munroe explained the powerful position of the oversman in the mines:

8. (Archie Munroe)
well in those days the oversman he was– he was like Christ
the manager was God
the oversman was Christ
I didn't know there was such a thing as an under-manager
I don't think there was
I think it was just the oversman
but this man was Jimmy Robb
and he had a very deep voice
and what he said
it was true
whether it was true or false
if he said it

Archie Munroe tells a story about how he persuaded his fellow workers, all older than him, not to do some extra work the oversman had told them to, unless they got paid for it. They succeeded in getting some extra pay but afterwards the oversman spoke to Munroe:

9. (Archie Munroe)
Robb come to me later
and he says "Munroe you're no going to get on very far in here sir
if you's carrying on like that"
I says "I'll get as far as you sir"

As in some other exchanges, the use of *sir* as an address term indicates distance rather than respect. Although Archie was much younger than Robb, he was willing to assert his independence. Despite the oversman being "like Christ", Archie had not been afraid to assert his equality. A comparison of the oversman with Christ comes up in another example.

Jock Bell was another miner who asserted his rights when the oversman told him he was being moved to a night shift that would have made it impossible for him to get back home at a reasonable hour after it:

10. (Jock Bell)
I says "Listen Davy   [*the oversman*]
I'm going to tell you something sir"
he says "What is that?"
"I widnae dae it for Jesus Christ"
and I says "and I widnae dae it for you"

Again, Jock Bell's tone is not that of one who feels inferior despite his subordinate position. Contrary to the oversman's instructions Bell ignored his new assignment and just turned up for his usual shift. When the oversman found that he was still on his old shift, he was surprised:

11. (Jock Bell)
he says "What in the hell are you daeing here sir?"
I says "Whit way?"
he says "You're the quarter past
you're on the continental"   [*the later shift*]
I says "Away and pu' up your kilt"
I says "No way am I going on the– I changed—"
"You will the morn"   [*tomorrow*]
I says "Aye my granny"

On this occasion the oversman makes his challenge in an aggressive face-threatening form: "What in the hell are you daeing here sir?" (as before, the use of the term *sir* does not reflect respect or higher rank). Since the oversman has opened the exchange in such a direct manner Bell can respond by two (even more face-threatening) insults: "Away and pu' up your kilt" and "Aye my granny". There is no respect for a person in authority who does not show respect for those under him.

Examples (10–11) illustrate another egalitarian belief:

E5:   I will not accept unreasonable working conditions

Examples (7–10) also illustrate a similar egalitarian belief:

E6:   I will not be bullied by someone in authority

When he was only seventeen, Archie Munroe got a place on the face line down the pit but his wages were still paid to him through the man who had supervised his apprenticeship. After a short time Archie went to him and said:

12. (Archie Munroe)
"Bobby I'm a man on my own now
and I want a pay line the same as the rest of the men
and there's no contractor going to be exploiting my lamp or my body"
he said "What are you worried about sir?
you're going to get your wages"
I says "Aye but I'm no making no wages for no contractor sir"
so that was the last time I worked for a contractor
and I started earning my own living

Although he was only seventeen, he was not going to have any contractor "exploiting" his lamp or his body.

E7:   I will resist any attempt to exploit my abilities

John MacDonald was a school attendance officer, interviewed as part of the Scottish Working People's Oral History. He told of one of his first visits to a house to enquire about why a young boy was not attending school. It turned out that the grandmother was keeping him at home for company and assistance. When he pointed out to her the risks she was taking, she gave the following response:

13. (John MacDonald)
She had a wee smile in the face
that you sometimes get with old buddies or with babies
and after I had finished my party piece
she put her hand on my shoulder
and she says "Och I wouldn't worry too much son if I was you"
she says "after all if it wasnae for the likes of us
you wouldn't have your good job now would you?"
so I left the door
thinking very seriously about how my next approach would be

Example (13) suggests another egalitarian belief:

E8:   I am not overawed by bureaucratic authority

The grandmother may have looked like an old buddy or a baby but she was not intimidated by the attendance officer or the authority he represented. She addresses him as a young man who does not have the experience that she does. Her manner is mildly patronising, although he was the one who had power over her.

Archie Munroe told a story about his father, who had also been a miner and a trade union representative:

14. (Archie Munroe)
after quite a period of time my father had a run in with the bosses
and it was something to do with a derailed mine car
and they wanted him to rail it without payment
and he wouldn't do that
so he had the men out on strike over this
so he told the story that the boss of the mine come on the scene
and he says to the manager when he had my father in
"You go away and leave Mr Munroe and I
and we'll settle this over a cigar"
my father always said "And I told him 'You never made a cigar big enough that you could buy me with'"

As with Willie Lang's story earlier, Archie's father is responding both to the attitude of the boss and the language in which the suggestion has been made. The implicit message of saying that they could settle the matter "over a cigar" is that Archie's father would be flattered at being treated as an equal. Instead, Archie's father finds the attitude patronising and offensive. Labour relations in the coal mines were often confrontational. Archie's father is not going to be "bought" over by anything as cheap as a cigar, but more importantly he needs to reject the implication that he would sit down on a friendly basis with the boss of the mine as if they could negotiate as equals. The boss is trying to undermine the confidence of the miners in their representative but Archie's father is alert to that danger and he is not afraid to reject that gambit in the most offensive way. Example (14) possibly exemplifies another egalitarian belief:

E9:   I will not be won over by flattery

In a very different kind of example of the language of equality, Hugh Gemmill talked about the daughter of one of the farmers who married into the aristocracy:

15. (Hugh Gemmill)
and the lassie she eventually mairried Lord G.
she's Lady G. nooadays
but she was a harer her
she tig-toyed aboot wi Lord I. and this kind of crowd
her mother used to say
that if it was the van boy that come up she'd be away wi him tae

Despite the considerable difference in their social status, Hugh Gemmill feels free to express his critical opinion of Lady G. by the use of such negative expressions as *a harer* and *tig-toyed*. He also implies that her mother treated Gemmill as enough of an equal to make her derogatory remark about her daughter to him, though in fact Gemmill may only have heard this from someone else.

Example (15) exemplifies another egalitarian belief:

E10: I am not impressed by rank

All these examples are relevant to McCrone's "racial characteristics" of egalitarianism. It is not simply that the speakers are willing to stand up for themselves; they express themselves with a directness and confidence that seems to come from a deep-seated ideology of basic equality. Those in authority may have more power and more money, but they are not "your masters".

McCrone's egalitarianism does not extend to gender equality. For women there is the additional problem that the world of work is dominated by men (Willis 1977, 1980). Bella K. often made clear her views on the position of women in relation to men in the workplace. She describes how in the shipyard the women used to tease the men who were "bursting for the lavvy" at five to twelve and looking for a place to urinate:

16. (Bella K.)
and it's a raw environment
and if you couldnae stick the raw environment

you couldnae stick anything
but it became a laugh
"Oh I saw him
look at them look at them aw"
at five to twelve all bursting for the lavvy
aw standing pissing in the corners
so they wouldnae need to piss in eh at dinner time in their dinner hour
and it– it was a great display of cocks all over the place
and and eh you either ignored it
or you made pass– you passed yourself rude remarks
and it became a game for to wait until they were at–
you would see them come down
you– you knew by the way that they were looking round about them
that they were looking for a place
and you would give it–
we used sit and count
and say "One two three four five six seven eight nine ten
yeah he's got his spaver open   [*trouser-fly*]
yes he's started
wait until he starts"
then we shouted "You dirty bugger"
and then he'd say "Oh Christ I didnae ken there was weemen here
What am I going to dae?
Well I cannae stop now I've started"

Willis (1977, 1980) points out that "[one] clear aspect of shop-floor culture is the distinctive form of language use and a highly developed form of intimidatory humour" (1980: 193). Willis cites this as evidence of the masculine attitude in the workplace but Bella K.'s example shows that women (at least in Dundee) were capable of intimidating the men. As Bella pointed out, it was a very raw environment and you had adapt to it. This extract shows one way in which the women managed to cope with that environment. She said that when she went back to the shipyard later, some of the men tried to shock her "but... I had wartime experience of it, and they couldnae shock me, I'm afraid they couldnae".

The following could be considered a as basic belief in equality for women:

EW1: As a woman, I will not be dominated by men in the workplace

In the masculine world of work Bella had learned to use a certain kind of language for survival but this did not mean that she had lost her femininity:

17. (Bella K.)
of course you're– you're coarsened off
but inside you are still female
you have still the ability to love your children and to love your husband
and to understand if your husband's no working
and he's willing to work
that it's not his fault
you're still willing
you're still feminine enough to know what love is
and to shelter and to shield and protect your own
and they're wrong when they say that we are coarse women
okay wer speech is coarse
we can swear
but four-letter words was left here behind with the Romans
and we– we didn't invent them
they were given to us to express werself
we're uneducated in lots of ways
and working women
what way are we going to express werself?

Too many accounts of gender differences are based on a middle-class perspective (e.g., Lakoff 1975; Coates 1996) in which it is claimed that women seldom use taboo language. (This is a good example of how claims based on limited research can lead to conclusions that many people know to be inconsistent with their own experience.) Bella takes pains to emphasise her "femininity" and reject the accusation of "coarseness" that had been levelled at women like her. Her whole interview is a counter-example to "coarseness" and inadequate language. However, in the "raw environment" of the shipyard she had learned the forms of speech she needed in order to survive. Bella makes it quite clear that it is quite common for women to swear in the workplace. Certainly, the women in the carpet factory in Ayr could swear like men but display their femininity with their painted nails (see Chapter Five). On the other hand, Ella and her mother did not approve of such language, so EW2 cannot be taken as a view that all the women would endorse.

EW2: As a woman I can swear like a man and still retain my femininity

Discussions of the differences between men's and women's speech tend to be heavily biased by middle-class norms. Men are said to be more competitive in their interactions and to indulge more in verbal games, such as teasing (Coates 1996, 2003; Holmes 1995). However, as Cameron (1997) points out, such judgements are problematic because the analyst may be influenced by prevailing stereotypes in classifying the behaviour. Cameron warns that "it is often the stereotype itself that underpins judgements that a certain form is cooperative rather than competitive [...] many instances of behaviour will support either interpretation, or both" (Cameron 1997: 55).

Bella's own speech and many of her stories show that women can handle situations where she was challenged by a man. She told me how on one occasion she was able to make a suitable response to a teasing question when she came into work in the shipyard one morning. This was when she was older and had returned to work in the shipyard as a middle-aged woman.

18. (Bella K.)
and the smell of drink would knock you on your backside
and eh one whose name was nickname was Mousey
and eh he was a burner
and eh he opened up the paper
and there it was "No virgins in the school"
and he was a man about my same age as myself
and he said "Ah that's bloody disgraceful
look at that
look at that"
he says "Look at that"
he says "I mean we didnae kerry on at that age did we?"
he says like "How auld was you?"
hm
and there was quietness went all round about
and I was stamping out a cigarette   [*demonstrates*]
coughing
and I thought "God I've got to answer this"
so I says "Well" like that
"I had a very unfortunate accident
you see when I was six month old
I sat on my dummy tit"

Later the foreman asked if she had really said that to Mousey ("because that went round the yard like wildfire you know") and he continued to enjoy the joke for weeks afterwards. Bella could also turn the tables on the men when they teased her about equality. When equal opportunity laws made it possible, she went back to the shipyard as (in her own words) "this fat grey-haired wifie", but she tells several stories that show she was not intimidated by the situation.

EW3: As a woman, I can deflect embarrassing questions through humour

She gave another example from the shipyard. In order to be able to get on the bus without having to force her way through the rush of men Bella was allowed to leave four minutes earlier, as had been the arrangement during the war. The men teased her about this:

19. (Bella K.)
there was a white line painted you know
where they werenae allowed to come beyond this line
they were all kept back
and through this line I used to march
and and they used to say eh "Equality
back behind the white line
equality"
and em I used to say "But you know my dear that's for safety
that's for safety"
"But Christ you can tak care of yourself"
I says "Oh but it's not done for my safety
it's done for yours
you see I'm no– I'm no frightened of you meddling with me
they're frightened of me meddling with you
what a shock you're going to get"
so I always had my answers for them

The men, of course, knew that the reason she was able to get a job in the shipyard was "equality", so they were keen to claim that it ought to work both ways. But, as Bella says, she always had her answers for them. The scene shows the way Bella was able to deal with what was still "a raw environment" – with humour, with spirit, and with a refusal to be intimidated. Smout cites a description of Dundee women in the 1920s as "tousled loud-voiced lassies with the light of battle in

their defiant eyes" (Smout 1986: 88) at a time when a quarter of the
married women in Dundee were working, compared with just over
five percent in Glasgow and Edinburgh. Bella K.'s examples thus
come from a long tradition of Dundee women showing their independence.

The examples in this section illustrate aspects of what may be a
common "cultural understanding" about egalitarianism, shown by listing the set of beliefs identified earlier.

E1:   I am as good as anybody else.
E2:   I do not have to accept someone as my "master".
E2a: It is no longer necessary to show respect by removing your cap
E3:   I deserve to be treated with respect
E4:   I am entitled to speak openly, even to those in a position of power
E5:   I will not accept unreasonable working conditions
E6:   I will not be bullied by someone in authority
E7:   I will resist any attempt to exploit my abilities
E8:   I am not overawed by bureaucratic authority
E9:   I will not be won over by flattery
E10: I am not impressed by rank

Although this set of beliefs has been illustrated by single examples from different speakers, there are enough examples elsewhere in
the interviews to suggest that these beliefs are more widely held:
namely that whatever your position in the working group, you deserve
to be treated politely and with respect, and that you are entitled to express your opinions. Attempts to enforce compliance by bullying tones
or direct criticism may be met with resistance. Of course, what we
have in the interviews are the examples of an independent attitude.
What we do not hear are the stories where the speaker was forced to
back down or remain acquiescent in the face of superior authority, and
we know that there must have been many more of those than of heroic
resistance. But the message that comes across from the examples is
that the myth of egalitarianism has strong roots in the way these
speakers illustrate their interactions with those in authority over them.
This is how they would like the world to be.

For women in the workplace, the evidence of one very independent-minded woman is not as representative, but it is possible that the

additional set of beliefs may be held by many other women in the workplace.

EW1: As a woman, I will not be dominated by men in the workplace
EW2: As a woman, I can swear like a man and still retain my femininity
EW3: As a woman, I can deflect embarrassing questions through humour

Ella Laidlaw's story (Chapter Five) does not support any of these ideas but instead illustrates her expectation that she should be treated with respect (E3) and not be bullied (E6), though her experience did not involve men.

One of the things that Bella K. did after she retired was to talk to young women and encourage them to stand up for themselves the way she had. In her interview with me she told me one of things she said to them:

20. (Bella K.)
You know if I die
when I go to heaven God will not ask me if I'm a man or a woman
he'll only ask me what I have done
and he'll say to me "Well you deserve your wings and your halo and your harp
off you go"
and if it is that I go down below he won't ask me
he'll just say to me "What've you done?"
and I'll say "Well I've done this and I've done that"
and he'll say "Right into the furni- furnace with you"
and I will be burnt.
and I says they never asked me if I'm a man or woman
they just asked me what I'd done
the only person that asks me if I'm a man or a woman is my employer
now I've got to ask myself
is he more godly than God
or is he more devilish than the Devil?
What is he?

It is not only women who may have wondered whether their employer was God or the Devil.

The world of work

The 1930s in Scotland were a period of extreme unemployment (Kellas 1980: 22; Smout 1986: 114). At one time more than a quarter of the adult population was classified as unemployed and on the Buroo (unemployment benefit). Thus, it is not surprising that, even for younger working-class speakers, the strongest sentiment is a belief in the value of work and the horror of being out of work. As Bella K. said:

21. (Bella K.)
and they say to you "What are you?"
you're unemployed
you're only an army
you're only one of an army
you're no nothing
you're nothing
if you're not– if you havenae got a job
you havenae got a trade
you're nothing

The key question is "What are you?" At an earlier time people often identified themselves by stating their geographical origin, but now it is your occupation that defines you. Bella makes it clear that she had been proud to be a welder and she enjoyed the recognition she had received as a skilled worker. Being unemployed does not give you a specific identity, it only makes you "one of an army". Bella herself had known what it was like to be "nothing" because she had been unable to get a job as a welder after the war ended. It was only in 1976, when as she said, "equality came out" (i.e., anti-discrimination legislation was passed) that she was able to get a job as a welder again in the shipyard. As she related in a story reproduced in Chapter Four (example 3), the lodgekeeper at the shipyard assumed that she had come in connection with a job as a cleaner. She had lost her identity as a skilled worker and fallen into the "army" of potential unskilled workers. Bella felt very strongly that much of her potential working life had been wasted because of discrimination against her as a woman. Her attitude in (21) can be represented as a general statement:

W1:   Without a job you have no place in society

Andrew Sinclair told me how he felt when he lost the job he had taken after he left the mines:

22. (Andrew Sinclair)
I mean I worked in the airport for six years
and I lost my job there
and I was idle for about eight twelve weeks
the first time I ever was idle in my life fae I left the school
because you know you come to a certain age
they don't want you or nothing like that
and –eh– it broke my heart really –eh–
I just couldnae get a job naewhere between the buroo
and going aboot lucking for a job myself and that

Instead of enjoying the period of eight to twelve weeks when he was living on unemployment benefit, it broke his heart not to be wanted. Having a job does not only mean earning money. It means that you are useful and that you are "wanted".

W2:   Losing your job is the worst thing that can happen

Although money is clearly the most important issue, the psychological aspect of being rejected may be even more distressing. Betty Simpson told me about her brother:

23. (Betty Simpson)
do you know Bill– Bill– Bill went for a job about a month ago
 went for an interview
 and mind you he's thirty-nine
and the man told him he was too old

Bill confirmed this

24. (Bill Finlay)
aye too old for the job
I says "I've got another twenty-five years to go"
he says "If you'd been thirty-five might've pushed you through"
he says "but thirty-nine no"
I felt terrible

Bill felt that he had another twenty-five years of a productive, useful life ahead of him. To be told that he was too old at the age of thirty-nine made him feel "terrible". As Betty said "Sort of it disnae give people much of a chance if they're paid off later on in life". After the war, because she was a woman, Bella K. was rejected for jobs similar to the one she had been doing during the war. Bill's and Bella's experiences illustrate another belief:

W3:   Age and gender discrimination is unjust

The greatest condemnation is for those who do not want to work. Willie Lang expressed this view strongly:

25. (Willie Lang)
it's a crying out shame
when you see so many being put on the scrap heap sort of thing
although there's a lot mind you that don't want to work
there's others
there's a lot that would work
but there's an awful lot that doesnae want to work
and these are the scroungers that are getting kept by the present-day government

Being laid off is "being put on the scrap heap", a metaphor that speaks for itself. For those who want to work nothing could be worse. However, there is "an awful lot" of scroungers "that doesnae want to work" and the implication is that they are quite happy to be "kept by the present-day government". Those who are out of work through no fault of their own do not want to be considered in the same category as the scroungers.

W4:   Those who do not want to work deserve no respect

James MacGregor had an example of one such individual:

26. (James MacGregor)
a youngster at school told Pat McCreath one of my assistants at school
when she was getting a row for not being dressed for gyms
and never taking part in things
and Pat said "What sort of job do you think you'll get
when you leave school?"

and she said "I'm not going to get a job
I'm going to let mugs like you support me"
and actually she has
that same girl has now two
she's unemployed
she can afford to pay somebody to look after her two kids
while she goes out to the bingo

James MacGregor is, of course, middle-class so he feels that it is his taxes that go towards her support, which makes him a "mug".

W5:   Those who do not want to work exploit the system at the expense of workers

For the speakers themselves, however, there is pride in being a good worker and a belief that you can get on if you are prepared to work hard. Andrew Sinclair made this point repeatedly:

27. (Andrew Sinclair)
I mean I never ever was feart to work
and many a time I might say I didnae feel like it
but – eh – I never ever was feart to work
and I mean this is how– just like life anywhere
I mean if you're prepared to do this and that
you'll get on and that you see

W6:   Being a good worker is a source of pride

In addition to the dislike of "scroungers", there was no respect for those who cheated at their work. Later in his career, Archie Munroe became a supervisor down the mine and caught a miner cheating. When he told the man that he would be deducting the extra from his pay, the miner called him a bastard. Archie Munroe did not like that and punched the man hard.

28. (Archie Munroe)
I hit him a punch
and I knocked him right over into the waste
and the only mistake I made was
there were another two men sitting at the time
well he sprung up
his nose was bleeding
and he said to the men "You seen that you seen that

I'm going to get you sacked"
and I was quite amazed
the two boys said "No we never seen anything"
and he says "You did you seen him hit me"
said "No no we never seen anything"

Afterwards the boys told him that the man had been boasting about how he was cheating. They had not approved, so they were quite pleased when Archie Munroe caught him.

W7:   Cheating at work is not accepted

Andrew Sinclair also claimed that the miners worked harder than other workers:

29. (Andrew Sinclair)
I've worked harder in a week in the pit
than I've done in twelve year oot of them

The clear implication is that hard work is something to value and to boast about.

W8:   Being able to work hard is a virtue

Mary Ritchie's father had been a miner and she was the widow of a woodcutter (Macaulay 1991a: 223–25). She told me about her first job:

30. (Mary Ritchie)
eh– fourteen– fourteen and a half by the time I started working
that was the age for leaving– fourteen
(RM: *What kind of job was it?*)
eh– carpet weaving
 it was– it suited– eh it suited me
my mother wasnae strong
and eh you had er – you only worked a half day on a Saturday
and that let me get home
to do the heavy work you know
and just so as my mother just had light work to do all week after it
but– eh– I wasnae in love with it either

I hated thon big gate clanking at the back of me
I felt as if I was in a prison

It might have been expected that a girl of fourteen would have wanted to spend her Saturday afternoons enjoying herself. Instead, she did "the heavy work" for her mother. Although she felt as if she "was in a prison" at work, she still said that the job suited her for this reason. This is the kind of stoicism many of the speakers exhibit, particularly when talking about their early work experiences.

W9: You don't complain about hard work

The miners were, as Andrew Sinclair said, "a close-knit community" and generally tried to help each other. He was quite explicit about his positive attitude:

31. (Andrew Sinclair)
but when you live and work among the mining community
I say you're living among the cream of human beings in the country
because they're a type of people
who will help one another

Willie Lang agreed with Andrew Sinclair that "the comradeship you have in the pit is amazing" compared with other working situations:

32. (Willie Lang)
I went to the stamp works
well there a difference with the stamp works and the pits a great difference
take– take going to the pit there
you got your pey on a Friday sort of thing
and you'd a piece-box and a bag with you ower your shooder
you put your pey-poke into your piece-box
stuck it in your bag
you stuck it doon in the side of the pad when you're going into the baths
you could come back oot you'd see your pey's there
but could you do that in the stamp works?
no way no way

W10: Being able to trust your fellow workers is valued

Part of the pride in being a miner probably came from the fact that many were following their father's footsteps. As Andrew Sinclair pointed out:

33. (Andrew Sinclair)
you see under the old system was your father was a joiner
and you automatically got to become a joiner the same as him
and you got a job with the firm that your father worked for
or through your father et cetera
I mean it was the same in the pit
your father was a miner you were a miner sort of thing
I mean there were very very few miners' sons or daughters there was then
that went oot of the pits
and some made careers
some turned doctors et cetera and that
you always get that
but the majority of them were that
and they were the better of it

Willie Lang reiterated this when he told me "of course your father had the contract and he got the money sort of thing you see". Willie Rae did not get down the mine at as young an age as some other boys because his father had been killed when he was young.

W11: Following your father's occupation is valued

The second part of Andrew Sinclair's statement in (33) refers to what McCrone (2001: 79) calls the "myth of egalitarianism", the belief that anyone can get ahead through talent and hard work. Ella Laidlaw gave me an example when she mentioned that the boy she had been equal with at school was now a professor of chemistry in Glasgow. However, as Andrew Sinclair observed "the majority" remained in a similar situation to that of their parents.

It was not only the working-class speakers who believed in the importance of work. Duncan Nicoll was forced to retire from a position he enjoyed because he had reached the organisation's retirement age. He described his feelings at the time:

34. (Duncan Nicoll)
and I was– ants in my pants

I was I– I don't like not working
I don't do– don't let me pretend I'm fond of work
don't let me kid you
but I – I can't do nothing

A friend of his arranged for him to get a supervisory job at Prestwick
Airport, checking that the dishwashers were doing their job properly
in preparing the dishes and cutlery to be used on board the aircraft. It
was not the kind of job he would have chosen but he needed the
money and he managed to find satisfaction even in that kind of work.

35. (Duncan Nicoll)
and I had nine happy months there
very happy months there doing a very menial job
but it was work
and I was enjoying people again
and imagining where that cup and saucer were going
and who was going to have them before it came back to us again

Duncan Nicoll would not have chosen such a very menial job "but it
was work", and he could not do "nothing". In addition to money that
he needed to earn, Duncan Nicoll "had nine happy months" at the airport because "it was work".

W12: Any kind of work is better than being unemployed

However, if you have a choice it is best to find job that is rewarding in itself. Bella K., for example, found her job satisfaction in the
shipyard. After unhappy experiences in the jute works and an ammunition factory she found herself doing work in which she could take
pride and where she could see the results of her efforts.

36. (Bella K.)
it was great building boats you know
[11 lines omitted]
and and the ships were beautiful
the ships were beautiful
[12 lines omitted]
it was to me– it was fulfillment of everything
and it did great for your ego
and great for your sense of achievement

it took away the drudgery out of the word work
all at once you were a creator

This is from one of the most eloquent passages in the whole set of interviews. (It will be examined in more detail in Chapter Eleven.) The transcript unfortunately cannot give an adequate impression of the enthusiasm with which Bella talks about working in the shipyard. This is the voice of someone who has known the drudgery of work and what it could do to those condemned to it. She made the same point in slightly different words when I interviewed her six years after the oral history interview.

37. (Bella K.)
to build a ship was like birth
it was creation
it was beautiful
and it was something personal belonging to you
and when it was launched
it *was* birth
and when it was finished
when you had completed the job
and it was all polished and in shape and decorated up
and you watched it going down the river
to me it was like my son going out to life
it was like the same as if he'd just graduated from the university
and there it was
and it would sail
and no matter where it went part of me was with it
and even if it sunk some of my work was still there

Bella's son had, in fact, graduated from university but it is not just her pride in his achievement that she is expressing here, it is also her satisfaction in the creative aspect of her work. Her work on the ship was like giving birth and the ship would take "part" of her with it wherever it went. This is a remarkable statement about work that was physically demanding, often uncomfortable, and sometimes even dangerous.

W13: Job satisfaction is highly valued

Conditions of work were not always ideal. Bella K. describes the conditions in the shipyard when she went back after the war in her response to a foreman who had complained about a young, newly-married man taking time off his work.

38. (Bella K.)
I says "Och you're too auld
you're really too auld
look roond this place
what dae you see?
you see a corrugated shed full of holes aw rust
look what you're working in
you havenae even got a kneeling pad to kneel on
you're lying in wet
you're lying in cats' piss
there's seagulls shitting on you
you're aboot blown away with draughts
there's fumes going up your nose"
I says "Now come on
now be honest
whaur would you rather be?
would you rather be lying on your back in this dirty hole
or in a warm bed with a bonny young lassie
whaur would you be?"
so maybe maybe we've got it roond the wrang wey
maybe we should work when we're auld
and no work when we're young
[*laughs*]
cause it's the best time of your life
and things are so unequal when you're old

W14: There is more to life than work

Bella K. was not the only one who spoke about humiliating work situations. As a farm labourer, Hugh Gemmill had been paid five pounds for six months with his keep though sometimes he did not get properly fed. He described the feeing fair where the farm labourers "fee'd on" for their next six month's spell:

39. (Hugh Gemmill)
and the Down Park that hall that used to be the dug's place at the show
they went there efter that
and it was like the cattle market
you had a number
and your number went up in the frame

and you paraded yoursel up and doon
the fermer he had a luck at you
that was a kinna cattle market kind of thing at the feenish of it
(RM: *You walked up and down?*)
that's right
there was this thing on the flair
and they shifted the numbers in it
and it was up to you to – if it was your number that was you aye
(RM: *They wanted to see how strong you were?*)
oh aye oh aye they had a look
och the maist of the fermers kent really whether you were genuine
or whether you werenae

Despite the fact that the feeing fair had turned into "a kinna cattle market", Gemmill did not complain about the work itself, no doubt because he himself was "genuine" and therefore presumably got taken on regularly for farm work.

Bella K. gives another example of treating workers like animals when she turns the comment of the supervisor in the Timex factory into a graphic description of the job:

40. (Bella K.)
and when the women went up
and asked in this Timex to Thompson for recognition
as– as– as eh skilled workers
he turned round and said "I could get chimpanzees to do the job"
and really I went on a machine in Timex
to be successful you would've had to be a fucking chimpanzee
because the machine was so made
that you would've needed at least four-feet-long legs six-feet-long arms and a two-
    feet body

The contrast here is between the women who thought that their work was "skilled" and Thompson, who saw it as so routine that chimpanzees could do it. The women wanted their work to be valued, but their employer was not interested in seeing it that way. Of course, both sides had a financial interest in the classification, since skilled workers would presumably expect to be paid more than unskilled workers, but there is also the psychological aspect of satisfaction in doing a difficult job well. McIvor (1996) in a chapter on women in Scottish society says: "Work performed by women was invariably labelled as unskilled, irrespective of objective elements such as task range, discretionary content and training period" (McIvor 1996: 200).

W15: Workers want their work to be properly evaluated

It was not only the working-class speakers who told about difficult working conditions. James MacGregor told me about his first teaching job in the 1930s at what they called the Buroo School in the Junior Instruction Centre, attended by boys who had left school and were unemployed. He had been able to control the boys because he taught physical education, but some of the other teachers were less fortunate:

41. (James MacGregor)
the woodwork teacher had to leave his class five minutes before the end
so that he could get out safely
eventually he had a nervous breakdown
they used to lean out the window and throw coal at him as he went past
and he was a very likeable person but he was soft just soft
and this is the way they treated him
the number of teachers in these Junior Instruction Centres
who had nervous breakdowns
was nobody's business

The message is that it is not enough to be "a very likeable person" if you are also "soft, just soft". In order to work, you have to be able to handle the situation, otherwise you may end up with a nervous breakdown.

W16: You have to be tough enough to survive in some adverse working conditions

While the emphasis was generally on work, there were occasional references to holidays, which were rare. Hugh Gemmill told me how the Tuesday after the feeing fair was "what they caw'd Duds Day, that's when you went to buy your claes [*clothes*] for the next six month".

Bella K. explained the choice of a day for her wedding:

42. (Bella K.)
Friday night the Dundee holiday week

well em em em it wasnae holiday weeks we had in these days
it was enforced idleness because we never got paid for it
but the work closed for a week let's put it that wey
so that when couples got married then
they were inclined to get married on the Friday night of the Dundee holiday week you
     see
because you werenae really allowed time off for to get married

W17: Employers are not considerate about workers' lives

    The above examples illustrate a general set of beliefs about work, as can be seen by listing them together.

W1:   Without a job you have no place in society
W2:   Losing your job is the worst thing that can happen
W3:   Age and gender discrimination is unjust
W4:   Those who do not want to work deserve no respect
W5:   Those who do not want to work exploit the system at the expense of workers
W6:   Being a good worker is a source of pride
W7:   Cheating at work is not accepted
W8:   Being able to work hard is a virtue
W9:   You don't complain about hard work
W10: Being able to trust your fellow workers is valued
W11: Following your father's occupation is valued
W12: Any kind of work is better than being unemployed
W13: Job satisfaction is highly valued
W14: There is more to life than work
W15: Workers want their work to be properly evaluated
W16: You have to be tough enough to survive in adverse working conditions
W17: Employers are not considerate about workers' lives

    These beliefs are set out as general statements, and although they are not completely compatible, they probably provide a good idea of the kind of cultural understandings the speakers share about work. The main theme that runs through this set of examples is that work is more than just a necessity in order to support oneself and one's family. Work can be both rewarding and virtuous and to be denied the opportunity to work is upsetting and demoralising. It is "normal" to work up to a certain age and it is seen as deprivation to be denied the opportunity to be able to work until that age. Those who do not share this view are considered to be "scroungers". However, as was apparent in the previous section, work is satisfying only under certain conditions, one of which is to be treated with respect by one's employer or superior. Money is not the most important factor, but it is important, as the next section will show.

Money

For the working-class, money was always a problem. Andrew Sinclair explained why did not accept the offer of an apprenticeship when he was boy in the mine:

43. (Andrew Sinclair)
and I was offered a job in the blacksmith's shop and aw
this they used to say "hauding the hammers for the blacksmiths"
well it was just more or less starting your apprenticeship and that
I never took it
I mean many a time noo I weeshed I had
and went to a trade et cetera and that
I mean a blacksmith's trade noo would have been a great thing
but it wasnae that
it was the wages
I mean at that time I was getting about seventeen and ten pence a week
for what I was doing
but to go back to start learning a trade
I would have lost aboot six or seeven shillings of my wages
I would have been back to about ten shillings to it
I mean that was just how it worked
and as I say one of thirteen well seeven shillings was a lot to your mother
at that time and these things

With hindsight, Sinclair can see that he might have done better as an adult if the family had been able to accept the loss of immediate income. He does not say to what extent it was his decision or his parents' but he does not imply that he resented the decision at the time.

M1:   Immediate financial needs may affect long-term decisions

Even serving an apprenticeship was no guarantee of better employment. Ellen Caldwell told me how her brother had had to go to England after he finished his apprenticeship as a plumber.

44. (Ellen Caldwell)
it used to be quite a regular thing
once your time was served you were just paid off
because the boss could take on another boy and start off again
it was cheaper
because once they were a journeyman they needed a certain wage
and the boss maybe couldn't afford that

So Andrew Sinclair's refusal of the apprenticeship may have been less significant than he suggested, though presumably Ellen Caldwell's brother got paid a better wage as a plumber in England than he would have as a labourer in Ayr.

M2:   Foregoing immediate income may not bring the expected long-term benefit.

Any time off work meant a loss of wages, whatever the reason. Willie Lang told me how had helped save a miner's injured hand because he had some knowledge of first aid and managed to bind it up securely.

45. (Willie Lang)
you ken I saved that man's haund
I went up the pit with him
and I lost time for going up the pit with him
I come hame
you see the ambulance come tae Ayr County [hospital]
and I was coming to Whitletts here you see
I steyed in twenty-three at that time
so my time was cut for coming to the hospital with him
my time was cut for that

Since his time was cut, he would get paid less. Lang later got a letter of commendation from the hospital for his first aid, but the mine did not compensate him for the loss of pay.

M3:   The system of payment may work against the individual

Hugh Gemmill told me about when he was out of work, he would go to the Buroo for his unemployment:

46. (Hugh Gemmill)
and they say "Gemmill one pound six shillings"
that was what I got – twenty-six bob
and oot of that I had to pey ten shillings a week for a room in Whiteletts
and you werenae left with much

When I asked him if there was anything he thought was better in the old days, he replied:

47. (Hugh Gemmill)
not that I ken of naw
the fact is you've got money noo that you hadnae
and money's– it's maybe the root of all evil
but it's a necessity tae at the same time

Hugh Gemmill had been a farm labourer when the wages were five pounds for six months plus your keep ("and you didnae get mony claes [*clothes*] you know then"). In one place he explained the labourers did not get fed properly and had to steal eggs and suck them. He never got overtime when he worked on the farms ("you were sorry for fermers in these days because there were nae money connected to the thing and everybody had to work and work dashed hard"). He had had to wait until he got some money on retirement to be able to put carpets on the floors ("that was handy"). He was comfortably off with his old age pension only because he did not drink or smoke.

M4: Money is a necessity

Jim Dyce in Aberdeen, living in more prosperous times, believed that money was less important for the kind of people he knew than it seemed to him was the case in the United States and Canada.

48. (Jim Dyce)
like here I think people
if they've got enough money to live here
they're nae oot to hae thoosands or millions
they're nae wanting big cars
they're wanting a car but nae necessarily a big car or necessarily a big hoose
to me uh– the majority of people that I ken onyway
I would say they're mair prepared to hae contentment
than to hae big money ken if they've enough money

Jim Dyce's nonchalance about money implies that "enough money" includes owning a car and having a house of one's own. This is very different from Andrew Sinclair's "seeven shillings" a week or Hugh Gemmill's "twenty-six bob". The prosperity of life in Aberdeen in the late 1970s has made "the necessity" of money a rather different matter.

M5:   You need only enough money to maintain a reasonable life style

Jim Dyce, however, wants to contrast his sense of contentment in Aberdeen with the situation in America:

49. (Jim Dyce)
maybe it's mair American than Canada
the impression I get
the pace of life is eh
ken eh ken like here you spick to the– the guys   [*speak*]
you ken they spick about fitbaa   [*football*]
they spick aboot their cars broken doon
when we went over to Canada
I dinna ken it's maybe me that's thinks of this
but every time you're spicking with Canadians
aathing seems to be money   [*everything*]

M6:   You should not be obsessed with the topic of money

At this point, Jim's father-in-law Bill Dalgleish intervenes to say that Jim would be more interested in money if he did the shopping. There is a general discussion in which it becomes clear that Jim has little idea of how much groceries cost. Jim and Bill eventually reach agreement that the difference is that in Scotland men give their wives their money and it is the women who pay the bills; "over there [i.e., in Canada] the men pay the bills" and "the wife has to gae to the man and ask him for dollars to get into a store". Jim concludes that men in Scotland are happy with what they've got, whereas "over there" the men have "got this burning ambition to make another dollar".

Jim is also critical of the notion of upward mobility because of the insecurity he senses both in Canada and the United States:

50. (Jim Dyce)
they're sitting ower there ken
the big cars, big hooses
and they've got aa this money   [*all*]
but when you listen to them spicking   [*speaking*]
the wey– I get the impression
they got a built-in fear of somebody's going to come along
and take it aall off of them
and they've got to start aa ower again   [*all over*]

Jim's attitude to money seems quite consistent. He is apparently satisfied with his standard of living and way of life. He is not envious of his transatlantic relatives with their big houses and big cars. He is not ambitious to move to a higher level that might produce feelings of anxiety.

M7:   It is not worth having more money if it makes you anxious about losing it

Archie Munroe also gave an example of how he was not interested in promotion in a kind of work he did not find rewarding. After the war he had resisted going back down the mine and he ended up working on road repairs, but he found his fellow workers impossible:

51. (Archie Munroe)
I had the local village idiot and another guy working with me
and it finished up I was just about getting as bad as them
so I goes up and I says "Give me my books"
"What's wrong?"
"Oh" I says "I'll be as daft as the boys I'm working with"
I says "if I carry on here"
"Oh" he says "we was going to give you promotion
we was going to send you to dig the big drain down at Crossgates"
I says "Oh thank you very much for that promotion
but no thanks"

M8:   Sometimes more money is not enough to make up for adverse working
      conditions

Bella K. gave an example of her grandmother's response to an offer of compensation. She told how her mother's youngest brother,

George, died at the age of twenty having developed pneumonia after helping to put out a fire at one of the jute mills:

52. (Bella K.)
it was weeks after that
the mill master came up to my granny's door with some money
and she threw it at him
and said "I don't want your bloody bloody money
stick it"

The fact that "it was weeks after" may help to explain Bella's grand-mother's response but there is perhaps a more basic rejection of the mill master's values.

M9:   There are some things that money cannot buy

Ella Laidlaw concluded her interview by reiterating that while money had always been a problem, it was not one that disheartened them:

53. (Ella Laidlaw)
so you see the world changes
as I say oor problems were very very small
compared with what they have nooadays
you had the problem of finding a pair of shoes for one of your family
 or something for the school for another yin
something for another yin
that's just how you planned it
and you got one of them something one week
the other yin another week another yin another week
and you got past
we've never died a winter yet have we?

M10: Money problems can usually be handled if you are careful

Money used to be a regular problem for the working-class, but it is not one that these speakers focus on as being a cause for resentment. It was normal to be poor, but "you got past". Jim Dyce can take a more cavalier attitude because as Hugh Gemmill said "you've got money noo that you hadnae", but even in less prosperous times,

Bella's grandmother could tell the mill master that she did not want his "bloody bloody money".

The speakers might not endorse all the statements about money listed here and the notions may be more idiosyncratic than the beliefs about egalitarianism or work, but collectively they represent an attitude that treats money as a necessity but not something to be pursued at all costs.

M1:   Immediate financial needs may affect long-term decisions
M2:   Foregoing immediate income may not bring the expected long-term benefit.
M3:   The system of payment may work against the individual
M4:   Money is a necessity
M5:   You need only enough money to maintain a reasonable life style
M6:   You should not be obsessed with the topic of money
M7:   It is not worth having more money if it makes you anxious about losing it
M8:   Sometimes more money is not enough to make up for adverse working conditions
M9:   There are some things that money cannot buy
M10: Money problems can usually be handled if you are careful

Other topics

It is largely through their stories that the speakers dramatise their values regarding equality, work, and money, and I have tried to articulate those values explicitly in the general statements. While stories of this kind occur frequently enough to indicate that they express community values, some other topics are addressed less frequently and it is more difficult to argue that the speakers present the same level of consensus in the community. For that reason, in this section, I will not suggest similar generalisations. Even so, in these stories the speakers provide an ideological position that the listener is invited to accept as common to the community. The topics covered are independence, religion, social class, and community loyalty.

Independence

As will have been obvious from many of the earlier examples, the speakers often manifest a fierce spirit of independence. Sometimes that spirit might seem to go too far. A spirited rejection of charity was displayed at a young age by a woman interviewed as part of the Scottish Working People's Oral Project:

54. (Mary Morrison)
when the miners were on strike
they had a soup kitchen
and they made Scotch broth
and it was taken up to the school
and set out for us
and I just couldn't look at it
the headmaster wasn't very pleased with me
and he said "Well it's either that or starve"
I said "Well I prefer to starve"

Although this example does not mention money, the reason for the soup kitchen was because the miners would not get paid while on strike. The headmaster's remark suggests little sympathy with the strikers. Mary's response showed that she was not going to be bullied into accepting something she did not want.

Sometimes, the determination can seem almost perverse. Willie Lang told me that his father was "a great man", although the meaning may be "remarkable" rather anything else. Here is an illustration he gave me of his father's "greatness".

55. (Willie Lang)
the bus come at twenty-five minutes to six in the morning
and he started at seven o'clock
twenty-five to six
now see if he didnae get that bus that was him
he wasnae oot
he needed to get the first one in the morning going doon the pit
or that's him slept in
so if the bus was by at twenty-five minutes to six that was him idle
no way would he go on the next bus
there were maybe three buses going
but no he had to get the first one

This shows a certain strength of character (or perhaps a damaging concern for his reputation of always being on time) but perhaps this was not the most useful attitude in someone who was supporting his family.

Harry Melrose, who later became a journalist, was interviewed as part of the Scottish Working People's Oral History. He told how he had lost a scholarship to Cambridge:

56. (Harry Melrose)
West Lothian Education Committee at that time had scholarships
for Cambridge for outstanding pupils from the County
I got it
but then they found out that I was appointed as a Labour candidate
after having been on the Council at Bathgate
for Moray and Nairn
not much chance of that
anyway having found that
they asked me to sever my connection with the Labour Party
during the tenure of the scholarship
I refused to do that
and the scholarship was withdrawn.

This is a principled refusal, unlike Willie Lang's father (55), but a similar stubborn determination is manifested.

What the examples in this section (like many of the examples in the previous sections) show is an independent spirit that is not going to be deflected by the opinion of others, even if the result might sometimes appear to be counterproductive. Underlying them seems to be a moral conviction that immediate self-interest is not the most important principle. There is no evidence that this attitude comes directly from religion.

Religion

There are only a limited number of comments with respect to religion. When I asked Nan Menzies whether she was aware of differences between Catholics and Protestants when she was growing up, she replied:

57. (Nan Menzies)
well no I can't say
we didn't –eh– know many Catholics actually
but it wouldn't have made any difference
I had a girl who– a Jew who was a friend at one point
I was very friendly [*laughs*] with her for a while a long time
and a girl who was a Catholic earlier on
but –eh– it didn't make any difference

Although Nan Menzies is saying that religion did not make any difference, she can remember two girls who *were* different, one a Catholic and the other a Jew. This suggests a tolerant attitude but also the view of someone who was not likely to encounter many challenges meeting people from different backgrounds. James MacGregor, who was being interviewed at the same time, had a similar kind of response.

58. (James MacGregor)
but I think that the– the– a Protestant accepted a person
and wasn't really interested in their religion at all
but I think that the Catholics had to find out
whether you were– the person they were playing with or talking to
was a Catholic or not
I don't know if it made any difference to them once they knew
but they had to establish that fact first
whereas it just didn't enter into the thoughts of a Protestant
you played with a person because he was there and you knew him
I was never conscious of –eh– the religion of anybody
eventually –eh– one of Dad's– one of the friends
who used to come and play solo with Dad
he and his wife came and played solo –eh– once a week
and he was– in fact two of his friends were both Roman Catholics
but it wasn't any source of wonder or anything
it was just–just– they were accepted as individuals

On the surface both sets of comments manifest tolerance and acceptance but they also reveal that religion was something that was noticed. He speculates about the attitude of Catholics, as if they were very different from Protestants. It may not have been "any source of wonder" but MacGregor bothers to point out that *two* of his father's friends were Roman Catholics, suggesting that in fact it was rare to have Catholics as friends.

John Wilson recalled the prevailing attitude when he was at school in Glasgow.

59. (John Wilson)
I recall when we were kids
somebody at school you know somebody would say
"Come on we'll go round and we'll throw stones at the Catholics" you know
and eh you– you didnae even know what a Catholic looked like
you still don't know what a Catholic looks like you know

Since there were separate schools for Protestants and Catholics in Glasgow, the boys would not necessarily be acquainted with any Catholics. Wilson's comment underlines the fact religion, unlike race, and perhaps also social class, is not easy to identify visually.

Willie Lang, as an adult, expresses a tolerant attitude to religious differences.

60. (Willie Lang)
but you don't need to be a good Christian to go to church
no you don't
and that's only yin of the two of them
either the Catholic or the Protestant church
there's guid and bad among everything
I would say that
(RM: *Not much conflict between Catholic and Protestant here?*)
naw oh naw
my best pal's a Catholic
my best pal's a Catholic
he's in the chip shop over there Tommy Rossi
aye he's like a brother to me
(RM: *It doesn't make any difference?*)
no no one bit of difference but we can talk aboot it
nothing to stop us talking aboot it
I'd say to him "Well thae fellows are only daeing a job aren't they?
the minister's daeing a job and the priest's daeing a job"
I mean that's how I look at it
it's a job that they're doing
so what are they there for?
they're there to get funds for the church
that's what their function is
they're there to get funds for the church
that's my opinion anyway

In his opening remark, Lang presumably means to say that you do not need to go to church to be a good Christian, rather than the more cynical perspective his actual words suggest. With his statements about the role of both churches, it is not surprising that Willie Lang can have a Catholic as his best friend. A much less tolerant attitude had been shown by Ella Laidlaw's grandparents:

61. (Ella Laidlaw)
my father's a French-Canadian
I never knew him
you see the way we put it was my father was
well what would you say?
my father was a Roman Catholic
my mother was of the opposite side
my grandfather was one of the sort of pillars of the Royal Orange Lodge
and mixed marriages didn't take place then not in those days
when it was found that my mother had made a mistake
it was decided he go his road and she go hers
and being what she was
she was only eighteen
she had to abide by the decision of her parents

At the start of an interview it is commonplace to begin with factual, neutral questions to put the speaker at ease before getting to what might be considered more personal queries. I had begun by asking Ella what her father had done and this was her response. The delicacy and understatement with which she told about the circumstances of her birth prevented any embarrassment I might have felt at having asked an awkward question. She lets me know about her illegitimacy by saying that she never knew her father, a Roman Catholic French-Canadian, because her grandfather was a pillar of the Royal Orange Lodge, which is an uncompromising Protestant organisation, and "mixed marriages [i.e., between Protestants and Catholics] didn't take place then" so "it was decided he go his road and she go hers". (Note the agentless passive, though it is obvious that it was the parents who had made the decision.) This is reported without rancour or complaint.

The values of the society are clearly expressed in this decision. There was no question of a Protestant young woman marrying a Catholic even if he might have taken her away to Canada, with the result that their married life need not have offended the local community. Avoiding this outcome was more important than acknowledging an illegitimate child, despite the stigma attached to illegitimacy. The parents had total authority in this situation over an eighteen-year-old woman.

Few of those I recorded had much to say about religion itself, though Hugh Gemmill remembered Sundays on the farm long ago.

62. (Hugh Gemmill)
I was in at High Keriston there
on a Sunday you got ta'en into the kitchen and set at this table
and the whole lot of femily roon aboot
the oldest son he said the prayers
and he started away wi some bit oot o the Bible
and he would read a verse
and whavever was next read the next one
and you had to watch what you were up to
because if you didnae
you didnae ken what verse you were going to read
so that was what happened
I think an awful lot of the ferms were the same as that
this is what they caw'd the Haw Bible

Despite the low pay and poor working conditions, the labourers were obviously assumed to be capable of reading aloud from the Bible.

Ellen Caldwell told me how in the tenements where she lived as a child, a lay missionary would come to conduct a service in somebody's house:

63. (Ellen Caldwell)
he would go to one of these houses
these people didn't go to church you see
in these days you had to be dressed to go to church
and they would have this kitchen meeting
and that served these people
there was a lot of trouble with poverty if there was any death in the family
there were a lot of deaths with children babies and that
and it must have been hard for them then
well if they didn't go to church
they wanted a minister to come down to the funeral
and it was usually maybe a missionary

This is the only example of such a report and it may be neither a general view nor an accurate one but it implies that the spiritual needs of the poor had to be addressed by lay members of the church, because the minister was too busy attending to his better-off parishioners. Ellen Caldwell's remark was uttered in a tone that gave no indication of complaint or condemnation.

Religious and social class differences may be salient in the community, but they are not frequent topics of conversation in the interviews. Most the examples from the middle-class speakers came in response to direct questions. Matters of religion and social class are not "events" and therefore not as likely to form the basis of narratives. Attendance at church in Scotland declined considerably during the twentieth century (Harvie 1998; Smout 1986) and it is unclear to what extent the convictions and attitudes of the speakers in this book have been influenced by traditional beliefs, but there are similarities to the uncompromising views of the founders of the Church of Scotland. Class identification is clearer, though not articulated in abstract terms. These speakers know on which side of the class divide they stand and it is so obvious that they do not need to state it expressly.

Social class

There are not many overt references to social class in the interviews and the picture they present is far from clear. Nan Menzies recalled how the washerwoman who worked for her mother got all their old clothes, and how distressed her mother was at the fact the washerwoman's family was so poor.

64. (Nan Menzies)
and I can remember seeing her with her shawl
you know wrapped in her shawl
and my mother was always upset after she had been
because you know she was comparing how lucky we were in comparison

With the universality of affordable clothing nowadays, it is only in photographs from the past that the clear social class differences in clothing can be seen. The washerwoman "wrapped in her shawl" remains a vivid reminder for Nan Menzies of what was a commonplace sight before World War II. Many middle-class Scots in the 1930s, like Nan Menzies' parents, were not prosperous but in comparison with the poor they were "lucky".

James MacGregor did not want to concede that class differences were particularly salient when he was young but he gave an indirect indication of middle-class attitudes towards these differences.

65. (James MacGregor)
no I don't think there was a consciousness of class particularly
but there was not far from where I was in Craigie
there were the red buildings
these were closes
they're still there I think
but I always thought that they weren't just quite the same
I think we didn't play with the boys from the red buildings

There is a difference between "a consciousness of class" and an awareness of differences. The fact that he and his friends did not play with the boys from the closes suggests that there was quite a strong class barrier. The boys in the red buildings might have been more conscious of the difference as one of social class.

Wallace Gibson reported on his own feelings about class when he was younger.

66. (Wallace Gibson)
I probably had a– an inferiority complex
but one– I always felt that my father was merely in insurance
compared with the lawyers' and the doctors' sons
and also when I was about fifteen
I became friendly with– oh a friend of my mother's had a shop
and this message boy –we struck it off rather well
completely different background
came from – a mining village in Whitletts
which was a mining village then
and– eh– it was refreshing to have somebody from a different background
I was interested
got on well
but even my parents – weren't happy about it
they– they thought it–
particularly father– mother was more understanding
one was made to feel you were stepping out of your class

in a way that [*clears throat*] if he had been– black or something
the same thing

This is a much keener sense of class consciousness, with a concern over the status of an insurance agent compared with that of a lawyer or a doctor. However, even the son of an insurance agent could not "step out of his class" to be the friend of a message boy. Gibson cleared his throat quite often during the interview and has many hesitation phenomena, but the throat clearing and hesitation before making the comparison between class and race suggests a slight embarrassment. Later he returned more confidently to the same comparison of class and race.

67. (Wallace Gibson)
but it's nonsense to say there isn't class
it's like saying that somebody isn't black when they are black
I remember a bloke I met [*draws in breath*]
and got friendly with–ah– an Indian
I– I said "Now look let's understand that I am interested in the fact
that you're– coloured
I'm not pretending– eh– that you're not coloured
and I'm a different colour to you
and it doesn't matter but it's there"
the same happens– eh– in class I think

If class differences are like racial differences, then it is hardly surprising that Gibson's parents did not want him to befriend the message boy, or that James MacGregor did not play with the boys segregated in the closes.

As was shown in Chapter Nine, the speakers are aware of class differences in speech. Nan Menzies, while denying that people were snobbish, mentioned one characteristic of a higher social class.

68. (Nan Menzies)
I don't think people were– didn't seem to be snobbish
they maybe talked a little differently
they had perhaps not just the local accent that we had
but –eh– I wasn't really aware of much

It would probably be people who had been educated at private schools that did not have "the local accent". Since Nan Menzies speaks what would be classified as Standard Scottish English (Aitken 1979), she is presumably referring to a form of RP (Received Pronunciation), but this form of speech is not recalled as being "snobbish".

Bella K. perhaps speaks for many of the others when she comments on the importance of class:

69. (Bella K.)
everything is class
it all– it all boils down to what class you belong to
and really there shouldnae be any class
there's only people
there's only people in the world

Community loyalty

Similar to their reluctance to change their speech (Chapter Nine), for many of the speakers there was no interest in leaving their own community. Andrew Sinclair had been in Canada during the war but had no interest in leaving Ayr.

70. (Andrew Sinclair)
I felt that the opportunities were here
I mean if you're prepared to work and everything in this country
you can make money just the same as you can abroad
and an awful lot of people that go abroad they go with a false impression

Ella Laidlaw's son had been in Canada and wanted to go back but Ella herself had no interest in moving:

71. (Ella Laidlaw)
I'm afraid it wouldnae excite me
I'm probably too– what would you say? settled– too old
to start and change my ways

When I told her that I like to come back to Scotland regularly she said:

72. (Ella Laidlaw)
you're quite right
there's something about Scotland never leaves you

At the bingo, Willie Lang had won a trip for himself and his family to go to New York on the Queen Elizabeth. He loved the boat trip but hated New York:

73. (Willie Lang)
terrible place
oh there a queer difference with New York and here
oh dear-a-dear
oh a terrible place
but that's me seen it
I would hardly go back to it

He had also won a trip to London to see the Miss World competition:

74. (Willie Lang)
oh aye London was aw right
oh aye it was all right
[RM: *Did you ever think of leaving?*]
no never ever gave it a thought
never thought of leaving this place at all
because I think it's one of the cleanest wee toons in Scotland
oh aye Ayr's the tidiest wee toon in Scotland

Scotland has lost many of its inhabitants to emigration (Harvie 1998; Smout 1986), but the speakers are among those who have chosen to stay, so it is perhaps not surprising that they should express their loyalty to their native land. The speakers for the most part also live in the place where they were born. Even those who have spent some time abroad, like Andrew Sinclair or Bella K., returned to their birthplace. For whatever reason, they are not restless or interested in moving elsewhere.

Conclusion

McCrone (1996) points out that class in Scotland "has to be interpreted in the frame of meaning, social, cultural and political. This means that class will carry its meanings within it, embedded in its culture" (McCrone 1996: 115). However, as Strauss and Quinn warn "we need to get away from ideas of culture as a single kind of thing" (Strauss and Quinn 1997: 251). The examples in this chapter have illustrated several aspects of cultural meanings that appear to be shared by some of the speakers. For example, there were various positions as regards work that were interpreted as a set of general statements. For convenience, they are repeated here.

W1: Without a job you have no place in society
W2: Losing your job is the worst thing that can happen
W3: Age and gender discrimination is unjust
W4: Those who do not want to work deserve no respect
W5: Those who do not want to work exploit the system at the expense of workers
W6: Being a good worker is a source of pride
W7: Cheating at work is not accepted
W8: Being able to work hard is a virtue
W9: You don't complain about hard work
W10: Being able to trust your fellow workers is valued
W11: Following your father's occupation is valued
W12: Any kind of work is better than being unemployed
W13: Job satisfaction is highly valued
W14: There is more to life than work
W15: Workers want their work to be properly evaluated
W16: You have to be tough enough to survive in adverse working conditions
W17: Employers are not considerate about workers' lives

Unlike the "lads" in Paul Willis's study of working-class adolescents (1977/1981), these speakers are not cynical about work and do not see all jobs as the same. The central feature is pride in work and doing work well. They want to use the talents that they have and to feel good about what they are doing. Willie Lang was proud that he could help when a miner got injured. Bella K. felt that "it was great building boats", Andrew Sinclair enjoyed being part of a rescue team down the mine wearing an oxygen mask:

75. (Andrew Sinclair)
and that was a great experience to me to go in there
and to be in the pit
you were wearing an apparatus
and you knew that if that come off you'd never be again you see

The satisfaction of doing the job outweighed the danger involved. The greatest disaster is to be out of work or to have to do work that is perceived to be, in Bella K.'s words, "soul destroying".

However, as Therborn observes, ideologies are "ongoing social processes" (Therburn 1980: 77) and these statements suggest an ideology that is shared by the speakers as members of the Scottish working class. It is possible to interpret some of these statements as indications of what Goldthorpe, Lockwood, Bechhofer and Platt (1969) consider the traditional working-class perspective:

> The basic conception of the social order is a dichotomous one: society is divided into "us" and "them". "They" are persons in positions in which they can exercise power and authority over "us". The division between "us" and "them" is seen as a virtually unbridgeable one; people are born on one side of the line and very largely remain there. (Goldthorpe *et al.* 1969: 118)

From the examples cited in this chapter it is possible to identify some underlying differences that characterise the dichotomy between "us" *vs.* "them".

Us	Them
We want to work	They don't always provide the opportunity
We work hard	They don't always recognise that
We want good working conditions	They don't always provide them
We want to be treated with respect	They don't always treat us with respect
We don't want to be bullied	They sometimes try to bully us

Like the examples themselves, this list does not suggest a revolutionary attitude towards society. The speakers do not look for a radical change in the power structure; they simply want to be treated fairly in the system that exists.

Goldthorpe *et al.* also state that in the traditional working-class perspective wants and expectations are relatively modest:

The major economic concern is with being able to *maintain* a certain standard and style of living, not with the continuous advancement of consumption norms and widening of cultural experience. (Goldthorpe *et al.* 1969: 118, emphasis in original)

This is a fairly good summary of the general statements about money that were listed earlier, and repeated below.

M1: Immediate financial needs may affect long-term decisions
M2: Foregoing immediate income may not bring the expected long-term benefit.
M3: The system of payment may work against the individual
M4: Money is a necessity
M5: You need only enough money to maintain a reasonable life style
M6: You should not be obsessed with the topic of money
M7: It is not worth having more money if it makes you anxious about losing it
M8: Sometimes more money is not enough to make up for adverse working conditions
M9: There are some things that money cannot buy
M10: Money problems can usually be handled if you are careful

Goldthorpe *et al.* cite a comment of Max Weber's: "A man does not by 'nature' wish to earn more and more money, but simply to live as he is accustomed to live and to earn as much as is necessary for that purpose" (Weber 1947: 59). To the extent that this is true it helps to explain why the working-class speakers do not attempt to adopt middle-class habits, including speech. In his introduction to a translation of Bourdieu's work Thompson explains:

One of the central ideas of Bourdieu's work, for which he is well known among sociologists of education, is the idea that there are different forms of capital: not only "economic capital" in the strict sense (i.e., material wealth in the form of money, stocks and shares, property, etc.), but also "cultural capital" (i.e., knowledge, skills and other cultural acquisitions, as exemplified by educational or technical qualifications), "symbolic capital" (i.e., accumulated prestige or honour), and so on. One of the most important properties of fields is the way in which they allow one form of capital to be converted into another– in the way, for example, that certain educational qualifications can be cashed in for lucrative jobs. (Thompson 1991: 14)

Since cultural capital, including the socially approved form of speech, can be converted into material wealth, upward mobility is potentially available to those willing to pay what McCrone might call "the weak language tariff" of learning to speak "proper". The fact that so many working-class Scots do not take advantage of this opportunity may be the result of their attitude to economic capital. In Bourdieu's society, as Jim Dyce said of Canada, "aathing seems to be money", with the assumption that everybody is similarly motivated by the desire for more and more money. But there are many conditions under which people, like Bella K.'s granny, do not want "your bloody bloody money". Mary Ritchie does not want to go back to the prison of the factory. Bella does not want to be "a fucking chimpanzee" counter-sinking eleven thousand five hundred number nine holes; she wants to be "a creator".

In many ways, therefore, the speakers' attitudes are consistent with Goldthorpe *et al.*'s view of the traditional working-class perspective. But there is a further set of attitudes that Goldthorpe *et al.* do not mention. These are the set of statements on egalitarianism, repeated below.

E1:   I am as good as anybody else
E2:   I do not have to accept someone as my "master"
E2a: It is no longer necessary to show respect by removing your cap
E3:   I deserve to be treated with respect
E4:   I am entitled to speak openly, even to those in a position of power
E5:   I will not accept unreasonable working conditions
E6:   I will not be bullied by someone in authority
E7:   I will resist any attempt to exploit my abilities
E8:   I am not overawed by bureaucratic authority
E9:   I will not be won over by flattery
E10: I am not impressed by rank
EW1: As a woman, I will not be dominated by men in the workplace
EW2: As a woman I can swear like a man and still retain my femininity
EW3: As a woman, I can deflect embarrassing questions through humour

Despite the obvious need to have a job and make money, the speakers are willing to speak up if the situation does not accord with their own self-esteem. They need work, they want to work, but there are limits to the indignities they will endure. What runs through their views is an absence of doubt. The speakers are not hesitant to say what they believe and they do not put forward their opinions tentatively. They are as uncompromising in their statements as they are in the unmistakably Scottish quality of their speech. In both senses, these are strong Scottish voices.

Chapter Eleven

The Poetry of Talk

When dealing with poetic function, linguistics cannot limit itself to the field of poetry. (Jakobson 1960: 356)

Literature is, and can be nothing other than, a kind of extension and application of certain properties of language. (Paul Valery)

Kenneth Burke comments on the similarity between aspects of formal art and social life.

Since social life, like art, is a *problem of appeal*, the poetic metaphor would give us invaluable hints for describing modes of practical action which are too often measured by simple tests of utility and too seldom with reference to the communicative, sympathetic, *propitiatory* factors that are clearly present in the procedures of formal art and must be as truly present in those informal arts of living we do not happen to call arts. (Burke 1935: 339–340, emphasis in original)

In other words, the parallels between art and social life are strong enough that we should look in everyday situations for the kind of qualities we associate with art. From a very different perspective, Wood and Kroger claim that discourse analysis "promotes a more positive view of persons in that it shows them to be more complex and accomplished than they often appear to be in conventional analyses" 2000: 190). They also cite Tracy who suggests that "a first criterion for interpretive analyses is that analyses be plausible and persuasive" (1995: 209). The present chapter presents evidence for the use of language by (mainly) working-class speakers that is more often associated with literary works. These go far beyond the kind of features illustrated by Tannen (1989) but the range and variety of examples should be plausible and persuasive evidence for the skills of these speakers. If Friedrich is correct in claiming that "it is the relatively poetic nature of language, formed and articulated through figures of speech, that most deeply and massively affects the imagination" (1986: 17), then it is not difficult to understand how effective these speakers are in presenting their views and attitudes.

Traditional studies of rhetoric provide a wide range of labels for poetic devices and figures of speech (Hiatt 1975; A. Quinn 1982; Wales 1989) and various linguists have applied these labels to different genres. It may seem unnecessary to employ such labels in looking at aesthetic features of ordinary language but there may be an added value in showing how appropriately these labels apply to speech that is not generally given recognition for its rhetorical values. As Leech points out:

Despite a tendency towards pedantry and arbitrariness in these rhetorical distinctions, it would be wrong to dismiss them as of merely historical interest, for the features they analyse belong to poetry of all ages. (Leech 1969: 81)

I would simply add that the features belong to all forms of language that exemplify what Roman Jakobson (1960) called the poetic function of language.

Jakobson's notion of the **poetic function** of language emphasises "focus on the message for its own sake" (1960: 356) and is similar to the Prague School notion of **foregrounding** (Mukarovsky 1964), in that both draw attention to aspects of the language used in communicating a particular message. Poetry employs devices such as rhyme and metre to create this poetic effect and such techniques are not part of talk-in-action. There are, however, other techniques employed by poets that sometimes occur in the kind of heightened language that speakers may use when communicating information of a personal nature or what Tannen calls **involvement**: "an internal, even emotional connection individuals feel which binds them to other people as well as to places, things activities, ideas, memories, and words" (Tannen 1989: 12).

The first feature that Tannen examines in a chapter subtitled "Toward a poetics of talk" (Tannen 1989: 36–97) is the use of **repetition** (see also Johnstone 1987; Labov 1972a; Ochs 1979; Coates 1996). Tannen shows the rhetorical function of repetition in everyday conversation, public speaking, oratory, and drama. Coates shows how repetition in the conversation of women friends "is a key component of the collaborative floor" and contributes to "patterns that *could* be called 'poetic'" (1996: 230, emphasis in original). The examples that follow will show the effective use of repetition even in what had been considered the "unnatural" (Wolfson 1976) context of recorded interviews.

For Jakobson the most important form of repetition was parallelism. In fact, he admitted that there had been no subject throughout his entire scholarly life that had interested him as much as parallelism, and he pointed out that "the role of parallelism extends far beyond the confines of poetic language" (Jakobson and Pomorska 1983: 106). Jakobson (1960) quotes Gerard Manley Hopkins on the importance of parallelism: "The artificial part of poetry, perhaps we shall be right to say all artifice, reduces itself to the principle of parallelism. The structure of poetry is that of continuous parallelism" (Jakobson 1960: 368)

Hiatt (1975) draws attention to the role of rhetorical devices in reinforcing parallelism:

Intimately associated with the whole subject of parallelism is a range of rhetorical devices of repetition. Parallelism itself is a pattern of emphasis; that is, parallel constructions are more noticeable than non-parallel constructions. But reinforcing the emphatic nature of parallelism are the classical rhetorical devices, rhetorical in that they also are emphatic or "persuasive". (Hiatt 1975: 5)

One of the commonest rhetorical devices employing repetition is **anaphora** or initial lexical parallelism (Leech 1969; Wales 1989). Hiatt defines anaphora as "repetition of the same word or words at the beginning of phrases or clauses in a sequence" (Hiatt 1975: 59).

Bella K. gives many examples of anaphora in her interview. In (1) she sums up what she had liked about working as a welder in the shipyard:

1.
it suited my personality
it suited my physique
it suited my outlook on life

Elsewhere Bella made it clear that she was strong both physically and psychologically. The parallel constructions here make the point that these qualities contributed to her positive attitude to life. She made the same point when explaining why working at a monotonously repetitive job in a munitions factory during the war did not suit her:

2.
I was young
I was full of life
I was strong

In describing the beauty of the kind of ship she helped build, she refers to aspects of the construction of the inside of the ship:

3.
how they put the wood on
how they put the furniture in
how they made their lounge

In the middle of what is a very enthusiastic and eloquent account why
she enjoyed "building boats", she follows (3) with the observation
"you knew at the back of that bonnie wood there was a pissy corner
where the men used to piss". The ability to combine a positive "outlook on life" with an awareness of the darker side of life is characteristic of Bella's interviews.

A more complex example is given in (4). Repetition can have
many functions, including that of reinforcing an image by repeating
the same word. Bella here uses repetition to make a comment on life
in general and her own life in particular.

4.
when you say to me "Think on a colour"
I think on grey
grey ashes in the grate
grey school uniform
grey is the colour
grey's the colour when you havenae got any money
I think on grey
grey days
grey rainy weather
grey
things are grey

The first two lines consist of an adjacency pair (Sacks 1992)
where Bella responds to the instruction "think on a colour" by saying
"I think on grey". (Incidentally, this pair is totally Bella's; the inter-

viewer had not said anything about colour.) Bella then produces two parallel verbless phrases

5.
grey ashes in the grate
grey school uniform

In addition to the repetition of the word *grey* itself, there is the alliteration with *grate* and the echoes of the vowel in *grate*.

6.
grey is the colour
grey's the colour when you havenae got any money

The initial response in the second line is repeated in the seventh line, followed by two more verbless phrases

7.
grey days
grey rainy weather

Again the vowel of *grey* is echoed in *days* and *rainy*. The second last line slows down the pace like a musical *rallentando* before the final phrase in the last line "things are grey". The ashes are grey in the grate when the fire is out, and when you have not got any money and it is raining, life can be very grey indeed. Bella had not enjoyed her time at school, so it was appropriate that she recalls that her uniform was grey.

After rhyme, one of the commonest forms of repetition in poetry is **alliteration**, sometimes known as "initial rhyme" (Wales 1989: 18), in which the initial consonant is repeated in two or more words. Ella Laidlaw made use of this device in describing the carpet factory where she had her first job (Chapter Five). As shown in that chapter, Ella's mother had got her into the finishing room because she thought it was the nicest part of the factory. The passage in which justification is presented is reproduced in (8).

8.
so– in the other places

the weft shed
the kiddering department
the dyehoose
and aw these places
they were wild
the women were
they werenae wild
they were workers
but they worked like men
and they swore like men

This passage is remarkable for the extreme use of alliteration:

9.
they *w*ere *w*ild
the *w*omen *w*ere
they *w*erenae *w*ild
they *w*ere *w*orkers

There is no need to speculate whether Ella herself was aware of the alliteration. The fact is that she was communicating a central part of her story and the alliteration is an expressive way of reinforcing the message for the listener the women both were wild and yet only in the way that workers (men and women) are affected by their environment.

Ella Laidlaw also makes use of the expressive device known as **apophony**, "variation in vowels where the consonants of the word or syllable remain constant" (Wales 1989: 31):

10.
they had pointed nails
well I never had seen pointed nails and painted nails

Since the nails feature at the climax of the story, the fact that they are both pointed and painted makes their importance even greater. The fact that they are painted makes them more salient. Their being pointed seems appropriate given their aggressive attitude towards Ella.

Ella had indicated her enthusiasm for the job by the parallel constructions

11.
I was going to get money among my fingers
I was going to get my pay

The repetition helps to bring out the point that Ella had entered the factory enthusiastically and not simply because her mother had arranged it. This is another example of anaphora but it is also similar to the traditional rhetorical device known as **isocolon** ("repetition of grammatical forms" A. Quinn 1982: 102).

Duncan Nicoll uses this device when he explains how he behaves when he goes as a church visitor to homes that he says were not "the best end of the district":

12.
and you've got to be able to talk bookie
you've got to be able to talk pub
to talk everything

Nicoll, in many places in the interview, made it clear that he liked to talk and that he felt comfortable talking with people from all walks of life.

Anaphora can be combined with **antithesis**, which is the "juxtaposition of contrasting or opposing ideas" (Hiatt 1975: 59; A. Quinn 1982: 67–68). When I interviewed Hugh Gemmill about his life as a farm labourer (Macaulay 1991a) he told me that the labourers were hired for six months at the feeing-fair. I asked if that was a chance to get more money. He replied:

13.
well whiles it was a chance to get mair money
and whiles it was a chance to get less

This laconic response from someone whose wages at one time had been five pounds for six months is consistent with his view that "money's– it's maybe the root of all evil but it's a necessity tae at the same time". He had never had much money and though he told me how he had often been badly paid, he did not complain about it. His response in (13) is characteristic of many he made during in the interview. When I asked him about ploughing he replied:

14.
the horse was the main piece of the business
and as long as you could keep your temper
and no faw oot with the horse
you were aw right
but if you fell oot wi the horse
you were aw wrong

Again the simple parallelism combined with contrast compresses a lot of experience into something like a proverbial saying.

Ella Laidlaw also uses partial repetition with amplification in (15).

15.
and she got me into one of the nicest
what she termed the nicest parts of the carpet works Gray's

The amendment from *one of the nicest* to *what she termed the nicest* is another example of what Ochs and Capps (2002) call **foreshadowing**, because the point of the story, as we have seen (Chapter Five), is that Ella's mother was wrong in the belief that the finishing room was one of the nicest parts of the factory as regards swearing. As Ina Solotti pointed out "we've nothing on them" when it came to swearing.

There are other examples of repetition in Ella's story with a notable example when she goes to tell her mother:

16.
and I says to her "I'm no going back in there"
she says "How are you no going back in ?"
I says "I'm no going back in"

The repetitions of *no going back* reinforce the message that despite her desire for money among her fingers, Ella was not going to continue working under those conditions.

Ending phrases or clauses with the same word or words in a parallel sequence is known as **epistrophe** (Hiatt 1975: 59; A. Quinn 1982: 85–86). Bella K. uses this rhetorical device in talking about a cousin of hers who had frequently been in trouble as a young man but who was deeply affected during the war when the ship he sailed in was unable to pick up the German survivors from a sinking ship:

17.
and it broke his heart
and he took to the drink
the birch never put him on the drink
the hard life of thieving never put him on the drink
but this compassion for a fellow man put him on the drink
and he died

The repetitions of *put him on the drink* are a clear example of epistrophe.

In Ella Laidlaw's example (4) above there is a good example of epistrophe in the last two lines:

18.
but they worked like men
and they swore like men

The parallel syntax produces the equation:

19.
(men) working $< = >$ (men) swearing

The combination of anaphora (initial repetition) and epistrophe (final repetition) is known as **symploce** (Hiatt 1975: 59; A. Quinn 1982: 86–87). Bella K. uses this device in describing how as children they used to search for objects of value in the midden or place where the rubbish was thrown:

20.
somebody had threw it oot
it had been sitting in the midden
stinking with ashes
there was ashes
there was shit
there was babies' shit
there was cat's shit
there was everything in that thing
oh boy

The lines *there was ashes/there was shit* exemplify anaphora and the lines *there was babies' shit/there was cat's shit* are an example of symploce. In addition to the repetition of the words there is the constant succession of [ɪ] vowels: *sitting, midden, stinking, shit, everything, thing.* Bella produces the sequence in (20) when explaining how as children they used to search in the midden (i.e., the rubbish tip) for "what we called a luckier", something that the children thought was worth saving. They would take it home, wash it, and say "Ma look look what I've got, I've got a braw ornament for your mantelpiece". Bella tells the interviewer about the midden after telling about the introduction of dustbins, observing "what a godsend it was a dustbin with a lid on it". Again, Bella manages to combine the negative aspect of the midden ("stinking") with the positive opportunity for the children to find "a luckier".

Sometimes parallelism can be employed with contrast, as when Bella went to take her welding test at the shipyard:

21.
and I could see the wee laddies running here
and the wee laddies running there

In describing the typical pattern for "folk in Dundee", Bella combines epistrophe in the first two lines of (22) with **chiasmus** (in which the syntactic function of the constituent is reversed) in the third line:

22.
they went to school with *that wee lassie*
and they sat next to *that wee lassie*
and *that wee lassie* remains their friend aw their life

She has another example. When she went back to the shipyard, the word had got around that a woman was coming to try out:

23.
and they're all expecting this young dolly bird to come doon
and doon comes this fat grey-haired wifie

This is a very clear example of chiasmus, the rhetorical device "in which two segments contain the same two parts with the order reversed" (Tannen 1989: 23): *X come doon, doon comes Y*. There is another example of chiasmus when Bella is describing her child:

24.
and he wasnae– he wasnae growing very well
so we decided he'd better come off the breast
and go on to the bottle
so on to the bottle he went

Duncan Nicoll uses chiasmus in conjunction with anaphora in describing himself:

25.
you see I'm a pig
I'm a pig for food
I don't drink
and I don't smoke
and I don't swear – anything very much any of these
I take a dram
and but food I love
I– I'm a glutton for food

The chiasmus is in the second last line *food I love* and reinforces the statement in the second line *I'm a pig for food*.

A more complex example of the use of different kinds of parallelism is Bella K.'s account of playing truant for a succession of days, which is given in terms of the scenery:

26.
so I went up the Law Hill
and I've seen the Law Hill in all its glory
I've seen the river there in all its silences and its roughness
I've seen the sun going down on it
and the sun come up on that River Tay
all from the days I played truant

It is not only the repetition of individual words that is effective but also the repetition of syntactic structures. There is the triple set of *I've seen X*. Dell Hymes (1996) has pointed out that in European stories things often come in threes: *I've seen the Law Hill, I've seen the river, I've seen the sun*. There is the parallelism of *in all its glory* and *in all its silences*, and the contrast of *silences* and *roughness* and between *going down* and *come up*.

27.

so	I went up	the Law Hill	
and	I've seen	the Law Hill	in all its glory
	I've seen	the river	in all its silences
			and its roughnesses
	I've seen	the sun	going down on it
and		the sun	come up

This is a remarkable way of evoking what was in fact a very unhappy and frightening episode in Bella's schooling.

Dubois and Sankoff (2001) draw attention to a process they call **enumeration**, which is "used to evoke some set larger than any of the components and generally larger than all of them put together" (2001: 289). Bella K. gives an example of this when reporting on a feature of her parents' house:

28.
that was another thing that was underneath our room– bed
it was FULL of musical instruments
there was a half-sized fiddle
a three-quarter-sized fiddle
and a full-sized fiddle
there was a banjo a G banjo
there was two banjo mandolines
there was a mandoline
and there was a one-stringed fiddle

The repetition of the words fiddle, banjo, and mandoline brings out clearly the force of the emphasised phrase "FULL of musical instruments".

Bella uses this device to imply a category that is not openly stated when talking about her friends:

29.
and it's funny how the crowd all divided up
because one did marry a Norwegian
I married a Dutchman

somebody else married an Englishman
you know they all married different

Here, although "they all married different", the implication is that they all married foreigners, putting the Englishman in the same category as the Norwegian and the Dutchman.

She uses a similar tactic in talking about the women she knew in Holland when she went there with her husband after the war:

30.
the women in Holland didnae work
their value was in being
to knit
and to sew
and to clean
and to be a willing servant to Papa

Here Bella sums up the qualities that made a good wife in Holland. Bella herself came from a place, Dundee, where the women had always had opportunities to work in the jute mills and elsewhere and often were the main wage-earner in the family. Bella herself hated (and resented) not being able to do the kind of work she had learned to do as a welder in the shipyard. The succession of infinitives in (30) is another example of isocolon.

Müller (1999) comments on the notion of **iconicity** in poetic and ordinary language:

Now if iconicity is always a latent possibility of aesthetic or poetic language and, further, if we take it for granted that aesthetic or poetic language exploits, develops, and heightens possibilities already inherent in ordinary, non-poetic discourse, the massive presence of iconic forms of expression in literature can be regarded as lending support to the theory of the iconic potential of language in general. (Müller 1999: 393–394)

Iconicity is found in many of the examples of eloquent speech in the data set. The most basic form of iconicity is auditory iconicity, more commonly known as **onomatopoeia**. There are many examples of this. Bella K. gives two examples is describing the sound of the looms in the jute mill:

31.
and I thought it was a very isolated job
white faces
same thing day in day out day in
clacketty-clack
no easy noise
clacketty-clack
and as you went to bed at night
the noise of the clacking of the shuttles was in your ears you know
you went to sleep with this clacketty-clack clacketty-clack in your ears
and I thought "Christ this is not– I'm going to go batty here"

The noise of the shuttles made it impossible for the women to talk to each other. When they needed to communicate for some practical reason they used signs. Later in the interview she suggests a different noise:

32.
and it was out of this shuttle going back and forward
"Dum dum dum dum"

But in both cases the noises ("clacketty-clack clacketty-clack" and "dum dum dum dum") suggest the repetitive nature of the noise and why she might "go batty" there.

Bella had a urinary tract problem that was not cured until she had an operation in middle age. She describes the agony of wetting herself as a young child in school:

33.
and I can remember sitting in the class
and at Hill Street it was on a slope
so that you had big broad steps
every step was another desk
and I can hear it yet to this day
trickling down these steps
trickle
trickle
trickle

The repetitions iconically reproduce the scene and evoke the embarrassment she must have felt. Bella describes how she managed not to wet herself at a slightly later age:

34.
I never done it during the day
because I was trained up to go according to the clock
you went afore you went to school
you went at ten o'clock at playtime
you went at twelve o'clock
you went at three o'clock
you went at four o'clock
there was times that you went to the toilet
you emptied your bladder by the clock
not according to how you felt

In addition to the anaphoric sequence of *you went*, the repetitions *ten o'clock, twelve o'clock, three o'clock, four o'clock* iconically reinforce the notion of how she had to regulate emptying her bladder.

John Wilson describes how he was sick on his first Atlantic voyage:

35.
and I'd be standing there scrubbing or cleaning pots
and every now and again I'd make a beeline for this chute
and be sick there you know
but wunst I got by the first day
keeping working
and keeping being sick and that
and eating
being made to eat

The succession of verbal forms in *-ing*, a poetic device known as **homoioteleuton** (Hiatt 1975; Leech 1969: 82), iconically recreates the scene:

36.
standing there *scrubbing* or *cleaning* pots
keeping working and *keeping being* sick and that
and *eating*
being made to eat

Hiatt observes that, unlike simple past tense endings as in *lasted* and *tasted*, "present participle endings are included in homoioteleuton because of the increased phonic emphasis of an 'ing' form" (1975: 56). In (35) the emphasis of the *-ing* forms helps to bring out the persistent feelings of seasickness.

Bella K. uses the same device in describing how her mother passed the time, because her father was a baker and worked on the night shift:

37.
and this is the way that she kept herself busy
by knitting
and sewing
and patching
and mending

This kind of repetition can have an even greater cumulative effect. Andrew Sinclair described for me his feeling the first time he went down the pit as a young coal miner:

38.
well I mean that's a thing I don't think I'll ever forget
I would never forget
I remember the first morning going in the cage and going down the pit
I mean the sensation of going down
I mean you go away
the cage goes away
and I mean you just feel your breath going away
I mean it's no like a lift
I mean it goes down at some tune
the sensation was
after you were maybe about halfway doon
you felt as if you were going back up
that was the kind of sensation it was you see

The account begins with the repetitive emphasis on memory, with the semantic parallelism of *not forget ~ remember* :

39.
I don't think I'll ever forget

I would never forget
I remember

Then there is the succession of repetitions of *go* with different prepositions and adverbs:

40.
*going **in*** the cage and *going **down*** the pit
the sensation of *going **down***
you *go **away***
the cage *goes **away***
you just feel your breath *going **away***
it *goes **down*** at some tune
you felt as if you were *going **back*** up

There are parallel structures:

41.
*going **in*** the cage
*going **down*** the pit

There is also elaboration:

42.
           *going **down***
the sensation of *going **down***

and also:

43.
           you *go **away***
      the cage *goes **away***
you just feel your breath *going **away***

There is also the emphatic repetition of the discourse marker *I mean*, used repeatedly to reiterate a point:

44.
I mean the sensation of going down
I mean you go away

and

I mean you just feel your breath going away
I mean it's no like a lift
I mean it goes down at some tune

There is the alternation of synonymous verbal and nominal constructions:

45.
the *sensation* of going down
you just *feel* your breath going away
the *sensation* was
you *felt* as if you were going back up
that was the kind of *sensation* it was

After all the emphasis on *going **down*** there is the rhetorical contrast in
the paradox of feeling as if one were *going **back up***.
   The rhetorical device known as **epizeuxis** (Hiatt 1975: 59; A.
Quinn 1982: 80–81) is a repetition of words with no words between.
Bella gives an example of this when describing work in the Timex
factory:

46.
ours was an eight-hour job
eight hours a day
the *hands hands hands* went the whole time

The repetition of *hands* suggests the constant movement.
   The omission of conjunctions in a series is known as **asyndeton**
(Hiatt 1975: 59; A. Quinn 1982: 7–10). When Bella refuses to blame
her pregnancy on the war conditions, she explains that along with her
innocence, ignorance, and curiosity, there was "a mixture of feelings":

47.
because alang with innocence and ignorance
there is also a great curiosity and em mixture of feelings
pity for the man perhaps
sorry that he was this sailor away fae hame
em love of the person himself
curiosity as to what it would be like

The last four lines of (47) are an example of asyndeton. The similarity between the third line "pity for the man" and the fifth "love of the person" makes the third line "sorry that he was this sailor away fae hame" and the sixth "curiosity as to what it would be like" seem more exactly parallel than they are because of the expectation set up.

Duncan Nicoll uses asyndeton with a succession of subjectless verbs to summarise his life when he first spoke to me:

48.
sixty-seven years of age
born in Ayr
didn't like the school
left at fourteen
came to work indentured
and served my time as a tailor with my father
sat on the bench and learned my craft
got tired of that
and went out into the insurance world
like people
quite fond of people
that'll come out as I talk to you

The succession of subjectless structures gives a staccato effect as well as providing a succinct summary of part of his working life.

The omission of the verb is known as **scesis onamaton** (A. Quinn 1982: 33). In describing her wayward uncle, Bella lists some of the characteristics that made him charming before summing up his type. She does this by a succession of verbless predicates, concluding with an antithetical final assessment:

49.
very tall
broad
good looking
dark wavy hair
terrific personality
but what a bugger
what a bugger that was

The list of positive qualities makes the final characterisation both surprising and effective.

In contrast to asyndeton, Hiatt defines the rhetorical device of **polysyndeton** as "repetitive use of conjunctions in triplets or series" (1975: 59). Bella K. illustrates this device in describing her welding test when she was about to return to the shipyard:

50.
as– as– you weld
you're– you start off with a rod
and it goes down and down and down
so your arm goes in and in and in

In addition to the polysyndetic use of *and*, there is the iconicity of *down and down and down* paralleled by *in and in and in*.

Bella K. can also use repetition to make a very serious statement, as in her perceptive, sympathetic description of the plight of married women whose husbands were away during the war:

51.
a terrible time for women whose husbands were away
young women
because they wanted to be faithful
they really did want to be faithful
but it's a long long time when your man's away
and it's awful wearisome
and oh you get tired of the washing
oh you'd get fed up with washing
you want something more than washing
than just feeding your weans
so you needed a wee bitty consolation
and they got consolation
they got consolation
they started going to the dancing
of course they did
they're human
they're natural
it was a natural instinct
it was a natural need of their human body
yes there was
there was a few
there was
I'm not saying all
I couldn't
you couldn't

you can't– you can't make a broad statement like that
you can't say all
but then I don't think they would be very natural women
if they could go five years
and never look at
never even look at another man
come on now
be reasonable
th– this is–
this is the other side of war
this is war

This is such an effective example that it deserves detailed examination. It is not only that there are numerous words repeated, e.g., *faithful, washing, consolation,* and *natural,* but there are also modifications in the repetitions, *women... young women, they wanted/they really wanted to be faithful, you get tired of /you'd get fed up with/ you want something more than washing, never look at/never even look at, they're natural/ it was a natural instinct/ it was a natural need of their human body* which reinforce the effect of the repetitions. Even in the third-last line where there is a false start *this is* the effect is more one of emphasis than of hesitation and this is reinforced by the condensation of *this is the other side of war* to *this is war.*

This passage came in response to the interviewer's question about people's attitude during the war. Bella began by telling a story about an old woman shouting abuse at a Polish soldier (which is amusing in a certain way), but then she goes on to say that generally the older women were very serious. She soon begins to tell about *the other ones:*

52.
there was the other ones
whose husbands were away
a terrible time for women
whose husbands were away
young women

As happens again and again in this passage Bella builds up the description with examples of epistrophe, repetition at the end of a phrase.

53.
the other ones whose husbands were away
women whose husbands were away
young women

Bella herself was just eighteen when the war broke out. She was not married but the father of her son, a Dutch sailor, "was away" (though as shown in Chapter Three he came back marry her after that war). So Bella was not just speaking about "the other ones" since she herself was also a young woman whose man was away. In her use of the pronouns *they* and *you* in (51) Bella distances herself from what was her own situation.

54.
they wanted to be faithful
they really did want to be faithful

In many other places in the interview Bella creates her effects by repetition and elaboration, and there are several here:

55.
oh you get tired of the washing
oh you'd get fed up with washing
you want something more than washing

The repetition of the word *washing* reinforces the notion that you would want "something more" than that.

56.
they're human
they're natural
it was a natural instinct
it was a natural need of their human body

One of the outstanding features of Bella's interview is her ability to talk about intimate bodily functions (e.g., her urinary problems) without any sense of embarrassment. Here she is able to talk about the women's sexual desire as a "natural need" because they are "human" and this is a "natural instinct". This is why they needed "consolation".

57.
so they needed a wee bitty consolation
and they got consolation
they got consolation

The final repetition is not redundant; it is emphatic, said in a low tone with reduced volume. The climax comes with a cumulative succession of negatives:

58.
I couldn't
you couldn't
you can't make a broad statement like that
you can't say all
but I don't think...
and never look at
never even look at another man

The women would not be "natural" if they could go for five years without even looking at another man. Later in the interview Bella more or less admitted that she herself had followed her "natural instinct". This might explain the appeal of the imperatives:

59.
come on now
be reasonable

Even the false start in the third-last line of (51) has a rhetorical effect as it helps to convey the emotion Bella was expressing:

60.
th– this is–
this is the other side of war
this is war

It was not only *the other side* of war, it was war itself. Again, in context, it is not redundant, but rhetorically reinforcing.

Hesitations such as that in (60) are sometimes classified as **disfluencies**, "generally described as interruptions of a speech plan, rather than deviations from this plan" (Postma, Kolk and Povel

1990: 19). For most of her interview Bella K. speaks very fluently but there are occasions when the flow of speech is interrupted in ways that would usually be classified as disfluencies. For example, in (61) the hesitation in the last line suggests that BK was thinking of mentioning the name of the orchestra but either could not remember it exactly or decided that it was not important:

61.
one of the girls that played the violin
she– she– she was good
she was really good
she played in– in– eh in the orchestras and that   <=

    Sometimes she seems to be searching for the right phrase:

62.
but em pictures was out of the– out of the– out of– out of wer– right out

This is a complicated example of **word search** (Schegloff, Jefferson, and   Sacks 1977; Moerman 1988). Bella seems to be on the point of saying "out of the question" or "out of wer reach" but either cannot recall the idiom or feels that it is inappropriate and begins an apparent repair to something like "beyond our means" (*wer* = "our") but ends up with "right out". Note that in her second repair the definite article is dropped before she comes out with the possessive in her third repair.

    It is, however, when Bella is most "involved" (Tannen 1989) that she uses hesitations as "contextualization cues" (Gumperz 1982, 1992). For example, she recalls her indignation when she had gone to consult a doctor about her pregnancy and all he had done was advise her to get married:

63.
I remember
I– I could've– could've knifed him   <=
could still knife him to this day eh Dr Gibson from Garland Place
I'll never forgive him

The hesitations and repetitions "perform" her anger. Bella utters the name of Dr Gibson with the tense, constricted muscles that (Fónagy 1999: 5) observes often accompany anger. She similarly expressed her frustration after the war at being denied work which she was well qualified to do just because she was a woman:

64.
I could see it
it was– it was so blatant
and em it– it– it– it–it annoyed– it annoyed me   <=
it got right up my nose

The repetitions of *it* in the third line suggest that the situation almost left her at a loss for words.

Bella K. uses hesitation in conveying other emotions than anger or irritation as when she describes the danger of falling from the side of the ship when welding:

65.
I'll be quite honest about it
it worried me
I– I was dead scared   <=
I mean I seen– I seen fellows falling   <=
I seen men falling
I seen men being killed in the yard

In these examples it is highly unlikely that Bella deliberately hesitates for effect, rather they are part of the paralinguistic aspect of her performance. There is one example that might have been more conscious. She is describing the way the men would simply urinate in odd corners of the ship rather than take the time out of their lunch hour to go the lavatory which was some distance away:

66.
at five to twelve all bursting for the lavie
aw standing pissing in the corners
so they wouldnae need to piss in eh eh at dinner time– in their dinner hour
and it– it was a great display of cocks all over the place   <=

The slight hesitation in the last line prepares the way for the punch line which produced appreciative laughter from the interviewer.

Another feature that occurs in the recordings is **litotes** or under-statement (Wales 1989: 282), as in Bella's reference to *a wee bitty consolation* in (50) above. Here is an example from Hugh Gemmill's interview. At one point, unprompted, he told me about his wife's death in understated terms:

67.
she just gied two gurgles
and that was– that was that

The slight hesitation in the second line suggests that Gemmill had perhaps considered alternative ways of saying that she had died before settling on the simplest.

Andrew Sinclair told me a story about a fall of coal in the mine that had almost totally blocked the way and he and another man had been sent in to investigate. He explained how he had difficulty crawling through a hole to get through "when this tremendous rumble started again":

68.
the first time when I got it out through
I mean it was kinna you know you'd to push yourself to make your way in
well when that rumble come
I went oot through it
and I guarantee I never touched the sides [*laughs*]
so these was wee kind of frights
that you got –eh – now and again

The danger is referred to only as "wee kind of frights" rather than being given greater emphasis. Similarly, Willie Lang responded to my question about dangerous situations down the pit by saying "I've had two or three skirmishes aye oh aye". In one of them:

69.
I was at a roadheid
and there was a taste of dirt fell away
and it got me in the back of the neck
I thought my neck was broken

It was a fall of earth that could have caused Lang serious injury but he refers to it as only "a taste of dirt" that fell away.

Bella K. also uses understatement in talking about her uncle:

70.
he'd been in Temperance– in the Temperance Society
and he was determined to be an M.P.
but the only M.P. he ever became was a member of pubs
never a member of parliament
and he liked a drappie

"And he liked a drappie" meaning that he drank quite a lot.

The examples in this chapter have illustrated the use of a wide range of rhetorical devices that have usually been studied in works of literature. These devices are:

alliteration	two or more words in close succession begin with the same initial consonant
anaphora	repetition of the same word or words at the beginning of phrases or clauses in a sequence
antithesis	the juxtaposition of contrasting or opposing ideas
apophony	variation in vowels where the consonants of the word or syllable remain constant
asyndeton	the omission of conjunctions in a series
chiasmus	two segments that contain the same two parts with the order reversed
enumeration	a list that evokes some set larger than any of the components
epistrophe	ending phrases or clauses with the same word or words in a parallel sequence
epizeuxis	a repetition of words with no other words between
homoioteleuton	a succession of verbal forms
iconicity	where the order of words parallels the order of events

isocolon	repetition of grammatical forms
litotes	understatement
onomatopoeia	the use of a word that sounds like its referent
polysyndeton	repetitive use of conjunctions in triplets or series
scesis onamaton	omission of the verb
symploce	the combination of anaphora (initial repetition) and epistrophe (final repetition)

It is highly unlikely that the speakers would have known the rhetorical terms to describe what they were doing, as these words are part of a recondite register of interest only to a small group of scholars. Yet they draw upon these devices in talking about their lives and things that are of interest to them. The evidence from these speakers validates Jakobson's view that the poetic function is not restricted to works of literature. The speakers used these devices not to impress the hearer with their literary skills but because they wished to communicate effectively the situation they were describing. As Norrman remarks, referring to literary works, "we must not regard rhetorical figures as something exclusively or primarily ornamental" (1986: 3). The speakers use what can be identified as rhetorical figures not as ornamental features but because that is the best way in which convey the meaning they wish to express, and they do it very successfully.

Chapter Twelve

Discover the People

Society is organized on the principle that any individual who possesses certain social characteristics has a moral right to expect that others will value and treat him in an appropriate way. (Goffman 1959: 13)

The previous chapters have shown that the individuals whose language has been examined are articulate, effective, and expressive speakers. They are good storytellers, they show that they are effective conversationalists, and they express their opinions clearly. The previous chapter showed that they can make good use of rhetorical devices, thus fully confirming Gibbs' comment:

It is a mistake, though, to think that using figurative language requires a special cognitive ability or that such language is encountered only in literary texts. Traditionally viewed as the tool of poets and politicians, figurative language is found not only in the treasured pages of literature but throughout ordinary speech and writing. (Gibbs 1994: 2–3)

Nor do the speakers simply use such devices to adorn their speech; they use them to express themselves effectively. To quote Gibbs again: "Metaphor, metonymy, irony, and other tropes are not linguistic distortions of literal mental thought but constitute basic schemes by which people conceptualise their experience and the external world" (Gibbs 1994: 1). The examples that have been given (and they are only a sample of possible extracts that could be cited) provide a window into the lives of the speakers, their attitudes and their experiences.

This is not a work of sociology or history, although I believe there is much information here that might be useful to either a sociologist or a historian, interested in twentieth-century Scotland. E.P. Thompson, author of *The Making of the English Working Class*, has observed: "If you want a generalization I would have to say that the historian has got to be listening all the time" (E.P. Thompson, cited in Johnson 1980: 215). One problem in "understanding Scotland" may have been a failure to listen. The nature of Scottish culture may have been misunderstood because the voices of the people have not generally been heard as clearly as they might, despite numerous oral history projects. It is ironic (but not surprising) that a volume entitled *Scottish Voices 1745–1960* (Smout and Wood 1990) should consist of extracts from *written* works. The examples that have been presented in this are actual "Scottish voices".

When Bella K. was interviewed once on television she was asked what she thought of Dundee. She told me that she had replied:

1. (Bella K.)
What is a town?
a town is people
discover the people
the people tell the story
we know the history of the courts
let's know the history of the people
jute jam and journalism
there's such a lot behind that three J's
there's such a lot of stories

"There's such a lot of stories" (*cf.* Barthes 1977, Habermas 1981, and White 1981). Shortly afterwards she said "ours is such a rich unedited history" and she used a very interesting simile.

2. (Bella K.)
well Shakespeare said it
all the world is a stage
and we all have wer part to play on it
but if you think on it like a clock
if you leave out one small wheel
you will never get the right time
and it's the same with history
if you leave out one small detail
you have lost the complete picture

Ochs and Capps make much the same point in rather different language: "To varying degrees, the silencing of alternative stories is a form of linguistic oppression" (Ochs and Capps 1996: 33).

The speakers that I have presented cannot provide "the complete picture" but they do provide a lot of small details. Many more details could have been included but my main purpose was not to create a social history based on oral testimony. That would require a different kind of book. What I have been looking at in the samples of speech examined in the previous chapters are not only the strategies, devices, or features which make these examples of successfully accomplished discourse. I have tried to draw attention to what makes them examples of Scottish speech rather than simply disembodied samples of "discourse", "conversation", or "English". The transcripts are "culturally contexted" (Moerman 1988) and ought to be evaluated in the context of the norms embedded in the community. The distribution of characteristic dialect features can best be understood in the context of their use in specific types of interaction.

As will have been obvious from the preceding chapters, the speakers, many of whom left school at the age of fourteen and received little or no formal education after that, showed remarkable skills in using language effectively. Scottish people are often said to be dull, shy, and inarticulate – "maybe it's just our dour natures" as one respondent in Glasgow observed to me (Macaulay 1977: 124), but the examples I have been dealing with show just the reverse. The speakers are energetic, involved, entertaining, and often moving. There are many ways in which the speakers create an emotional atmosphere even in the situation of a dyadic interview with a stranger, though it is also true that the "social aesthetic" (Brenneis 1987) is usually a somewhat restrained one. Billy Kay mentions a BBC internal report on a series of interviews with working-class speakers that praised his ability to make "inarticulate people" talk. Kay comments: "In the six months I had been conducting the interviews, I had met nothing but highly articulate characters – the kind of folk that made the series such compelling listening" (Kay 1993: 20).

Similarly, the examples examined in the present study show that urban speech in Scotland, far from being impoverished or "hopelessly corrupt" (Grant| 1931: xxvii), has an eloquence, a vigour, and a beauty that deserve recognition and provide a refutation of the low evaluation of working-class speech by Bernstein (1971) and others. Elsewhere (Macaulay 1991, forthcoming) I have shown that there is no reason to accept Bernstein's accounts of "a restricted code" with simpler syntax and a more limited lexicon used by working-class speakers contrasted with "an elaborated code" available to middle-class speakers. There is no evidence in my Ayr study (Macaulay 1991a) or in a later Glasgow study (Macaulay, forthcoming) for the claim that complex differences of this kind present a sharp dichotomy that polarises the two social class groups in Scotland. On the contrary, in both studies the sharp polarisation of the two social class groups is mainly in phonological and morphological features, not in syntactic, lexical, and discourse features that are affected by topic, genre, and interactive factors.

In the Ayr volume (Macaulay 1991a: 266–67) I argued against Wolfson's (1976: 195) claim that interviews could not provide good examples of ordinary speech. Wolfson was apparently arguing from her own unhappy experience in interviewing, but it is disturbing to find her views on interview speech echoed at a more theoretical level:

members of the lower classes who, lacking the means to exercise the liberties of plain speaking, which they reserve for private usage, have no choice but to opt for the broken forms of a borrowed and clumsy language or to escape into abstention and silence. (Bourdieu 1991: 83)

How Bourdieu manages to find evidence for this in Labov's research baffles me, but it suggests either that Bourdieu has never spoken meaningfully with a member of the lower classes or that things are very different in France.

Alas, even those who have championed regional and social variety in language may sometimes fail to appreciate the value of everyday discourse:

Some people enjoy language the way others enjoy food; they relish neat turns of phrase, picturesque figures of speech, puns, riddles, and word games. Others look upon it as a necessary evil, something we have to use for communication, the more's the pity. Perhaps related to this difference is the great range of variation among individuals in the skill with which they use language. This is a matter which has not been given much attention by theoretical linguists, who tend to think of linguistic competence as more or less uniform among the members of a speech community. Nothing could be further from the truth. The range of skill from a Winston Churchill, Martin Luther King, Jr, or Adlai Stevenson to the inarticulate speaker who gropes for words, mixes up his sentence structure, and interlards his phrases with "you know", "I mean" and "actually" is as great as the range of skill in any other common occupation. (Francis 1983: 45–46)

As will have become obvious from the preceding chapters many of the working-class speakers display rhetorical skills similar to those of Churchill, King, and Stevenson and it is equally clear that the use of discourse markers such as *you know* and *I mean* is not necessarily a sign of inarticulateness. On the contrary, the use of such features is systematic (Schiffrin 1987; Macaulay 2002b) and may actually be a mark of eloquence (Östman 1981, 1982). That even a dialectologist can display such apparent prejudice underlines the need for the kind of illustration of the expressiveness of folk speech that has been presented in this volume.

Even from the transcripts, which give only limited information as to how the speakers sound, it will have been obvious that these are Scottish voices. From the tapes themselves, none of the speakers could ever have been mistakenly classified as English. Irvine (2001) examining the ideological and cultural implications of stylistic differentiation observes:

Styles in speaking involve the ways speakers, as agents in social (and sociolinguistic) space, negotiate their positions and goals within a system of distinctions and possibilities. Their acts of speaking are ideologically mediated, since those acts necessarily involve the speaker's understandings of salient social groups, activities, and practices, including forms of talk. (Irvine 2001: 23–24)

It has been demonstrated repeatedly in earlier chapters that the speakers are aware of the salient differences in speech and behaviour that can be found in Scotland. Irvine goes on to point out that sociolinguists have not paid enough attention to such factors:

Most sociolinguistic work, too, has appealed to some notion of social evaluation, attitudes, scales of prestige, or schemes of values, and/or has alluded to speakers' conceptions of social identity, and the like. Many sociolinguists, however, have placed these evaluative schemes in the background, as if they could be taken as obvious, or were but one "factor" among many, or, especially, as if they could be read off the distributions of sociolinguistic facts (i.e., as if they needed no independent investigation). (Irvine 2001: 24)

In Chapter Nine, it was shown that the speakers are aware of social differences in language and know that there are occasions on which it is necessary to modify one's speech, yet they manifested no desire to change their normal way of speaking on a more permanent basis. On the contrary, they prefer to "talk wer ain tongue wer ain wey among werselves" and they admire those that have not lost "their tongue" after years away from Scotland. The attitudes displayed in Chapter Ten showed an independent spirit and often a stubborn determination in the face of adverse circumstances. T.C. Smout in the introduction to his *A Century of the Scottish People 1830–1950* observes:

If I have dwelt excessively upon the dark exterior of life, it is inevitably so in a book concerned with working-class experience in an age when most Scots were working-class and when their experience was, to the modern eye, bad. (Smout 1986: 1)

Smout was mostly dealing with an earlier period than the lives of the speakers whose voices were quoted in the preceding chapters but there is some overlap. However, as the speakers themselves made clear the "dark exterior" did not manage to crush their spirit.

It remains a puzzle as to why scholars such as McCrone (1992, 2001) and Kellas (1980) downplay the importance of language in understanding the situation in Scotland. Irvine (2001) uses the deconstructionist term *erasure* to describe situations where some form of language is ignored:

Erasure [...] is the process in which an ideology simplifies the sociolinguistic field. Attending to one dimension of distinctiveness, it ignores another, thereby rendering some sociolinguistic phenomena (or persons or activities) invisible. So, for example, a social group, or a language, may be imagined as homogeneous, its internal variation disregarded or explained away. (Irvine 2001: 33–34)

Attempts to identify and define working-class culture have shown that it is a complex notion (Clarke, Critcher, and Johnson 1980; Johnson 1980). When writers such as McCrone (1996, 2001) and Beveridge and Turnbull (1989) refer to Scottish "culture" their examples include the "Kailyard School" and the Scottish Renaissance under Hugh MacDiarmid. In the works of these two groups the language of ordinary Scots is effectively "erased". It is only relatively recently that the work of writers such as Tom Leonard, Alasdair Gray, and James Kelman has provided a more realistic literary representation of the

speech of working-class Scots. The effectiveness of this kind of representation can be seen in an extract from James Kelman's *How late it
was, how late*. Sammy, who has been blinded, is trying to find his way
home without help. The extract gives his thoughts as he, as it were,
talks to himself, trying to encourage himself to keep going.

3.
He was gony be fine. Across the big junction and onto the bridge and that was him, so
okay, so that's that, ye just fucking that's all ye do, step by step, ye walk step by step,
by step, ye keep going, ye just don't cave in man that feeling, hanging there, but ye
don't let it cover ye ye keep going christ the times he had had, the times he had been
through man he had been through the fucking worst man he had been through it man
and this wasnay it, it fucking wasnay, it wasnay, it just fucking wasnay, he had seen it,
the worst man he had fucking seen it, cunts fucking dying, getting fucking kicked to
death, the fucking lot man he had seen it. Fucking Charlie! Ye didnay fucking need
Charlie to tell ye man ye kidding! Get to fuck. Fucking bastards. Sammy had fucking
seen it, he had seen it. All he wanted was his due, that was all man his fucking due.
He had copped for it; copped for this and copped for that. Fucking alright, okay, okay;
fuck yez! (Kelman 1995: 57)

Kelman uses conventional punctuation and line arrangement but
it is possible to set out the passage in the same format as the transcripts in the present volume. This gives the display in (4).

4.
he was gony be fine
across the big junction and onto the bridge
and that was him
so okay
so that's that
ye just fucking
that's all ye do
step by step
ye walk
step by step by step
ye keep going
ye just don't cave in
man that feeling
hanging there
but ye don't let it cover ye
ye keep going
christ the times he had had
the times he had been through man

he had been through the fucking worst man
he had been through it man
and this wasnay it
it fucking wasnay
it wasnay
it just fucking wasnay
he had seen it
the worst man
he had fucking seen it
cunts fucking dying
getting fucking kicked to death
the fucking lot man
he had seen it
fucking Charlie!
ye didnay fucking need Charlie to tell ye man
ye kidding!
get to fuck
fucking bastards
Sammy had fucking seen it
he had seen it
all he wanted was his due
that was all man
his fucking due
he had copped for it
copped for this
and copped for that
fucking alright
okay okay
fuck yez!

As presented in (3), the most salient aspect for many readers may be the frequent use of taboo expressions. When the same text is set out as in (4), we can see more clearly the parallel expressions and the repetitions, similar to those used by the speakers in this book, and the rhythm of speech is brought out. Kelman's great achievement lies not in his use of taboo expressions but in his ability to reproduce the pattern and rhythm of actual speech.

The international success of Kelman's (and Irvine Welsh's) work shows that representations of Scottish speech are no barrier to comprehension, even to people who have never heard anyone talk like that. However, until very recently such forms of speech were effectively "erased" from Scottish "culture". This was presumably because of the attitude that Tom Leonard portrayed in the poem about all the people who told him that his language was "disgraceful" (Leonard 1984: 120; Macaulay 1988d). It is not that writers such as McCrone and Kellas are unaware of Scottish working-class speech, but they appear to consider it too "disgraceful" to form part of Scottish culture. So, the most salient aspect of Scottish identity is ignored and its typical speakers become invisible. The "weak language tariff which people have to pay to be 'Scots'" (McCrone 2001: 177) consists of the vowels and consonants of Standard Scottish English and the few "overt Scotticisms" (Aitken 1984a: 107) that middle-class speakers use, particularly to confuse English English speakers.

All Scots are aware of English English forms of speech (Trudgill 1984) from the radio and television but it is usually only the upper-class Scots who have been educated at public schools that speak RP or anything closely approaching it. Middle-class Scots usually speak Scottish Standard English (Aitken 1984), which is distinguished from RP by a number of features: it is rhotic (i.e., *r* is pronounced in final position, as in *car*, and before a consonant, as in *card*); there is no neutralisation of vowels before *r*, so *fir* and *fur* are distinct, as are *tern* and *turn*; there is no distinction between long and short *a*, so *Sam* and *psalm* are the same; there is no distinction in the high back rounded vowels so *food* rhymes with *good*; there are other differences in vowel quality and length, including a contrast between *tide* and *tied*, and Scottish intonation is markedly different from southern English. It is generally very easy for Scots speakers to identify fellow Scots from even very short overheard utterances. It is a highly focused form of speech.

The lower-class Scots speakers show even greater differences from southern English. The Great English Vowel Shift operated differently north of the border and produced a very different system. The most salient feature is that the Middle English long high back rounded vowel *u* did not diphthongise, with the result that lower-class Scots speakers can be heard saying *doon, oot,* and *hoose* for *down, out,* and *house*. Another consequence of the difference in the vowel shift is that lower-class speakers will sometimes use forms such as *hame, mair,* and *stane* for *home, more,* and *stone*. However, all Scots know the standard forms and can use them when they wish. The use of forms such as *doon* and *hame* is not because of ignorance of the standard forms or an inability to produce them. There are many other vowel differences, and some consonantal differences, many of them varying from one part of the country to the other. There is also a fairly rare but very salient use of the velar fricative in words such as *night* and *bought*, which may be pronounced *nicht* and *bocht*.

In these features, Scottish English, as spoken by many ordinary people today, is on several counts a very conservative form of English, with some forms (e.g., *doon, oot, nicht, bocht*) which have remained almost unchanged since the days before English was a separate language but which were lost or altered in most varieties of English by the sixteenth century (Murison 1979). The persistence of these forms is all the more remarkable in that they are not generally used in education, in the mass media, in the institutionalised bureaucracy, or by the more prosperous sector of Scottish society (Ryan 1979; Macaulay 1988b). This conservatism is not political but a traditionalism; it is the standard language that adopted innovations such as the loss of the velar fricative and the Great Vowel Shift.

There are a number of factors that probably contribute to this conservatism: the desire of a minority group to maintain its distinctness from the dominant majority group; a relatively low level of prosperity which limited social mobility and contributed more to emigration than immigration; a cultural traditionalism that takes many forms; the Scots' view of their own national character; and no doubt many others. However, none of these alone nor all combined explain why Scots forms of speech should be so resilient, despite the pressures of education, employment, and the media.

The situation is complicated by social class differences. While most Scots reveal their Scottishness through their speech, it is the working-class speakers who display the most marked features. Working-class solidarity has been (at least until recently) much stronger in Scotland than in England (e.g., in the trade union movement and in voting patterns). The working-class speech is thus indexical (Hanks 1996; Silverstein 1996) in two respects. In the first place it asserts their Scottishness and separateness from the English. Secondly, it affirms their working-class loyalty and rejection of middle-class values. This is significant because too often the speakers of non-prestige varieties are believed to accept the values of the dominant group or class (Gal 1989: 353–54).

The cultural understandings (Strauss and Quinn 1997) that have been demonstrated in this book (particularly by the examples in Chapter Ten but also in other chapters) present a picture of people who believe themselves to be hard-working, independent-minded, and deserving of respect, whatever their status. They do not manifest insecurity or feelings of inferiority. They are perceptive about the world they live in and able to talk about their lives in an eloquent and dignified manner.

As Le Page observes:

The primary function of language is that of enabling each of us, initially as children and then throughout our lives, to emerge from collectivities as individuals, claiming an identity by relating ourselves to others as we perceive them. We may try to establish solidarity without distance from others. (Le Page 1994: 118)

The speakers in this book have demonstrated the "primary function of language" in vivid and eloquent terms.

Appendix A

Len M.'s Trip to Russia as a Boy

(Len M.)
we went to– sailed the boat through the Kiel Canal right up through the
    Baltic into Leningrad
we disembarked in Leningrad
and stayed a few days in Leningrad
and went to Moscow
and eh while I was there the young lass– the girl– the girl I was with
a person called Violet Dunbar
her fa– her brother was killed in the Spanish republican war
he eh– she took homesick
and eh they had to send her home
and eh I think they were in a corner wondering what to do with me
but I wasna homesick
I had twa or three– me being a political– coming up I was more settled with the
    situation
and eh so she was sent home
and the rest of the big delegation they were eh they were going to see the Dnieper
    Dam
this was the great thing that was happening at that time in Russia
building this Dnieper Dam on the– the Dnieper eh Dnie– eh Dnieper Dam
and they went to see that
well they thought
well with it being on my own there was no point in me going there
because of the eh it was more for grown-ups
it was not for a child
like you know I was only twelve year old
so they kept me
eh I went round all the schools and places like that
and while I was there
[9 *lines omitted*]
and em while we're there
Stalin's first wife had died
and eh I remember looking out the windae at the funeral procession
and eh they pointed out Stalin
that was the only time eh I saw Stalin in eh in eh the thingy
cause eh I'd saw him just a bit of him
when I was there for the seventh of November celebrations
and he was on the Red Square in Lenin's mausoleum
and em we saw him– I saw him there

but the fellas went till eh– the older people they went till a big meeting
and he– he addressed the meeting
so they would see him better
I have a photograph of that meeting
but I was at another meeting
and eh Lenin's widow was the main speaker at that thing
but I wasn't introduced to her–
I was introduced to her but not as Lenin
and as I say I'm named after her husband
so she probably never knew
who I was as regards the situations as regards Lenin
but that was Krupskaya
she was at at that meeting
and it was on the radio
and eh in fact I went
I come back
and the headmaster– well my second headmaster Mr McIntosh of Rockwell School he
        eh told us– told us
that he'd heard us on the– the radio

This is an unusual narrative. Len has a really interesting story to tell: going to Russia at the age of twelve, seeing Stalin, and meeting Lenin's widow. Yet he fails to make it effective. He tells about *not* going to see the Dnieper Dam, about barely seeing Stalin, and about Lenin's widow *not* being told he was named after her husband. It is all negative. Then the positive part is that his headmaster had heard him on the radio. Somehow Len manages to make the narrative uninteresting when it should have been one of the high points of his interview because he has a unique experience to recount.

Two versions of "The road and the miles to Dundee"

(These stories are discussed in Chapter Six.)

(Bella K.)
and there's a song "The road and the miles to Dundee"
about a girl walking from some place to Dundee
and in Dun– on her way she meets a man
she lost her way
and he tells the road to Dundee
now I always believed

that somehow or other my granny was connected with this song
for em she– she did walk from Aberdeen to Dundee for a job
she went– big story in it
she– she walked with her sister
but her sister run away at Montrose with a soldier
[*laughs*]
left her on her own
but she was just a wee lassie
she was barely fourteen
and she did lose her way
and somebody did give her–
and in the song it says
that he ga–he took the gold brooch
my gran had a brooch that wasn't gold
but it was sort of like pewter-like stuff with two pansies enamelled on it
one mauve and one yellow
and she got that from somebody who showed her on the road to Dundee
and when she landed in Dundee
the first house she came to
she asked for a drink of water
and when the woman came out my granny had fainted on her doorstep
and the woman took her in
and she lived with that woman until the day she was married

(Len M.)
eh my grandmither– my mother's mother they reckon
Bella was telling me
she's heard
my mother must've told her a tune
"The Miles– the Road and the Miles to Dundee" was written for her situation
she'd left–
my mother's mother born in Aberdeen
and eh about fifteen and her and her aulder sister
there's no work up there
and the works here were starting women in the eighteen hundreds– eighteen probably
    well eighteen sixties or round about that
and they were booming here
and eh they said that they walked all the way
and eh they stayed in Montrose
and Montrose at that time was eh a soldiers' depot
and eh my granny she was just young
she was eh as I say probably about fourteen fifteen maybe younger
I don't know but probably maybe older
cause I remember eh the young people in the mills
they eh and her sister was a lot older than her
and her sister got in tow with a soldier in Montrose

and she stayed in Montrose for a while with her older sister
but eh the older sister was expecting
course that was a terrible thing
she wasna married or anything at that time
and she looked– the older sister looked as if she was staying in Montrose with the soldier
and my granny decided to go to Dundee herself
and she– instead of taking the coast road
as you know in Montrose you come over a bridge
now I don't know what like the bridge was that time
but the road for eh Montrose across the Esk
eh the bridge here
road here for Forfar
and the coastal road for Dundee
and she took the wrong road
she took the Forfar Road
and eh this is how the eh she had to walk the– walked all the way
I don't know what they are never
coorse she died with–
I remember my granny quite well
but she wasna old enough for me to find out about a lot of things
which you would find out now you know what I mean
older now you would be able to say
"Well what happened then?"
I could build a picture a story of the whole situation
but they reckon that was there she was lost
she was completely lost
cause she'd ended up in probably Forfar or Glamis
or something like that you know
and I think she walked over the Sidlaws
cause that was the road
that would probably be– that was one of the roads to– to go over the hills at that time
the Forfar road would probably just be a trough you know
and eh at that time
so she eh–
that's where they reckoned the same song came fae
but they don't know
we don't know
it's only family history family thingy
but it's–
looking on it I can see it's possible

Appendix B

Bill Dalgleish's story

(See Chapter Eight)

well that was in wartime
but eh– a boat– a port ship blew up with 500-pound bombs in it
and the whole warehouses– the– the pillars that held up the warehouses
just got cut right through
and everything fell down on top of it   5
fellows that we knew that was working
and we'd to go in about and try and–
and all that was left of the ship was the number one hatch
so I marched this squad round in into this docks to give a hand
and we're standing playing a hose on to this ship   10
and at the back of the ship was a floating crane
and there'd been ammunition landed on this floating crane which was burning
we played wer hoses
all that we could hear was the bullets passing us "Waaa! wooo!"
so the boy says to me   15
one of the sappers says to me "Hey sarge somebody's shooting"
"Don't be silly there naebody shooting"
so we got a ladder
another sergeant and I got a ladder and went aboard this ship
what was left of it   20
and eh directed the hoses on to where it was burning
but when we passed this hatch
see I've got concussional deafness
I had to come from the gunnery
I was a gunner   25
but I was downgraded B6 when I took this job
being in the railway and that you know this stevedore battalion
when I'm passing this hatch
I hear "Venire qua" in Italian see
I say "Aw it must be in my ears   30
cannae be naebody doon there"
but the ither fellow says to me "Here Jock there's somebody doon there"
so we goes away doon the hatch
feart?
I was feart to pit my fit on the bombs you know   35
there was still bombs in the ship down the hatch
we found one Italian in between decks with his rosary

well we felt him
oh he was just aboot gone
but we goes down   40
we could see a hand waving in amongst the bombs
so I was the first doon [*short pause*]
I didn't know if I had put my– [*slight cough*] my foot on this bomb or no
but it was a piece of metal
but unknown to me   45
of course I'm coming doon the ladder this way
and I could see it
[*bangs table*]
I pits my fit on this piece of metal
when I looked roond it's across a fellow's throat you know   50
but this young chap he had got thrown
he either lay or got thrown in the space where the bombs had been taken out
and the timber was underneath with a girder across his head across his neck
and he couldnae get out or in
so we went up and got medical aid down to him and that you know   55
and then we got him on my back with a rope round his arm
we took him oot of the hatch
but I was never so feart in aall my life
no kidding
and the Brigadier Clark that was there   60
we hears him telling the captain "Put the two men away"
this is this to the other sergeant and that
so he put his hand to his cheek
he said "Now you'll go back and you'll have a bath
and you'll go right to bed"   65
but we had wer shower and that
but we says "Aw we'll go for a pint of beer"
into the mess
"A pint"
I takes up the pint like that aff the table   70
[*Demonstrates hand shaking badly, rest of the family laughs*]
so there I was
"Steady up with you Jock"
I says "Lift your pint"
[*Demonstrates again; more laughter*]   75
I said "Hey come on the reaction's setting in
let's go to bed"
but you never felt nothing until you took a weight in your hand
aa the beer was aall over
you didn't know what to do with your hand   80
that's the only time I was afraid by putting my fit on that bomb
I says "If this thing goes I'm away– away to heaven"

This story fits the Labov and Waletzky model very well. The first fourteen lines are orientation, and the complicating action begins at line 15 with the connective *so*, followed by another example in line 18. Lines 23–27 add explanatory background information about Bill's deafness which explains his reluctance to trust his ears (lines 30–31). The other soldier, however, had heard the voice too so they go down the hatch (another episode introduced by *so*, line 33, with the narrative present tense *goes*). Lines 34–36 are evaluative explaining the reason for his fear in the unexploded bombs on the ship. Lines 37–39 provide the results of their first search, the dying Italian "with his rosary", evoking the idea of prayer.

Lines 40–54 contain the climax of the narrative, finding the young man alive but trapped by a girder across his neck. Again the episode begins in a clause with the narrative present tense, introduced this time by *but*. In this section, Bill makes a significant pause at the end of line 42 ("so I was the first doon"), iconically reflecting his own ignorance of what would happen. This increases the suspense of the narrative. His gesture of banging the table (line 48) heightens this suspense by alerting the hearers to the coming discovery. In contrast, the resolution (lines 55–57) is described very simply. Lines 58–80 are a long evaluative section, underlining the danger and the fear. Lines 81–82 are the coda, indicating that the story is complete.

The language in which Bill's story is told confirms Gal's (1979) view that "Danger of Death" stories do not always affect the style in a single direction. Bill begins by using only standard forms for words such as *warehouses, pound, down, top, about*, and *round*. It is not until line 18 that he uses the form *naebody* but that is in quoted dialogue. In line 26 he uses the form *downgraded* but it is possible that this word is not normally found with a monophthong (cf. Macaulay 1991a: 43). Then in the central episode of the story lines 28–57 standard forms become less common but they are not absent: *doon* lines 31, 32, 33, 42, 45 (but *down* lines 36, 40, 55), *aboot* line 39, *roond* line 50 (but *round* line 56), *oot* line 57 (but *out* lines 52, 54); *cannae* lone 31, *couldnae* line 54 (but *didn't* line 43) and *naebody* line 31; *feart* lines 34, 35); *pit my fit* lines 35, 49 (but *put my foot* line 43). There is also the narrative present tense (Macaulay 1991a: 60–62) in *we goes* in line

33, which is used again in line 40, and in line 49 *I pits*, line 61 *we hears*, and line 70 *I takes*.

The interesting point is at line 43 where he uses the forms *didn't, put* and *foot*. This is not a narrative clause in Labov and Waletzky's (1967) sense though it is central to the story which is not just about the danger but also about Bill's fear. Between line 42 *so I was the first doon* and line 43 *I didn't know* there is a noticeable pause and he coughs slightly after the first *my* on line 43. The whole effect is one of underlining the importance of what he is saying in these lines. It may not be a coincidence that he should use standard forms for emphasis, particularly in addressing someone who used only standard forms. But this is not accommodation in any simple sense. Bill Dalgleish knows that I can understand him just as well when he says *pit my fit* as when he says *put my foot*.

Appendix C

Bella K.'s Father

In the oral history interview and in her interview with me, Bella K. spoke a lot about her father. She told me "it's my father that was the biggest influence on me". When the oral history interviewer at the end of the interview asked Bella to sum up her life, this is how she responded:

I wish I had paid more attention to what my father said
I wish I had taken advantage of the opportunities that he gave me
but as they say you can't put an old head on young shoulders
if I was to sum up
I would say– take something from my father's book
and I would say
I need not be missed if another succeed me
to reap down the fields which in spring I have sowed
he who ploughs and sows is not missed by the reaper
they are only remembered by what they have done
and I think for women's equality I threw a pebble in the water
it was a very very small wave
but it was my wave
and I feel I achieved something

The following extracts from the two interviews are only a sample of the things Bella said about her father but they are enough to give a strong indication of the kind of man he was. They also are further evidence of Bella's linguistic skills. (I have simplified the transcripts slightly for ease of reading.):

we could never ever forget what class we belonged to
because my father was a strict teetotaler
he did not drink
so every New Year for–
to let you know how the Scottish custom was
everything had to be cleaned before twelve o' clock
and to let my mother get on with the housework
and get the last things done
father used to take us to the pictures

the only time that my father was ever really up
that he had a free night
the only night he had free was Hogmanay
and he used to take us to the pictures
and take us round the town
and see the stands that were there for selling first foots
and all the shops were open till twelve o' clock at night
butchers and bakers and em father was a baker
that was another thing for the New Year
you used to go all round the baker's shops
and look at the shortbread
because it was a great work of art to get a thistle
a good clear thistle on a cake of shortbread
and we were able to judge the shortbread
by the clearness of this thistle
if he was a good baker yes or no
if he wasn't a good baker the thistle wasn't a clear emblem of a thistle
and then we used to come up past the Hill Street Dairy
where my father would buy three bottles of milk
three children three bottles of milk
and we all got a bottle of milk each to carry
and we had a box of biscuits– chocolate biscuits for my mother
from my father you know
and when anybody shouted across the road
"Happy New Year to you when it comes
have you got your bottle in?"
he used to hold up the bottle of milk
and say "Yeah I've got my bottle in"
it was his bottle of milk
and we all had fruit cordial
and my father used to lift his glass
and the words that he said was
"Here's to a working class New Year"
and that's the way we could never ever forget
what class that we belonged to
it was a working class New Year that we were wished
always loads and loads to eat
course my father was a baker
and mind you he bought everything
there was no such a thing as this stealing it from the bakehouse
my father could never do that never ever

and we had an old gramophone with a great big horn on it
and a one-sided record–
it was about a half inch thick and it was only–
you played on the one side

it only played one song on the one side
and it was– I can hear it yet in my head
it was "A Guid New Year to yin and aw and many may you see"
and father used to lift up the window
and put out this horn
and wished the whole street a Happy New Year
it was simple good fun

but I'm afraid my father had too big a heart for to be a businessman
because he gave all his bread away to poor town people
so he had to go out and work himself
and eh he just gave his money away
he was a worker but he wasnae a businessman
I'm afraid that our opinion of a businessman
you've got to be a bit of a killer
my father was too much of a Christian to be a killer

and of course my father was a disciple
can I put "disciple" not in a religious sense
he was a disciple in his beliefs
because he believed in socialism
and he worked for socialism
all his life he gave for socialism
I would say yes he would've died for socialism
and he came to the conclusion
that Christ must have been a communist
that Christ wasn't what they portrayed him
to be a man of God– of spirit
he was a man who saw a better way of life
and if it was
"Do unto others as you'd have them to do on yourself"
yes my father lived that life
and in that form he was a Christian
and you didn't tell lies
and to call anybody a liar was fighting talk
and you never laughed at anybody's disabilities
if anybody had clothes that was outlandish or didn't suit
he used to say "Well they either think
that they're braa looking with it
or that's aw they've got to put on"
so there was a humility and generosity and a love of children
and every newborn baby that was put in his arms
wrapped in a white shawl as they used to be
they lay wrapped in a white shawl with a white hat
and he would– he could handle it when it was that way see
and he would take it

and he would look down at the baby
and he had such a strong face
he was so aware of the indignities that man has to suffer
that his mouth had a permanent scowl on it
and he had a manner of speaking that was aggressive
because it was an aggressive life
and he would down at this baby
and the whole face would soften off
and he would look down
and say "Ah well maybe this yin will prove a blessing to mankind"
and that was the man

and he used to– he had my mother on a pedestal
he really adored this woman
there was nobody could look after children like her
nobody could nurse children like her
nobody could make a pot of soup like her
nobody– there was nobody could do anything like my mother
if your child was sick "You tak it to my wife
and my wife'll sort your bairn" you know

after my father come out of prison
of course couldnae get a job for love nor money you know
two year idle
and then eh when he did get a job
eh my father was in a position like what women are
in that you've got sort of like prove yourself better than anybody else
so he was in the position that he had to prove
though he was a socialist
that he could work better than anybody else
and he was a strict teetotaler
and eh when he went– when he got this job in Elders in Lochee
they phoned up to say "Do you know that man you've working for you has been a
        political prisoner?"
and he said "Well if all men could work like Tammy M.
I'd fill the bakehoose with them"

he demonstrated during the General Strike
and he had his navy blue serge suit
and his homburg hat and his watch and chain on
and they said "Why is this well-dressed man leading the demonstration?"
and that was his reply
 "Because I don't want to come down to your level
I want you up to mine"

there was trouble brewing one time
and eh he saved this policemen's life you know
just with his protection
and the man never forgot it
well it was a detective really says to him
"Tammy M. I'll never forget you
you saved my life"
and that was the first I had heard of it you know
[*RM: This was during the strike?*]
during the strikes
during the baton charges and things like that
and he got cornered
he got cornered
my father saved him from getting murdered you know
but at the same time he'd a big rolling pin in his troosers
and a bag of pepper
my mother never went oot withoot a bag of pepper
during these– the baton charges times
and that was to throw in the horses' faces

my father run guns to Ireland
not because he was a Catholic
but because he was against imperialism–
that he thought from the start
that nobody has any right in another man's country
and eh it's funny how things comes back
because he used to get–
it was the guns from the fourteen eighteen war you see
and the soldiers still had a few guns
but they all had their number on them
so father used to get and file off the numbers
hand-filing off the numbers
and when hostilities ceased
he was left with a few guns
so what he did was
the old-fashioned range grate that we had in our house
we lived in Elm Street
it's probably still in the papers yet
he took out the fire
and he cemented the guns at the back of the fire
and years later my mother picked up the *Courier*
and she said to me
they used to run little snippets you know
"A woman's had her grate removed
and found two guns at the back
the address was twenty-one Elm Street"

she says "That's your father and his guns to Ireland"
he also eh he run– the way that he did it was
he would go to a chemist
and he would get bandages ointment pills
and the chemist would put them in his dustbin
my father'd go round and pick them out
and that was what he sent to Ireland
but that– it wasn't for– because he was a peace loving man
he really loved peace
we were brought up to believe in peace
and not to take part in
what my father described as an imperialistic war
it was very very strong influence as regards to politics beliefs

he was such an honest man
there was guile
there was no deviousness in the man
he was intelligent
he was what you could almost say self-educated
and his upbringing made him what he was
and my father sat by candlelight sewing jute bags for a penny
while his father was out getting drunk
and the father at the hinder end– my grandfather
I suppose it was a nervous breakdown the man took
but he landed out in the asylum
well what he said about his father
I can just remember the atmosphere in the home
my mother begging him to go to the funeral
and my uncle sitting there saying to him–
my mother saying "Tam it's your father
you've got to go"
and he said he stood up
and he said "No you honour your father and your mother
but you don't honour them if they were bloody weeds
and my father was a weed"

Glossary

I have listed all the forms that might be unfamiliar to some readers, though the meaning of most of them is usually obvious from the context. I have listed them all so that readers who are in doubt may consult this list. My second reason for listing them all is to show the extent to which these speakers are using a form of Scots. There are about 200 Scots forms here that are not found in Standard English. There are many more Scots forms used by the speakers that are not indicated by the spelling, so this is a minimal list.

aa	—	all
aabody	—	everybody
aafy	—	awful
aald	—	old
aall	—	all
aathing	—	everything
aboot	—	about
aff	—	off
ain	—	own
alloo	—	allow
aul(d)	—	old
aw	—	all
awaa	—	away
awfie	—	awful
aye	—	yes
aye	—	always
bade	—	stayed (past of *bide*)
bairn	—	child
baists	—	beasts
baith	—	both
bobbie	—	policeman
borrowt	—	borrowed
braa	—	splendid
brae	—	hill
brose	—	porridge
buroo	—	employment office (also, unemployment benefit)
caaing	—	calling
cairt	—	cart
cannae	—	can't
caw'd	—	called
chap aff	—	chop off

cheek	—	be insolent
cissies	—	effeminate males
claes	—	clothes
councilors	—	councillors
coont	—	count
coorse	—	course
cotman	—	farm labourer
couldnae	—	couldn't
crabbit	—	bad-tempered
croon	—	crown
dae	—	do
daffing	—	doffing, taking off
dee	—	do
deid	—	dead
didnae	—	didn't
doon	—	down
drappie	—	a little drop
draps	—	drops
duds	—	clothes
dug	—	dog
dummy tit	—	pacifier
dyehoose	—	dyehouse
eediot	—	idiot
een	—	one
efter	—	after
eicht	—	eight
eil	—	oil
fae	—	from
faever	—	wherever
faither	—	father
far	—	where
feart	—	afraid
fee'd on	—	signed on
feeing fair	—	hiring fair
feenish(ing)	—	finish(ing)
femily	—	family
fen	—	when
ferm	—	farm
fermer	—	farmer
fit	—	what
fit	—	foot
fitbaa	—	football
Fitdee	—	Footdee
flair	—	floor
forbye	—	in addition to
gaa	—	go

gaaing	—	going
gaes	—	goes
gie	—	give
gied	—	gave
gi'en	—	gave
ging	—	go
gled	—	glad
goodherted	—	goodhearted
guid	—	good
hadnae	—	hadn't
hae	—	have
haeing	—	having
hale	—	whole
hame	—	home
harer	—	wild young person
haud(ing)	—	hold(ing)
haund	—	hand
havenae	—	haven't
heid	—	head
hert	—	heart
hervest	—	harvest
hid	—	had
hinging	—	hanging
hoose	—	house
hut	—	hit
ither	—	other
jeckit	—	jacket
joab	—	job
ken	—	know
kenning	—	knowing
kent	—	known
kerry	—	carry
kirk	—	church
lassie	—	girl
lavvy	—	lavatory
lend	—	loan
lucking	—	looking
lucks	—	looks
mair	—	more
maist	—	most
maks	—	makes
meenit	—	minute
messages	—	grocery shopping
micht	—	might
midden	—	refuse dump
mither	—	mother

mony	—	many
nae	—	no
naebody	—	nobody
naw	—	no
neeghbour	—	neighbour
no	—	not
noo	—	now
nooadays	—	nowadays
oer	—	over
ony	—	any
onyway	—	anyway
oot	—	out
oot of my road	—	out of my way
outside	—	outside
ower	—	over
pey	—	pay
piecebox	—	lunchbox
pit	—	put
poke	—	bag
prood	—	proud
pu	—	pull
redd up	—	cleared out
retirt	—	retired
roon(d)	—	round
sae	—	so
seen	—	saw
seeven	—	seven
shooder	—	shoulder
snaa	—	snow
spaver	—	trouser–fly
spick	—	speak
stanes	—	stones
staunin	—	standing
steyed	—	stayed (i.e., lived)
ttert	—	start
ta'en	—	taken
tacketty baits	—	boots with metal studs
tae	—	too
tae	—	to
ta'en	—	taken
tap	—	top
tatties	—	potatoes
telt	—	told
thae	—	those
thegether	—	together
theirsel(s)	—	themselves

thon	—	those
thoosand	—	thousand
tig-toyed	—	played games
troosers	—	trousers
waiting on	—	waiting for
wasnae	—	wasn't
wat	—	wet
weans	—	children
wee	—	small
weemen	—	women
weeshed	—	wished
weet	—	wet
wer	—	our
werenae	—	weren't
werselves	—	ourselves
wey	—	way
whaur	—	where
whawever	—	whoever
whit	—	what
wifie	—	woman
winna	—	won't
wouldnae	—	wouldn't
wrang	—	wrong
wuman	—	woman
wunst	—	once
yin	—	one
yon	—	that

Bibliography

Aitken, Adam J. 1979. "Scottish speech: a historical view with special reference to the Standard English of Scotland" in Aitken, A.J. and Tom McArthur (eds) *Languages of Scotland*. Edinburgh: Chambers. 85–118.

—. 1981. "The Scottish vowel-length rule" in Benskin, M. and M.L. Samuels (eds) *So Meny People Longages and Tonges*. Edinburgh: Middle English Dialect Project. 131–57.

—. 1984a. "Scottish accents and dialects" in Trudgill, Peter (ed.) *Language in the British Isles*. Cambridge: Cambridge University Press. 94–114.

—. 1984b. "Scots and English in Scotland" in Trudgill, Peter (ed.) *Language in the British Isles*. Cambridge: Cambridge University Press. 517–32.

—. 1985. "A history of Scots" in Robinson, Mairi (ed.) *The Concise Scots Dictionary*. Aberdeen: Aberdeen University Press. ix–xli.

Aronoff, Mark and Janie Rees-Miller (eds). 2001. *The Handbook of Linguistics*. Oxford: Blackwell.

Atkinson, J. Michael and John Heritage (eds). 1984. *Structures of Social Action: Studies in Conversational Analysis*. Cambridge: Cambridge University Press.

Bakhtin, Mikhail. 1973. *Problems of Dostoevsky's Poetics* (tr. R.W. Rotsel) Ann Arbor: Ardis.

—. 1981. *The Dialogic Imagination: Four Essays by M.M. Bakhtin* (ed. Michael Holquist, tr. Caryl Emerson and Michael Holquist). Austin: University of Texas Press.

Bamberg, Michael G.W. (ed.). 1997. *Oral Versions of Personal Experience: Three Decades of Narrative Analysis* [Special Issue of *Journal of Narrative and Life History* 7(1–4)]. Mahwah. N.J.: Lawrence Erlbaum.

Barthes, Roland. 1977. *Image, Music, Text*. New York: Hill and Wang.

Bauman, Richard. 1986. *Story, Performance, and Event: Contextual Studies of Oral Narrative*. Cambridge: Cambridge University Press.

—. 1996. "'Any man who keeps more'n one hound'll lie to you': A contextual study of expressive lying" in Brenneis, Donald and Ronald K.S. Macaulay (eds) *The Matrix of Language: Contemporary Linguistic Anthropology*. Boulder, Colo.: Westview Press. 160–81.

—. 2001. "The ethnography of genre in a Mexican market: Form, function, variation" in Eckert, Penelope and John R. Rickford (eds) *Style and Sociolinguistic Variation*. Cambridge: Cambridge University Press. 57–77.

Bell, Allan. 1984. "Language style as audience design" in *Language in Society* 13: 145–204.

—. 2001. "Back in style: Reworking audience design" in Eckert, Penelope and John R. Rickford (eds) *Style and Sociolinguistic Variation*. Cambridge: Cambridge University Press. 139–69.

Bernstein, Basil. 1962. "Social class, linguistic codes, and grammatical Elements" in *Language and Speech* 5: 31–46. [Reprinted in *Class, Codes and Control*. 1971. 1: 95–117. London: Routledge and Kegan Paul.]

—. 1971. *Class, Codes and Control*. London: Routledge and Kegan Paul. vol. 1.

Beveridge, C. and R. Turnbull. 1989. *The Eclipse of Scottish Culture: Inferiorism and the Intellectuals*. Edinburgh: Polygon.

Biber, Douglas. 1986. "Spoken and written textual dimensions in English" in *Language* 62: 384–414.

——. 1988. *Variation across Speech and Writing*. Cambridge: Cambridge University Press.

Biber, Douglas and Edward Finegan (eds). 1994. *Sociolinguistic Perspectives on Register*. New York: Oxford University Press.

Bisseret, Noëlle. 1979. *Education, Class Language, and Ideology*. London: Routledge and Kegan Paul.

Bloomfield, Leonard. 1927. Review of *The Philosophy of Grammar* by Otto Jespersen, in *JEGP* 26: 444–46.

——. 1933. *Language*. New York: Holt.

Blum-Kulka, Shoshana. 1997. *Dinner Talk: Cultural Patterns of Sociability and Socialization in Family Discourse*. Mahwah, N.J.: Lawrence Erlbaum.

Bourdieu, Pierre. 1977. *Outline of a Theory of Practice* (tr. R. Nice). Cambridge: Cambridge University Press.

——. 1991. *Language and Symbolic Power*. Cambridge: Polity Press.

Bourdieu, Pierre and Loic J.D. Wacquant. 1992. *An Invitation to Reflexive Sociology*. Chicago: University of Chicago Press.

Brazil, David C. 1985. *The Communicative Value of Intonation* [Discourse Analysis Monographs, no. 8]. Birmingham: English Language Research, University of Birmingham.

Brenneis, Donald. 1978. "The matter of talk: Political performances in Bhatgaon" in *Language in Society* 7: 159–70.

——. 1986. "Shared territory: audience, indirection and meaning" in *Text* 6: 339–47.

——. 1987. "Performing passions: Aesthetics and politics in an occasionally egalitarian community" in *American Ethnologist* 14: 236–50.

——. 1988. "Telling troubles: narrative, conflict and experience". Paper presented at the American Ethnological Society Spring Meeting.

Brockmeier, Jens and Donal Carbaugh (eds). 2001. *Narrative and Identity: Studies in Autobiography, Self and Culture*. Amsterdam: John Benjamins.

Brockmeier, Jens and Rom Harré. 2001. "Narrative: Problems and promises of an alternative paradigm" in Brockmeier, Jens and Donal Carbaugh (eds) *Narrative and Identity: Studies in Autobiography, Self and Culture*. Amsterdam: John Benjamins. 39–58.

Brown, Colin and Penelope Fraser. 1979. "Speech as a marker of situation" in Scherer, Klaus R. and Howard Giles (eds) *Social Markers in Speech*. Cambridge: Cambridge University Press. 33–62.

Brown, Penelope and Stephen Levinson. 1987. *Politeness: Some Universals in Language Usage*. Cambridge: Cambridge University Press.

Bruner, Jerome. 1987. "Life as narrative" in *Social Research* 54: 11–32.

——. 2001. "Self-making and world-making" in Brockmeier, Jens and Donal Carbaugh (eds). 2001. *Narrative and Identity: Studies in Autobiography, Self and Culture*. Amsterdam: John Benjamins. 25–37.

Burke, Kenneth. 1935. *Permanence and Change*. New York: New Republic.

Cameron, Deborah. 1997. "Performing gender identity: young men's talk and the construction of heterosexual masculinity" in Johnson, Sally and Ulrike Meinhof (eds) *Language and Masculinity*. Oxford: Blackwell.

Carr, David. 1986. "Narrative and the real world" in *History and Theory* 25: 117–31.

Chafe, Wallace. 1982. "Integration and involvement in speaking, writing, and oral literature" in Tannen, Deborah (ed.) *Spoken and Written Language: Exploring Orality and Literacy*. Norwood, N.J.: Ablex. 35–53.

—. 1994. *Discourse, Consciousness, and Time: The Flow and Displacement of Conscious Experience in Speaking and Writing*. Chicago: University of Chicago Press.

—. 1995. "Adequacy, user-friendliness, and practicality in transcribing" in Leech, Geoffrey, Greg Myers, and Jenny Thomas (eds) *Spoken English on Computer*. London: Longman. 54–61.

Chambers, J.K. 1988. "Acquisition of phonological variants" in Thomas, Alan R. (ed.) *Methods in Dialectology*. Clevedon, Avon: Multilingual Matters. 650–65.

Cheshire, Jenny. 1982. *Variation in an English Dialect*. Cambridge: Cambridge University Press.

Chomsky, Noam. 1965. *Aspects of the Theory of Syntax*. Cambridge, Mass.: MIT Press.

Clarke, John, Chas Critcher, and Richard Johnson (eds). 1979. *Working-Class Culture: Studies in History and Theory*. New York: St. Martin's Press. 185–98.

Clegg, Stewart R. 1993. "Narrative, power, and social theory" in Mumby, Dennis K. (ed.) *Narrative and Social Control: Critical Perspectives*. Newbury Park, Calif.: Sage Publications. 15–45.

Coates, Jennifer. 1996. *Women Talk: Conversation between Women Friends*. Oxford: Blackwell.

—. 2003. *Men Talk: Stories in the Making of Masculinities*. Oxford: Blackwell.

Cole, Roger W. 1986. "Literary representation of dialect: A theoretical approach to the artistic problem" in *The USF Language Quarterly* 14: 3–8.

Cook, Guy. 1994. *Discourse and Literature: The Interplay of Form and Mind*. Oxford: Oxford University Press.

—. 1995. "Theoretical issues: transcribing the untranscribable" in Leech, Geoffrey, Greg Myers, and Jenny Thomas (eds) *Spoken English on Computer*. London: Longman. 35–53.

Coombs, Clyde Hamilton. 1964. *A Theory of Data*. New York: Wiley.

Cooper, Barry. 1976. *Bernstein's Codes: A Classroom Study* [University of Sussex Education area occasional paper, no. 6]. Brighton: University of Sussex.

Coulmas, Florian (ed.). 1986. *Direct and Indirect Speech*. Berlin: Mouton de Gruyter.

Coupland, Nikolas. 1980. "Style-shifting in a Cardiff work setting" in *Language in Society* 9: 1–12.

—. 1988. *Dialect in Use: Sociolinguistic Variation in Cardiff English*. Cardiff: University of Wales Press.

—. 2001. "Language, situation, and the relational self: Theorizing dialect-style in sociolinguistics" in Eckert, Penelope and John R. Rickford (eds) *Style and Sociolinguistic Variation*. Cambridge: Cambridge University Press. 185–210.

Crystal, David. 1969. *Prosodic Systems and Intonation in English*. London: Cambridge University Press.

D'Andrade, Roy G. and Claudia Strauss (eds). 1992. *Human Motives and Cultural Models*. Cambridge: Cambridge University Press.

Devine, T.M. and R.J. Finlay (eds). 1996. *Scotland in the Twentieth Century*. Edinburgh: Edinburgh University Press.

Dines, Elizabeth R. 1980. "Variation in discourse – 'and stuff like that'" in *Language in Society* 9: 13–31.

Dittmar, Norbert. 1988a. Foreword to the series "Sociolinguistics and language contact" in Dittmar, Norbert and Peter Schlobinski (eds) *The Sociolinguistics of Urban Vernaculars: Case Studies and their Evaluation*. Berlin: de Gruyter. ix–xii.

—. 1988b "Introduction" in Dittmar, Norbert and Peter Schlobinski (eds) *The Sociolinguistics of Urban Vernaculars: Case Studies and their Evaluation*. Berlin: de Gruyter. xiii–xviii.

Donnachie, Ian and Christopher Whatley (eds). 1992. *The Manufacture of Scottish History*. Edinburgh: Polygon

Dorian, Nancy C. 1985. *The Tyranny of Tide*. Ann Arbor: Karoma.

Dorian, Nancy. 1994. "Stylistic variation in a language restricted to private-sphere use" in Biber, Douglas and Edward Finegan (eds) *Sociolinguistic Perspectives on Register*. New York: Oxford University Press. 217–32.

Douglas, Sheila. 1998. "Sir James Wilson and his commonsense approach to the Scots language" in *Scottish Language* 17: 16–21.

Dressler, Richard A. and Roger J. Kreuz. 2000. "Transcribing oral discourse: A survey and a model system" in *Discourse Processes* 29: 25–36.

Drew, Paul and John Heritage (eds) 1992. *Talk at Work: Interaction in Institutional Settings*. Cambridge: Cambridge University Press.

Du Bois, John W. 1980. "Beyond definiteness: the trace of identity" in Chafe, Wallace L. (ed.) *The Pear Stories*. Norwood, N.J.: Ablex. 203–74.

—. 1987. "The discourse basis of ergativity" in *Language* 63: 805–55.

DuBois, John W., Stefan Schuetze-Coburn, Susanna Cumming and D. Paolino. 1993. "Outline of discourse transcription" in Edwards, Jane A. and Michael D. Lampert (eds) *Talking Data: Transcription and Coding in Discourse Research*. Hillsdale, N.J.: Lawrence Erlbaum. 3–31.

Dubois, Sylvie and David Sankoff. 2001. "The variationist approach towards discourse structural effects and socio-cultural dynamics: The quantitative analysis of enumeration in oral speech" in Schiffrin, Deborah, Deborah Tannen, and Heidi E. Hamilton (eds) *Handbook of Discourse Analysis*. Oxford: Blackwell. 282–303.

Duranti, Alessandro. 1981. *The Samoan Fono: A Sociolinguistic Study*. Canberra: The Australian National University, Department of Linguistics, Research School of Pacific Studies.

—. 1994. *From Grammar to Politics: Linguistic Anthropology in a Samoan Village*. Berkeley: University of California Press.

Duranti, Alessandro and Charles Goodwin (eds). 1992. *Rethinking Context: Language as an Interactive Phenomenon*. Cambridge: Cambridge University Press.

Eckert, Penelope. 1989. *Jocks and Burnouts: Social Categories and Identity in the High School*. New York: Teachers College.
—. 2000. *Linguistic Variation as Social Practice: The Linguistic Construction of Identity in Belten High*. Oxford: Blackwell.
—. 2001. "Style and social meaning" in Eckert, Penelope and John R. Rickford (eds) *Style and Sociolinguistic Variation*. Cambridge: Cambridge University Press. 119–26.
Eckert, Penelope and John R. Rickford (eds). 2001. *Style and Sociolinguistic Variation*. Cambridge: Cambridge University Press.
Edwards, Jane A. 1995. "Principles and alternative systems in the transcription, coding and mark-up of spoken discourse" in Leech, Geoffrey Greg Myers, and Jenny Thomas (eds) *Spoken English on Computer*. London: Longman. 19–34.
Edwards, Jane A. and Michael D. Lampert (eds). 1993. *Talking Data: Transcription and Coding in Discourse Research*. Hillsdale, N.J.: Lawrence Erlbaum. 3–31.
Eggins, Suzanne and Diana Slade. 1997. *Analyzing Casual Conversation*. London: Cassell.
Emerson, Caryl. 1986. "The outer word and inner speech: Bakhtin, Vygotsky, and the internalization of language" in Morson, Gary Saul (ed.) *Bakhtin, Essays and Dialogues on His Work*. Chicago: University of Chicago Press. 21–40.
Erbaugh, Mary S. 1987. "Psycholinguistic evidence for foregrounding and backgrounding" in Tomlin, Russell S. (ed.) *Coherence and Grounding on Discourse*. Amsterdam: John Benjamins. 109–30.
Ervin-Trip, Susan. 2001. "Variety, style-shifting, and ideology" in Eckert, Penelope and John R. Rickford (eds) *Style and Sociolinguistic Variation*. Cambridge: Cambridge University Press. 44–56.
Fabb, Nigel. 1997. *Linguistics and Literature: Language in the Verbal Arts of the World.* Oxford: Blackwell.
—. 2002. *Language and Literary Structure: The Linguistic Analysis of Form in Verse and Narrative*. Cambridge: Cambridge University Press.
Feagin, Crawford. 1979. *Variation and Change in Alabama English: A Sociolinguistic Study of the White Community*. Washington, D.C.: Georgetown University Press.
Ferrara, Kathleen and Barbara Bell. 1995. "Sociolinguistic variation and discourse function of constructed dialogue introducers: The case of be+like" in *American Speech* 70: 265–89.
Fillmore, Charles J. 1979. "On fluency" in Fillmore, Charles J., Daniel Kempler, and William S-Y. Wang (eds) *Individual Differences in Language Ability and Language Behavior*. New York: Academic Press. 85–101.
Finegan, Edward and Douglas Biber. 1994. "Register and social dialect variation: An integrated approach" in Biber, Douglas and Edward Finegan (eds) *Sociolinguistic Perspectives on Register*. Oxford: Oxford University Press. 315–47.
—. 2001. "Register variation and social dialect variation: The Register Axiom" in Eckert, Penelope and John R. Rickford (eds) *Style and Sociolinguistic Variation*. Cambridge: Cambridge University Press. 235–67.
Fleischman, Suzanne. 1990. *Tense and Narrativity: From Medieval Performance to Modern Fiction*. Austin: University of Texas Press.

—. 2001. "Language and medicine" in Schiffrin, Deborah, Deborah Tannen, and Heidi E. Hamilton. (eds) *Handbook of Discourse Analysis*. Oxford: Blackwell. 470–502.

Fónagy, Ivan. 1999. "Why iconicity?" in Nänny, Max and Olga Fischer (eds) *Form Miming Meaning: Iconicity in Language and Literature*. Amsterdam: John Benjamins. 3–36.

Francis, Nelson W. 1983. *Dialectology*. London: Longman.

Freeman, Derek. 1999. *The Fateful Hoaxing of Margaret Mead: A Historical Analysis of her Samoan Research*. Boulder, Colo.: Westview Press.

Friedrich, Paul. 1986. *The Language Parallax: Linguistic Relativism and Poetic Indeterminacy*. Austin: University of Texas Press.

Gal, Susan. 1979. *Language Shift: Social Determinants of Linguistic Change in Bilingual Austria*. New York: Academic Press.

—. 1989. "Between speech and silence: the problematics of research on language and gender" in *Papers in Pragmatics* 3(1): 1–38.

Garfinkel, Harold. 1967. *Studies in Ethnomethodology*. Englewood Cliffs, N.J.: Prentice-Hall.

Gee, James Paul. 1990. *Social Linguistics and Literacies: Ideology in Discourses*. London: Falmer.

—. 1992. *The Social Mind: Language, Ideology, and Social Practice*. New York: Bergin and Garvey.

—. 1999. *An Introduction to Discourse Analysis*. London: Routledge.

Gibbs, Raymon W., Jr. 1994. *The Poetics of Mind: Figurative Thought, Language, and Understanding*. Cambridge: Cambridge University Press.

Giddens, Anthony. 1979. *Central Problems in Social Theory*. London: Macmillan.

—. 1981. *New Rules of Sociological Method*. London: Macmillan.

—. 1984. *The Constitution of Society: Outline of the Theory of Structuration*. Berkeley: University of California Press.

—. 1991. *Modernity and Self-Identity: Self and Society in the Late Modern Age*. Stanford: Stanford University Press.

Giles, Howard. 2001. "Couplandia and beyond" in Eckert, Penelope and John R. Rickford (eds) *Style and Sociolinguistic Variation*. Cambridge: Cambridge University Press. 211–19.

Giles, Howard and Nikolas Coupland. 1991. *Language: Contexts and Consequences*. Pacific Grove, Calif.: Brooks/Cole.

Giles, Howard and Peter E. Powesland. 1975. *Speech Style and Social Evaluation*. New York: Academic Press.

Goffman, Erving. 1959. *The Presentation of Self in Everyday Life*. Garden City, N.Y.: Doubleday.

—. 1974. *Frame Analysis*. New York: Harper.

—. 1981. *Forms of Talk*. Philadelphia: University of Pennsylvania Press.

Goldthorpe, J.H., D. Lockwood, F. Bechhofer, and J. Platt. 1969. *The Affluent Worker in the Class Structure*. Cambridge: Cambridge University Press.

Goodwin, Charles. 1981. *Conversational Organization: Interaction between Speakers and Hearers*. New York: Academic Press.

Goodwin, Margaret H. 1982. "'Instigating': storytelling as social process" in *American Ethnologist* 9: 799–819.

Grant, William. 1931. *The Scottish National Dictionary*. Edinburgh: Scottish National Dictionary Association. Vol.1.

Gregersen, Frans and Inge Lise Pedersen (eds) 1991. *The Copenhagen Study in Urban Sociolinguistics*. 2 vols. Copenhagen: C.A. Reitzels Forlag.

Grice, H.P. 1975. "Logic and conversation" in Cole, Peter and Jerrold Morgan (eds) *Speech Acts*. New York: Academic Press. 41–58.

Gumperz, John J. 1982. *Discourse Strategies*. Cambridge: Cambridge University Press.

—. 1992. "Contextualization and understanding" in Duranti, Alessandro and Charles Goodwin (eds) *Rethinking Context*. Cambridge: Cambridge University Press. 229–52.

Haeri, Niloofar. 1996. *The Sociolinguistic Market of Cairo: Gender, Class, and Education*. London: Kegan Paul International.

Halliday, Michael A.K. 1964. "The users and uses of language" in Halliday, M.A.K., A. Mcintosh, and P. Strevens (eds) *The Linguistic Sciences and Language Teaching*. London: Longmans. 75–110.

Hanks, William F. 1990. *Referential Practice: Language and Lived Space among the Maya*. Chicago: University of Chicago Press.

—. 1996. *Language and Communicative Practices*. Boulder, Colo.: Westview Press.

Harvie, Christopher. 1998a. *Scotland and Nationalism: Scottish Society and Politics 1707 to the Present*. 3rd edn. London: Routledge.

—. 1998b. *No Gods and Precious Few Heroes: Twentieth-Century Scotland*. 3rd edn. Edinburgh: Edinburgh University Press.

Heath, Shirley Brice. 1983. *Ways with Words: Language, Life, and Work in Communities and Classrooms*. Cambridge: Cambridge University Press.

Heritage, John. 1990. "Oh-prefaced responses to inquiry". Paper presented at the International Pragmatics Conference (Barcelona, July).

Herman, David. 1999. *Narratologies: New Perspectives on Narrative Analysis*. Columbus: Ohio State University Press.

—. 2002. *Story Logic: Problems and Possibilities of Narrative*. Lincoln: University of Nebraska Press.

Hiatt, Mary P. 1975. *Artful Balance: The Parallel Structures of Style*. New York: Teachers College Press.

Hill, Jane H. 1986. "The refiguration of the anthropology of language" in *Cultural Anthropology* 1: 89–102.

Horvath, Barbara. 1985. *Variation in Australian English*. Cambridge: Cambridge University Press.

Hughes, Geoffrey. 1991. *Swearing: A Social History of Foul Language, Oaths, and Profanity in English*. Oxford: Blackwell.

Hymes, Dell. 1974. *Foundations in Sociolinguistics: An Ethnographic Approach*. Philadelphia: University of Pennsylvania Press.

—. 1979. "Sapir, competence, voices" in Fillmore, Charles J., Daniel Kempler, and William S-Y. Wang (eds) *Individual Differences in Language Ability and Language Behavior*. New York: Academic Press. 33–45.

—. 1980. *Language in Education: Ethnolinguistic Essays.* Washington, D.C.: Center for Applied Linguistics.

—. 1981. *"In vain I tried to tell you" – Essays in Native American Ethnopoetics* [Studies in Native American Literature, no. 1]. Philadelphia: University of Pennsylvania Press.

—. 1996. *Ethnography, Linguistics, Narrative Inequality: Toward an Understanding of Voice.* London: Taylor and Francis.

Irvine, Judith. T. 1990. "Registering affect: Heteroglossia in the linguistic expression of emotion" in Lutz, Catherine A. and Lila Abu-Lughod (eds) *Language and the Politics of Emotion.* Cambridge: Cambridge University Press. 126–61.

—. 2001. "'Style' as distinctiveness: The culture and ideology of linguistic differentiation" in Eckert, Penelope and John R. Rickford (eds) *Style and Sociolinguistic Variation.* Cambridge: Cambridge University Press. 21–43.

Jakobson, Roman. 1960. "Closing statement: Linguistics and poetics" in Sebeok, Thomas A. (ed.) *Style in Language.* New York: MIT and Wiley. 350–77.

Jakobson, Roman and Krystyna Pomorska. 1983. *Dialogues.* Cambridge, Mass.: MIT Press.

Jassem, Wiktor and Grazyna Demenko. 1986. "Extracting linguistic information from F_o traces" in Catherine Johns-Lewis (ed.) *Intonation in Discourse.* London: Croom Helm. 1–17.

Johansson, Stig. 1995. "The approach of the Text Encoding initiative to the encoding of spoken discourse" in Leech, Geoffrey, Greg Myers, and Jenny Thomas (eds) *Spoken English on Computer.* London: Longman. 82–98.

Johnston, Paul A. 1997. "Regional variation" in Jones, Charles (ed.) *The Edinburgh History of the Scots Language.* Edinburgh: Edinburgh University Press. 443–513.

Johnson, Richard. 1980. "Three problematics: elements of a theory of working-class culture" in Clarke, John, Chas Critcher, and Richard Johnson (eds) *Working-class Culture: Studies in History and Theory.* New York: St. Martin's Press. 201–37.

Johnstone, Barbara. 1987. "'He says ... so I said': Verb tense alternation and narrative depictions of authority in American English" in *Linguistics* 25: 33–52.

—. 1990. *Stories, Community and Place: Narratives from Middle America.* Bloomington: Indiana University Press.

—. 1996. *The Linguistic Individual.* New York: Oxford University Press.

Kay, Billy. 1993. *Scots: The Mither Tongue.* Darvel: Alloway Publishing.

Keenan (Ochs), Elinor. 1974. "Norm-makers, norm-breakers: Uses of speech by men and women in a Malagasay community" in Bauman, Richard and Joel Scherzer (eds) *Explorations in the Ethnography of Speaking.* London: Cambridge University Press. 125–43.

Kellas, J.G. 1968. *Modern Scotland.* New York: Praeger.

Kellas, James G. and Peter Fotheringham. 1976. "The political behaviour of the working class" in MacLaren, A. Allan (ed.) *Social Class in Scotland: Past and Present.* Edinburgh: John Donald. 143–65.

Kelly, J. and J.K. Local. 1989. "On the use of general phonetic techniques in handling conversational material" in Roger, Derek and Peter Bull (eds) *Conversation: An Interdisciplinary Perspective*. Clevedon: Multilingual Matters. 197–212.

Kelman, James. 1995. *How late it was, how late*. London: Minerva.

Kendon, Adam. 1990. *Conducting Interaction: Patterns of Behavior in Focused Encounters*. Cambridge: Cambridge University Press.

Kumpf, Lorraine E. 1987. "The use of pitch phenomena in the structuring of stories" in Tomlin, Russell S. (ed.) *Coherence and Grounding on Discourse*. Amsterdam: John Benjamins. 189–216.

Labov, William. 1966a. *The Social Stratification of English in New York City*. Washington, D.C.: Center for Applied Linguistics.

—. 1966b. "Hypercorrection by the lower middle class as a factor in linguistic change" in Bright, William (ed.) *Sociolinguistics*. The Hague: Mouton. 84–113.

—. 1972a. *Language in the Inner City*. Philadelphia: University of Pennsylvania Press.

—. 1972b. *Sociolinguistic Patterns*. Philadelphia: University of Pennsylvania Press.

—. 1981. *Field Methods of the Project on Linguistic Change and Variation* [Sociolinguistic Working Paper, no. 81]. Austin: Southwest Educational Development Laboratory.

—. 1982. "Speech actions and reactions in personal narrative" in Tannen, Deborah (ed.) *Analyzing Discourse: Text and Talk*. Washington, D.C.: Georgetown University Press. 219–47.

—. 1984. "Intensity" in Schiffrin, Deborah (ed.). *Meaning Form and Use in Context: Linguistic Applications*. Washington, D.C.: Georgetown University Press. 43–70.

—. 1986. "On not putting two and two together: the shallow interpretation of narrative". Paper presented at Pitzer College Forum (March 1986).

—. 1997. "Some further steps in narrative analysis" in Bamberg, Michael G.W. (ed.) *Oral Versions of Personal Experience: Three Decades of Narrative Analysis*. Mahwah, N.J.: Lawrence Erlbaum. 395–415.

—. 2001a. "The anatomy of style-shifting" in Eckert. Penelope and John R. Rickford (eds) *Style and Sociolinguistic Variation*. Cambridge: Cambridge University Press. 85–108.

—. 2001b. "Uncovering the event structure of narrative" in Tannen. Deborah and James E. Alatis (eds) *Linguistics, Language, and the Real World: Discourse and Beyond*. Washington, D.C.: Georgetown University Press. 63–83.

—. 2004. "Ordinary events" in Fought, Carmen (ed.) *Sociolinguistic Variation: Critical Reflections*. New York: Oxford University Press. 31–43.

Labov, William and David Fanshel. 1977. *Therapeutic Discourse: Psychotherapy as Conversation*. New York: Academic Press.

Labov, William and Joshua Waletztky. 1967. "Narrative analysis: Oral versions of personal experience" in Helm, June (ed.) *Essays on the Verbal and Visual Arts*. Seattle: University of Washington Press. 12–44.

Lakoff, Robin. 1975. *Language and Woman's Place*. New York: Harper and Row.

Langellier, Kristin M. and Eric E. Peterson. 1993. "Family storytelling as a strategy of social control" in Mumby, Dennis K. (ed.) *Narrative and Social Control: Critical Perspectives*. Newbury Park, Calif.: Sage. 49–76.

Lavandera, Beatriz. 1981. "Sociolinguistics" in Posner, Rebecca and John N. Green (eds) *Trends in Romance Linguistics and Philology, Vol. 2: Synchronic Romance Linguistics*. The Hague: Mouton. 129–228.

Leech, Geoffrey. 1969. *A Linguistic Guide to English Poetry*. London: Longmans.

Le Page, Robert B. 1994. "The notion of 'linguistic system' revisited" in *International Journal of the Sociology of Language*. 109: 109–20.

Leonard, Tom. 1984. *Intimate Voices: Selected Work 1965–1983*. Newcastle: Galloping Dog Press.

Leonard, Tom, A. Hamilton, and J. Kelman. 1976. *Three Glasgow Writers*. Glasgow: The Molendinar Press.

Levinson, Stephen C. 1988. "Conceptual problems in the study of regional and cultural style" in Dittmar, Norbert and Peter Schlobinski (eds) *The Sociolinguistics of Urban Vernaculars: Case Studies and their Evaluation*. Berlin: de Gruyter. 161–90.

Lewis, David K. 1978. "Truth in fiction" in *American Philosophical Quarterly* 15: 37–46.

Li, Charles N. 1986. "Direct and indirect speech: A functional study" in Florian Coulmas (ed.) *Direct and Indirect Speech*. Berlin: Mouton de Gruyter. 29–45.

Linde, Charlotte. 1993. *Life Stories: The Creation of Coherence*. New York: Oxford University Press.

—. 1996. "Whose story is this? Point of view variation and group identity" in Arnold, Jennifer, Robert Blake, Brad Davidson, Scott Schwenter, and Julie Solomon (eds) *Oral Narrative Sociolinguistic Variation: Data, Theory and Analysis*. Stanford: CSLI.

Linell, Per. 1982. *The Written Language Bias in Linguistics*. Linköping: University of Linköping.

—. 1998. *Approaching Dialogue: Talk, interaction and Contexts in Dialogical Perspectives*. Amsterdam: John Benjamins.

Lutz, Catherine A. and Lila Abu-Lughod (eds). 1990. *Language and the Politics of Emotion*. Cambridge: Cambridge University Press.

Macafee, Caroline. 1988. *Some Studies in the Glasgow Vernacular*. PhD thesis. University of Glasgow.

—. 1994. *Traditional Dialect in the Modern World: A Glasgow Case Study*. Frankfurt: Peter Lang.

—. 2000. "The demography of Scots: The lessons of the census campaign" in *Scottish Language* 19: 1–44.

Macaulay, Ronald K.S. 1977. *Language, Social Class, and Education: A Glasgow Study*. Edinburgh: Edinburgh University Press.

—. 1984. "Chattering, nattering and blethering: informal interviews as speech events" in Enninger, Werner and Lilith M. Haynes *Studies in Language Ecology*. Wiesbaden: Franz Steiner Verlag. 51–64.

—. 1985. "The narrative skills of a Scottish coal miner" in Görlach, Manfred (ed.) *Focus on: Scotland*. Amsterdam: John Benjamins. 101–24.

—. 1987a. "The sociolinguistic significance of Scottish dialect humor" in *International Journal of the Sociology of Language* 65: 53–63.

—. 1987b. "Polyphonic monologues: quoted direct speech in oral narratives" in *IPRA Papers in Pragmatics* 1: 1–34.

—. 1988a. "A microsociolinguistic study of the dialect of Ayr" in Thomas, Alan R. (ed.) *Methods in Dialectology*. Philadelphia: Multilingual Matters. 456–63.

—. 1988b. "Linguistic change and stability" in Ferrara, Kathleen, Becky Brown, Keith Walters, and John Baugh (eds) *Linguistic Change and Contact*. Austin: University of Texas. 225–31.

—. 1988c. "What happened to sociolinguistics?" in *English World-Wide* 9: 153–69.

—. 1988d. "Urbanity in an urban dialect: the poetry of Tom Leonard" in *Studies in Scottish Literature* 23: 150–56

—. 1989. "He was some man him: Emphatic pronouns in Scottish English" in Walsh, Thomas J. (ed.) *Synchronic and Diachronic Approaches to Linguistic Variation and Change*. Washington, D.C.: Georgetown University Press. 179–87.

—. 1990. "The essential meaningfulness of ordinary discourse: Evidence from mistranscription". Paper presented at NWAVE XIX (University of Pennsylvania, October 1990).

—. 1991a. *Locating Dialect in Discourse: The Language of Honest Men and Bonnie Lasses in Ayr*. New York: Oxford University Press.

—. 1991b. "'Coz it izny spelt when they say it': Displaying dialect in writing" in *American Speech* 66: 280–91.

—. 1995. "The adverbs of authority" in *English World-Wide* 16: 37–60.

—. 1996. "A man can no more invent a new style than he can invent a new language". Paper given at Sociolinguistics Symposium 11 (Cardiff, September 1996).

—. 1999. "Is sociolinguistics lacking in style?" in *Cuadernos de Filologia inglesa* 8: 9–33.

—. 2001. "The question of genre" in Eckert, Penelope and John R. Rickford (eds) *Style and Sociolinguistic Variation*. Cambridge: Cambridge University Press. 78–82.

—. 2002a. "Discourse variation" in Chambers, Jack C., Peter Trudgill, and Natalie Schilling-Estes (eds) *Handbook of Language Variation and Change*. Oxford: Blackwells. 283–305.

—. 2002b. "You know, it depends" in *Journal of Pragmatics* 34: 749–67.

—. 2002c. "Extremely interesting, very interesting, or only quite interesting: Adverbs and social class" in *Journal of Sociolinguistics* 6: 398–417.

—. (Forthcoming). *Talk that Counts: Age, Gender, and Social Class Differences in Discourse*. New York: Oxford University Press.

Macaulay, Ronald K.S and G.D. Trevelyan. 1973. *Language, Education and Employment in Glasgow, Final Report to the Social Science Research Council*. 2 vols. Edinburgh: The Scottish Council for Research in Education.

McCafferty, Kevin. 2001. *Ethnicity and Language Change: English in (London) Derry, Northern Ireland*. Amsterdam: John Benjamins.

McClure, J. Derrick. 1985. The debate on Scots orthography" in Manfred Görlach (ed.) *Focus on: Scotland*. Amsterdam: John Benjamins. 203–9.

—. 1988. *Why Scots Matters*. Edinburgh. The Saltire Society.

—. 1996. *Scots and its Literature.* Amsterdam: John Benjamins.

McCrone, David. 1992. *Understanding Scotland: The Sociology of a Stateless Nation.* London: Routledge

—. 1996. "We're a' Jock Tamson's bairns: Social class in twentieth-century Scotland" in Devine, T.M. and R.J. Finlay (eds) *Scotland in the Twentieth Century.* Edinburgh: Edinburgh University Press. 102–21.

—. 2001. *Understanding Scotland: The Sociology of a Nation.* 2nd edn. London: Routledge.

McCrone, David, Angela Morris, and Richard Kiely. 1995. *Scotland – the Brand: The Making of Scottish Heritage.* Edinburgh: Edinburgh University Press.

McIllvanney, William. 1975. *Docherty.* London: Allen and Unwin.

McIvor, Arthur. 1996. "Gender apartheid?: Women in Scottish society" in Devine, T.M. and R.J. Finlay (eds) *Scotland in the Twentieth Century.* Edinburgh: Edinburgh University Press. 188–209.

MacLaren, A. Allan (ed.). 1976. *Social Class in Scotland: Past and Present.* Edinburgh: John Donald.

Mandler, Jean Matter. 1984. *Stories, Scripts, and Scenes: Aspects of Schema Theory.* Hillsdale, N.J.: Lawrence Erlbaum.

Margolin, Uri. 1999. "Of what is past, is passing, or to come: Temporality, Aspectuality, Modality, and the nature of literary narrative" in David Herman (ed.) *Narratologies: New Perspectives on Narrative Analysis.* Columbus: Ohio State University Press. 142–66.

Markova, Ivana and Klaus Foppa (eds). 1990. *The Dynamics of Dialogue.* Hemel Hempstead: Harvester Wheatsheaf.

Maté, Ian. 1996. *Scots Language GRO(S). A Report on the Scots Language Research Carried Out by the General Register Office for Scotland in 1996.* Edinburgh: The General Register Office for Scotland.

Mathis, Terrie and George Yule. 1994. "Zero quotatives" in *Discourse Processes* 18: 63–76.

Mead, Margaret. 1928. *Coming of Age in Samoa: A Psychological Study of Primitive Youth for Western Civilization.* New York: Morrow.

Menn, Lise and Suzanne Boyce. 1982. "Fundamental frequency and Discourse structure" in *Language and Speech* 25: 341–83.

Menzies, J. 1991. "An investigation of attitudes to Scots and Glasgow dialect among secondary school pupils" in *Scottish Language* 10: 30–46.

Miller, Jim. 2003. "The grammar of urban Scots" in Corbett, John, Derrick M. McClure, and Jane Stuart-Smith (eds) *The Edinburgh Companion to Scots.* Edinburgh: Edinburgh University Press. 72–109.

Miller, Jim and Regina Weinert. 1998. *Spontaneous Spoken Language: Syntax and Discourse.* Oxford: Oxford University Press.

Milroy, James and Lesley Milroy. 1977. "Speech and context in an urban setting" in *Belfast Working Papers in Language and Linguistics* 2: 1–85.

—. 1985. *Authority in Language: Investigating Language Prescription and Standardisation.* London: Routledge and Kegan Paul.

Milroy, Lesley. 1980. *Language and Social Networks.* Oxford: Blackwell.

—. 1987. *Observing and Analysing Natural Language: A Critical Account of Socio-linguistic Method*. Oxford: Blackwell.

—. 2001. "Conversation, spoken language, and social identity" in Eckert, Penelope and John R. Rickford (eds) *Style and Sociolinguistic Variation*. Cambridge: Cambridge University Press. 268–78.

Moerman, Michael. 1988. *Talking Culture: Ethnography and Conversation Analysis*. Philadelphia: University of Pennsylvania Press.

Morson, Gary Saul. 1999. "Essential narrative: Tempics and the return of process" in Herman, David (ed.) *Narratologies: New Perspectives on Narrative Analysis*. Columbus: Ohio State University Press. 277–314.

Müller, Wolfgang G. 1999. "The iconic use of syntax in British and American fiction" in Nänny, Max and Olga Fischer (eds) *Form Miming Meaning: Iconicity in Language and Literature*. Amsterdam: John Benjamins. 393–408.

Mukarovsky, Jan. 1964. "Standard language and poetic language" in Garvin, Paul L. (ed.) *A Prague School Reader on Esthetics, Literary Structure, and Style*. Washington, D.C.: Georgetown University Press. 17–30.

Murdoch, Steve. 1995. *Language Politics in Scotland*. Aberdeen: Aberdeen University Scots Leid Quorum.

Murison, David. 1979. "The historical background" in Aitken, A.J. and Tom McArthur (eds) *Languages of Scotland*. Edinburgh: Chambers. 2–13.

Nänny, Max and Olga Fischer (eds). 1999a. *Form Miming Meaning: Iconicity in Language and Literature*. Amsterdam: John Benjamins.

—. 1999b. "Introduction: Iconicity as a creative force in language use" in Nänny, Max and Olga Fischer (eds) *Form Miming Meaning: Iconicity in Language and Literature*. Amsterdam: John Benjamins. xv–xxxvi.

Norrman, Ralf. 1986. *Samuel Butler and the Meaning of Chiasmus*. Basingstoke: Macmillan.

—. 1999. "Creating the world in our image: A new theory of love of symmetry and iconicist desire" in Nänny, Max and Olga Fischer (eds) *Form Miming Meaning: Iconicity in Language and Literature*. Amsterdam: John Benjamins. 59–82.

Ochs, Elinor. 1979. "Transcription as theory" in Ochs, Elinor and Bambi B. Schieffelin (eds) *Developmental Pragmatics*. New York: Academic Press. 43–72.

—. 1988. *Culture and Language Development: Language Acquisition and Language Socialization in a Samoan Village*. Cambridge: Cambridge University Press.

—. 1996. "Linguistic resources for socializing humanity" in Gumperz, John J. and Stephen C. Levinson (eds) *Rethinking Linguistic Relativity*. Cambridge: Cambridge University Press. 407–37.

—. 1997. "Narrative" in van Dijk, Teun A. (ed.) *Discourse as Structure and Process*. Thousand Oaks, Calif.: Sage. 185–207.

Ochs, Elinor and Lisa Capps. 1996. "Narrating the self" in *Annual Review of Anthropology* 25: 19–43.

—. 2001. *Living Narrative: Creating Lives in Everyday Storytelling*. Cambridge, Mass.: Harvard University Press.

O' Connell, Daniel. 1988. *Critical Essays on Language Use and Psychology*. New York: Springer-Verlag.

Östman, Jan-Ola. 1981. *You Know: A Discourse-Functional Approach* [Pragmatics and beyond II: 7]. Amsterdam: John Benjamins.

—. 1982. "The symbiotic relationship between pragmatic particles and impromptu speech" in Enkvist, Nils E. (ed.) *Impromptu Speech: A Symposium*. Åbo: The Åbo Akademi Foundation. 147–77.

Philips, Susan U. 1992. "The routinization of repair in courtroom discourse" in Duranti, Alessandro and Charles Goodwin (eds) *Rethinking Context: Language as an Interactive Phenomenon*. Cambridge: Cambridge University Press.

Pittinger, Robert E., Charles F. Hockett, and John J. Danehy. 1960. *The First Five Minutes: A Sample of Microscopic Interview Analysis*. Ithaca: Martineau.

Polanyi, Livia. 1982. "Literary complexity in everyday storytelling" in Tannen, Deborah (ed.) *Spoken and Written Language: Exploring Orality and Literacy*. Norwood, N.J.: Ablex. 155–70.

—. 1985. *Telling the American Story: A Structural and Cultural Analysis of Conversational Storytelling*. Norwood, N.J.: Ablex.

Pomerantz, Anna. 1978. "Compliment responses: Notes on the co-operation of multiple constraints" in Scheinkein, Jim (ed.) *Studies in the Organization of Conversational Interaction*. New York: Academic Press. 79–112.

Postma, Albert, Herman Kolk, and Dirk-Jan Povel. 1990. "On the relation among speech errors, disfluencies, and self-repairs" in *Language and Speech* 33: 19–29.

Preston, Dennis R. 1982. "'Ritin' fowklower daun 'rong': Folklorists' failures in phonology" in *Journal of American Folklore* 95: 304–26.

—. 1985. "The Li'l Abner syndrome: Written representations of speech" in *American Speech* 60: 328–36.

—. 2001. "Style and the psycholinguistics of sociolinguistics: the logical problem of language variation" in Eckert, Penelope and John R. Rickford (eds) *Style and Sociolinguistic Variation*. Cambridge: Cambridge University Press. 279–304.

Quastoff, Uta M. and Kurt Nikolaus. 1982. "What makes a good story? Towards the production of conversational narratives" in Flammer, August and Walter Kintsch (eds) *Discourse Processing*. Amsterdam: North-Holland. 16–28.

Quinn, Arthur. 1982. *Figures of Speech: 60 Ways to Turn a Phrase*. Salt Lake City: Peregrine Smith.

Quinn, Naomi. 1982. "'Commitment' in American marriage: A cultural analysis" in *American Ethnologist* 9: 755–89.

Reah, K. 1982. "The Labovian interview: A reappraisal" in *Lore and Language* 3.7: 1–13.

Rickford, John R. 1987. *Dimensions of a Creole Continuum: History, Texts, and Linguistic Analysis of a Guyanese Creole*. Stanford: Stanford University Press.

Rickford, John R. and Faye McNair-Knox. 1994. "Addressee- and topic-influenced style shift: A quantitative sociolinguistic study" in Biber, Douglas and Edward Finegan (eds) *Sociolinguistic Perspectives on Register*. New York: Oxford University Press. 235–76.

Robinson, Mairi. 1985. *The Concise Scots Dictionary*. Aberdeen: Aberdeen University Press.

Romaine, Suzanne. 1975. *Linguistic Variability in the Speech of some Edinburgh Schoolchildren.* MLitt thesis. University of Edinburgh.
—. 1980. "A critical overview of the methodology of urban British sociolinguistics" in *English World-Wide* 1. 163–98.
—. 1982. *Socio-historical Linguistics: Its Status and Methodology.* Cambridge: Cambridge University Press.
—. 1984. *The Language of Children and Adolescents: The Acquisition of Communicative Competence.* Oxford: Blackwell.
—. 1989. *Bilingualism.* Oxford: Blackwell.
Ryan, Ellen Bouchard. 1979. "Why do low-prestige language varieties persist?" in Giles, Howard and Robert N. St. Clair (eds) *Language and Social Psychology.* Baltimore: University Park Press. 145–57.
Sacks, Harvey. 1992. *Lectures on Conversation* (ed. Gail Jefferson). 2 vols. Oxford: Blackwells.
Sacks, Harvey, Emanuel Schegloff, and Gail Jefferson. 1974. "A simplest systematics for the organization of turn-taking for conversation" in *Language* 50: 696–735.
Sankoff, Gillian. 1980. *The Social Life of Language.* Philadelphia: University of Pennsylvania Press.
Sapir, Edward. 1921. *Language.* New York: Harcourt, Brace and World.
—. 1949. *Selected Writings of Edward Sapir in Language, Culture and Personality* (ed. by David G. Mandelbaum). Berkeley: University of California Press.
Saussure, F. de. 1922. *Course de linguistique générale.* 2nd edn. Paris: Payot. [(Tr. W. Baskin 1959) New York: McGraw-Hill. (tr. Roy Harris 1986) La Salle, Ill.: Open Court.]
Schank, Roger C. and Robert P. Abelson. 1977. *Scripts, Plans, Goals and Understanding: An Inquiry into Human Knowledge Structures.* Hillsdale, N.J.: Lawrence Erlbaum.
Schegloff, Emmanuel A, Gail Jefferson, and Harvey Sacks. 1997. "The preference for self correction in the organisation of repair in conversation" in *Language* 53: 361–82.
Schieffelin, Bambi B. 1990. *The Give and Take of Everyday Life: Language Socialization of Kaluli Children.* Cambridge: Cambridge University Press.
Schiffrin, Deborah. 1981. "Tense variation in narrative" in *Language* 57: 45–62.
—. 1984. "How a story says what it means and does" in *Text* 4: 313–46.
—. 1987. *Discourse Markers.* Cambridge: Cambridge University Press.
—. 1988. "Sociolinguistic approaches to discourse: topic and reference in narrative" in Ferrara, Kathleen, Becky Brown, Keith Walters, and John Baugh (eds) *Linguistic Change and Contact: Proceedings of NWAV XVI* Austin: University of Texas. 1–17.
—. 1994. *Approaches to Discourse.* Oxford: Blackwell.
Schiffrin, Deborah, Deborah Tannen, and Heidi E. Hamilton (eds). 2001. *Handbook of Discourse Analysis.* Oxford: Blackwell.
Schuetze-Coburn, Stephan, Marian Shapley, and Elizabeth G. Weber. 1991. "Units of intonation in discourse: A comparison of acoustic auditory analyses" in *Language and Speech* 34: 207–34.

Shapley, Marian. 1989. *Fundamental Frequency Variation in Conversational Discourse*. PhD thesis. UCLA.

Shuy, Roger W., Walter A. Wolfram, and William K. Riley. 1968. *Field Techniques in an Urban Language Study*. Washington, D.C.: Center for Applied Linguistics.

Silverstein, Michael. 1996. "Monglot 'Standard' in America: Standardization and metaphors of linguistic hegemony" in Brenneis, Donald and Ronald K.S. Macaulay (eds) *The Matrix of Language: Contemporary Linguistic Anthropology*. Boulder, Colo.: Westview Press. 284–306.

Sinclair, John M. 1991. *Corpus, Concordance, Collocation*. Oxford: Oxford University Press.

—. 1995. "From theory to practice" in Leech, Geoffrey, Greg Myers, and Jenny Thomas (eds) *Spoken English on Computer: Transcription, Markup and Application*. London: Longman.

Smith, Barbara Herrnstein. 1978. *On the Margins of Discourse: The Relation of Literature to Language*. Chicago: University of Chicago Press.

Smout, T.C. 1986. *A Century of the Scottish People 1830–1950*. London: Collins.

Smout, T.C. and Sydney Wood. 1990. *Scottish Voices 1745–1960*. London: Fontana.

Stone, Elizabeth. 1988. *Black Sheep and Kissing Cousins: How our Family Stories Shape us*. New York: Penguin Books.

Strauss, Claudia and Naomi Quinn. 1997. *A Cognitive Theory of Cultural meaning*. Cambridge: Cambridge University Press.

Stuart-Smith, Jane. 1999. "Glasgow" in Foulkes, Paul and Gerry Docherty (eds) *Urban Voices: Variation and Change in British Accents*. London: Arnold. 203–22.

—. "The phonology of modern Urban Scots" in Corbett, John, Derrick M. McClure, and Jane Stuart-Smith (eds) *The Edinburgh Companion to Scots*. Edinburgh: Edinburgh University Press. 110–37.

Tabakowska, Elzbieta. 1999. "Linguistic expression of perceptual relationships: Iconicity as a principle of text organization (A case study)" in Nänny, Max and Olga Fischer (eds) *Form Miming Meaning: Iconicity in Language and Literature*. Amsterdam: John Benjamins. 409–22.

Tagliamonte Sali and Rachel Hudson. 1999. "*Be like* et al. beyond America: The quotative system in British and Canadian youth" in *Journal of Sociolinguistics* 3: 147–72.

Tannen, Deborah. 1989. *Talking Voices: Repetition, Dialogue, and Imagery in Conversational Discourse*. Cambridge: Cambridge University Press.

Tedlock, Dennis. 1983. *The Spoken Word and the Work of Interpretation*. Philadephia: University of Pennsylvania Press.

Thakerar, Jitendra N., Howard Giles and Jenny Cheshire. 1982. "Psychological and linguistic parameters of speech accommodation theory" in Fraser, Colin and Klaus R. Scherer (eds) *Advances in the Social Psychology of Language*. Cambridge: Cambridge University Press. 205–55.

Therborn, Göran. 1980. *The Ideology of Power and the Power of Ideology*. London: Verso and NLB.

Thibault, Pierrette. 1988. "Discourse analysis in sociolinguistics" in Dittmar, Norbert and Peter Schlobinski (eds) *The Sociolinguistics of Urban Vernaculars: Case Studies and their Evaluation*. Berlin: de Gruyter. 154–60.

Thompson, E.P. 1963. *The Making of the English Working-Class*. London: Gollancz.

Thompson, John B. 1991. "Editor's introduction" in Bourdieu, Pierre *Language and Symbolic Power*. Cambridge: Polity Press.

Thornborrow, Joanna. 2002. *Power Talk: Language and Interaction in Institutional Discourse*. Harlow: Pearson Education.

Todorov, Tzvetan. 1984. *Mikhail Bakhtin: The Dialogical Principle* (tr. Wlad Godzich). Minneapolis: University of Minnesota Press.

Tracy, K. 1995. "Action-implicative discourse analysis" in *Journal of Language and Social Psychology* 14: 195–215.

Traugott, Elizabeth and Suzannne Romaine. 1985. "Some questions for the definition of 'Style' in sociohistorical linguistics" in *Folia Linguistica* 6: 7–39.

Trudgill, Peter. 1974. *The Social Differentiation of English in Norwich City*. Cambridge: Cambridge University Press.

—. 1984. "Introduction" in Trudgill, Peter (ed.) *Language in the British Isles*. Cambridge: Cambridge University Press. 2–4.

—. 1990. *The Dialects of England*. Oxford: Blackwell.

Tsitsipis, Lukas D. 1995. "The coding of linguistic ideology in Arvanitika (Albanian) language shift: Congruent and contradictory discourse" in *Anthropological Linguistics* 37: 541–77.

van Dijk, Teun A. 1987. *Communicating Racism: Ethnic Prejudice in Thought and Talk*. Newbury Park, Calif.: Sage.

—. 1993. "Stories and racism" in Mumby, Dennis K. (ed.) *Narrative and Social Control: Critical Perspectives*. Newbury Park, Calif.: Sage Publications. 121–42.

Voloshinov, V.N. 1928. "Novejshie techenija lingvisticheskoj mysli na Zapade" [The most recent currents of linguistic thought in the West] in *Literature i marksizm* 5.

—. [1929] 1986. *Marxism and the Philosophy of Language* (tr. by L. Matejka and I.R. Titunik). Cambridge, Mass.: Harvard University Press.

Wales, Kathleen. 1988. "Back to the future: Bakhtin, stylistics and discourse" in van Peer, Willie (ed.) *The Taming of the Text: Explorations in Language, Literature and Culture*. London: Routledge. 176–92.

Wales, Katie. 1989. *A Dictionary of Stylistics*. London: Longman.

Weber, Max. 1947. *The Protestant Ethic and the Spirit of Capitalism* (tr. Talcott Parsons). London: Allen and Unwin.

Weiyun He, Agnes. 2001. "Discourse analysis" in Aronoff, Mark and Janie Rees-Miller (eds) *The Handbook of Linguistics*. Oxford: Blackwell. 428–45.

Wertsch, James V. 1991. *Voices of the Mind: A Sociocultural Approach to Mediated Action*. London: Harvester Wheatsheaf.

White, Allon. 1993. *Carnival, Hysteria, and Writing: Collected Essays and Autobiography*. Oxford: Oxford University Press.

White, Hayden. 1981. "The value of narrativity in the representation of reality" in Mitchell, W.J.T. (ed.) *On Narrative*. Chicago: University of Chicago Press. 1–23.

Williams, Raymond. 1958. *Culture and Society, 1780–1950*. New York: Columbia University Press.

Willis, Paul. [1977] 1981. *Learning to Labor: How Working-Class Kids get Working-Class Jobs*. New York: Columbia University Press.

—. 1979. "Shop-floor culture, masculinity and the wage-form" in Clarke, John, Chas Critcher, and Richard Johnson (eds) *Working-class Culture: Studies in History and Theory*. New York: St. Martin's Press. 185–98.

Wilson, John. 1989. *On the Boundaries of Conversation*. Oxford: Pergamon Press.

Wilson, Sir James. 1923. *The Dialect of Robert Burns as Spoken in Central Ayrshire*. Oxford: Oxford University Press.

Wolfowitz, Clare. 1991. *Language Style and Social Space: Stylistic Choice in Suriname Javanese*. Urbana: University of Illinois Press.

Wolfram, Walt. 1969. *A Sociolinguistic Description of Detroit Negro Speech*. Washington, D.C.: Center for Applied Linguistics.

Wolfson, Nessa. 1976. "Speech events and natural speech: some implications for sociolinguistic methodology" in *Language in Society* 5: 189–211.

—. 1982. *CHP: The Conversational Historical Present in American English Narrative*. Dordrecht: Foris.

Wood, Linda A. and Rolf O. Kroger. 2000. *Doing Discourse Analysis: Methods for Studying Action in Talk and Text*. Thousand Oaks, Calif.: Sage.

Yaeger-Dror, Malcah. 2001. "Primitives of a system for 'style' and 'register'" in Eckert, Penelope and John R. Rickford (eds) *Style and Sociolinguistic Variation*. Cambridge: Cambridge University Press. 170–84.

Index

Scotland in Theory.
Reflections on Culture & Literature.

Edited by Eleanor Bell and Gavin Miller.

Amsterdam/New York, NY 2004. 287 pp. (SCROLL 1)
ISBN: 90-420-1028-2   € 60.-/US$ 75.-

Scotland in Theory offers new ways of reading Scottish texts and culture within the context of an altered political framework and a changing sense of national identity. With the re-establishment of a Parliament in Edinburgh, issues of nationality and nationalism can be looked at afresh. It is timely now to revisit representations of Scottish culture in cinematography and literature, and also to examine aspects of gender, sexuality and ideology that have shaped how Scots have come to understand themselves. Established and younger critics use a variety of theoretical approaches here to catch an authentic sense of a post-modern Scotland in the process of change.
Literature and the arts provide radical ways of knowing what Scotland, in theory, could become.

The collection will be of interest to teachers and students of Scottish and English literature, literary theory, cultural and media analysis, and the history of ideas. Contributors include Eleanor Bell, Kasia Boddy, Cairns Craig, Thomas Docherty, Christopher Harvie, Ellen Raïssa-Jackson, Willy Maley, Gavin Miller, Tom Nairn, Sarah Neely, Laurence Nicoll, Berthold Schoene, Anne McManus Scriven, A.J.P. Thomson, Ronald Turnbull, Christopher Whyte.

USA/Canada: One Rockefeller Plaza, Ste. 1420, New York, NY 10020,
Tel. (212) 265-6360, Call toll-free (U.S. only) 1-800-225-3998,
Fax (212) 265-6402
All other countries: Tijnmuiden 7, 1046 AK Amsterdam, The Netherlands.
Tel. ++ 31 (0)20 611 48 21, Fax ++ 31 (0)20 447 29 79
Orders-queries@rodopi.nl   **www.rodopi.nl**
Please note that the exchange rate is subject to fluctuations

Beyond Scotland
New Contexts for Twentieth-Century Scottish Literature

Edited by Gerard Carruthers, David Goldie & Alastair Renfrew

Amsterdam/New York, NY 2004. 267 pp. (Scroll 2)

ISBN: 90-420-1883-6   € 54,- /US $ 70.-
ISBN: 90-420-1893-3   € 24,- /US $ 31.-
Textbook Edition (with a minimum of 10 copies)

Scottish creative writing in the twentieth century was notable for its willingness to explore and absorb the literatures of other times and other nations. From the engagement with Russian literature of Hugh MacDiarmid and Edwin Morgan, through to the interplay with continental literary theory, Scottish writers have proved active participants in a diverse international literary practice. Scottish criticism has, arguably, often been slow in appreciating the full extent of this exchange. Preoccupied with marking out its territory, with identifying an independent and distinctive tradition, Scottish criticism has occasionally blinded itself to the diversity and range of its writers. In stressing the importance of cultural independence, it has tended to overlook the many virtues of interdependence.

The essays in this book aim to offer a corrective view. They celebrate the achievement of Scottish writing in the twentieth century by offering a wider basis for appreciation than a narrow idea of 'Scottishness'. Each essay explores an aspect of Scottish writing in an individual foreign perspective; together they provide an enriching account of a national literary practice that has deep, and often surprisingly complex, roots in international culture.

USA/Canada: One Rockefeller Plaza, Ste. 1420, New York, NY 10020,
Tel. (212) 265-6360, Call toll-free (U.S. only) 1-800-225-3998,
Fax (212) 265-6402
All other countries: Tijnmuiden 7, 1046 AK Amsterdam, The Netherlands.
Tel. ++ 31 (0)20 611 48 21, Fax ++ 31 (0)20 447 29 79
Orders-queries@rodopi.nl   www.rodopi.nl
Please note that the exchange rate is subject to fluctuations

Rodopi

History and Representation
in Ford Madox Ford's Writings

Edited by Joseph Wiesenfarth

Amsterdam/New York, NY 2004. XI, 241 pp.
(International Ford Madox Ford Studies 3)

ISBN: 90-420-1613-2   € 50,-/US $ 63.-

History and Representation in Ford Madox Ford's Writings explores the idea of history across various genres: fiction, autobiography, books about places and cultures, criticism, and poetry. 'I wanted the Novelist in fact to appear in his really proud position as historian of his own time', wrote Ford. The twenty leading specialists assembled for this volume consider his writing about twentieth-century events, especially the First World War; and also his representations of the past, particularly in his fine trilogy about Henry VIII and Katharine Howard, *The Fifth Queen*. Ford's provocative dealings with the relationship between fiction and history is shown to anticipate postmodern thinking about historiography and narrative. The collection includes essays by two acclaimed novelists, Nicholas Delbanco and Alan Judd, assessing Ford's grasp of literary history, and his place in it.

USA/Canada: One Rockefeller Plaza, Ste. 1420, New York, NY 10020,
Tel. (212) 265-6360, Call toll-free (U.S. only) 1-800-225-3998,
Fax (212) 265-6402
All other countries: Tijnmuiden 7, 1046 AK Amsterdam, The Netherlands.
Tel. ++ 31 (0)20 611 48 21, Fax ++ 31 (0)20 447 29 79
Orders-queries@rodopi.nl   www.rodopi.nl
Please note that the exchange rate is subject to fluctuations

The Swarming Streets
Twentieth-Century Literary Representations of London

Edited by Lawrence Phillips

Amsterdam/New York, NY 2004. VI, 227 pp.
(Costerus NS 154)

ISBN: 90-420-1663-9   € 47,-/US $ 61.-

Ranging from the turn of the nineteenth century to the last few years of the twentieth century, *The Swarming Streets* explores the representation of London in the last century through some of the major writers who have made it the foundation of their work. The natural companion to recent major histories and biographies of the metropolis, students and researchers alike will find major new essays on Virginia Woolf, Dorothy Richardson, Storm Jameson, E. Nesbit, Julian Barnes, Iain Sinclair, Graham Swift, B. S. Johnson, and Andrea Levy and others. Drawing on a rich variety of critical approaches, each essay is distinct as well as contributing to an overall analysis of literary representations of twentieth-century London.

USA/Canada: One Rockefeller Plaza, Ste. 1420, New York, NY 10020,
Tel. (212) 265-6360, Call toll-free (U.S. only) 1-800-225-3998,
Fax (212) 265-6402
All other countries: Tijnmuiden 7, 1046 AK Amsterdam, The Netherlands.
Tel. ++ 31 (0)20 611 48 21, Fax ++ 31 (0)20 447 29 79
<u>Orders-queries@rodopi.nl</u>   <u>www.rodopi.nl</u>
Please note that the exchange rate is subject to fluctuations